NUMBER 57

NUMBER 57

The History of a House

Maxwell Hutchinson

headline

First published in 2003
by HEADLINE BOOK PUBLISHING

10 9 8 7 6 5 4 3 2 1

British Library Cataloguing in Publication Data
0 7553 1147 7

Designed by designsection
Special photography by Paul Bricknell
Reprographics by Radstock Reproductions, Midsomer Norton, Bath
Printed and bound in Great Britain by Butler and Tanner

HEADLINE BOOK PUBLISHING
A division of Hodder Headline
338 Euston Road
London NW1 3BH

www.headline.co.uk
www.hodderheadline.com

This book accompanies the series *Number 57*, produced by Flashback/TwoFour for Channel 4.
Executive producers: David Edgar, Jill Lourie and Charles Wace
Series producer: Hannah Wyatt

ACKNOWLEDGMENTS

This book would not have come about without the television series it accompanies.

My thanks goes to all those involved in this daunting but hugely rewarding project – Ben Frow, commissioning editor for Channel 4; David Edgar, executive producer for Flashback and Jill Lowrie, executive producer for Two Four. Also to Hannah Wyatt, series producer and her entire staff: Clare Anderson, Geoff Dunlop, Hilary Jelbert, Zazie Mackintosh, Tom Mikulin, Alice Norris, Juliette Otterburn, Rebecca Parkinson and Roseanna Westwood.

I could not have written this book without the support and help of Emma Tait of Headline, who commissioned this book, her editor Christine King; my agent Francine Fletcher; my personal researcher Marianne Butler; and also Paul Bricknell, Sarah Gavetna, Carole McDonald, Charlotte Mullins, Jonathan Ruffle, Kath Smith and Gary Walters.

My love and thanks to Georgina Burrell, my partner for her support and tolerance throughout the entire project.

CONTENTS

INTRODUCTION

Most of us can remember the house in which we grew up. I was born in what appeared to be a Georgian house. It was, in fact, only Georgian-fronted. This only goes to prove that nothing in history can or should be taken for granted except the absolute coordinates of date and time. How many great names in history can be viewed either as hero or tyrant, depending on whether the victor or the vanquished wrote the history? We even play games with our memories. Through a process of selective amnesia, all childhood summers were warm and sunny; snow was crisper and deeper; first loves were the royalty of romance. Events that hurt or jar us today may be wiped from the tape of time, even if they are among the most important events that shape our lives.

My first home was in Grantham, Lincolnshire, the birthplace of Isaac Newton and, lest we forget, our first female prime minister. Our house stood in the shadow of the great St Wulfram's Church. I could see the faint glow of the church's sanctuary lamp from my window and was rattled by the pealing bells for the first seven years of my life. I entered its community when I was baptised at a font designed by Sir George Gilbert Scott, the famous Victorian architect (who designed, among other buildings, St Pancras Station).

Behind the façade of the house were a host of Georgian features, but much of it was older. There was Jacobean panelling and a trace of medieval wall painting in the sitting room. Of course, the Victorians had had their way with it too, adding the inevitable red-brick extensions at the rear to accommodate an elementary kitchen and scullery. When I arrived in 1948 to play my small part in the history of this venerable place, there were stone flags, an outside toilet and open fires. We had gas for cooking and a scattering of 15-amp sockets placed with no sensitivity on the original Georgian and Victorian skirtings. It was a house to love, a very atmospheric home. Growing up in a building like that was one of the reasons I became an architect.

Today I live in a converted public house in London within easy walking distance of St Paul's Cathedral and Covent Garden. Its name, The Rose, is picked out in terracotta on the gable end of the building. When I started asking around the neighbourhood about the reputation of The Rose, and looking it up in the records and on old maps, I was researching the genealogy of a building; I was putting its roles, location and inheritance in the context of today. This highly enjoyable pursuit was just like researching a family tree. I discovered that the pub, built in 1899 (the date is proudly emblazoned on another panel on the side elevation), had a rather naughty reputation as a striptease establishment in the 1960s. What is now my living room was once the hang-out of local villains who, rumour has it, enjoyed a somewhat fuller service. Everything I have found out enriches my experience of a personal and unique structure. Any one of us can do the same, even if at first sight a particular dwelling may seem to be undistinguished, it has something unique to tell in the way that all our lives have at least one story worth telling.

The *Number 57* project is the story of a house in Kingsdown Parade, Bristol. It reveals how a similar investigation can be undertaken on any house. In the case of Number 57, for the purpose of the television series that inspired this book, we had a hunch that it had more than a few stories to tell. We were rewarded with a rich and varied history that exceeded our expectations.

When the television series was first proposed to me – the study of a house over the last 200 years – I thought this was an architectural project and a history of interiors. I was soon to discover that everything I thought I knew about domestic architecture was inextricably linked to social history, because design is a response to our changing needs. This was to be an examination of a house as a manifestation of social change. My enthusiasm was fired. I am always interested in finding out something new; especially something that I can integrate into what I already know.

Having been given the challenge of the series, the hunt was on. We needed a comparatively unassuming house to show how the dust in our homes could tell us more about ourselves than we dare to imagine. Television is a medium that needs to balance reality with cost. Television's traditional answer to this problem is to build a set in a studio. Lights, technicians, director and presenter are all to hand. Sets are immensely flexible; they are designed to serve whatever the programme-makers are trying to show, regardless of their veracity. Cameramen do not have to lean round a tricky chimney breast to get a shot, they simply roll the offending piece of plywood architecture out of their way. When the idea of turning back time in a real house was suggested, applause for courage was certainly due. In television terms, we were looking at a cumbersome and tricky way to tell our story with a multitude of technical problems to overcome.

I am not sure where the process of making television programmes ranks in the indices of stress, but it has to be near the top. This project threatened to be unusually difficult, because any delay by the builders – and 'builders' and 'delay' are two words that seem inseparable – would shatter the delicate historical schedule of the programme. The bonuses of redesigning a real house had to be legion to outweigh these difficulties. The overriding advantage was integrity. Give a production team a programme that could be a real aid to the understanding of social history, that could open up a whole area of architecture and design for the third of the British population who live in a house built before 1914, and you will have a team that will work all hours to get it right. Integrity is costly. Insistence on doing it the right way is always more expensive. But it shows, it tells, and it thrills.

The team of which I was part would be doing something unique. We would be addressing the problems of living in a particular space just as the original occupants had done over seven generations. There would be no portable, plywood chimneys. Instead, real, awkward chimneys would be needed to serve real fires – chimneys that during their lives could have been blocked up, re-routed or removed altogether, only to return several decades later. We would have to put ourselves in the minds of those who had made those changes and see how they had formulated their solutions. This way, their solutions would become our solutions.

This project, to search out the soul of a house, has been one of the most demanding and rewarding challenges I have ever been involved with and I have been a practising architect in my own right for thirty years, working in television and radio for twenty. Mine was a small part to play – I simply had to tell the story that was being painstakingly pieced together by a dedicated team of researchers. The art and construction departments struggled, on a fortnightly schedule, to transform comparatively small rooms into the most accurate recreation of the past – six times. The director, cameraman, sound recordist, electrician and half a houseful of more crew had to squeeze themselves into a beautifully lit and expertly dressed room while I tried to conjure up the spirit of the past, to tease the truth from silent walls and make our chosen house sing. Here was an opportunity to go through the complex logistics of a real and dynamic learning experience: problems addressed, problems solved and problems left hanging for a later builder to scratch his head about. I am an expert on matters architectural, and would claim a strong working knowledge of the political history of the late eighteenth century, but the insertion of a whole layer of social history into my understanding of a building was completely new.

As we were going to explore over 200 years of daily change, there was no point in choosing a grand home. The rich can solve problems immediately, adopting new ideas, techniques and products as soon as they become available. If they choose, they can replace everything in the house in one fell swoop. However, the old money of the aristocracy and the upper classes tends to lead not to profligacy but to the gradual build-up of increasingly valuable artefacts from the past. Whenever I visit the homes of those whose wealth has built up over time, I am struck by the way in which successive generations have held on to furniture, pictures, porcelain and silver that reinforce their sense of ancestral history – quite literally, they will not sell the family silver. In contrast, the *nouveau riche* want to show off their wealth with enthusiastic extravagance, changing their homes at will as a means of displaying their wealth.

A dwelling at the other end of the scale, lived in by the truly poor, would not suit our purposes either. People in such circumstances were involved in a desperate struggle for survival, where it was enough to have a roof over their heads – never mind such luxuries as fixtures and fittings and decoration. As a result it was decided that we should find what we called a 'middling' home, an everyday house of what we now call the middle classes. One that would hold up a mirror to the day-to-day aspirations of ordinary people who were living out their lives in history, through history, but who were unlikely to make an individual impact on history. So, we were looking for a middling, unremarkable eighteenth-century house, preferably with its rooms still laid out as they were originally. Where would we find such a house, and how old should it be? What should distinguish it from its next-door neighbours?

Wherever this house was going to be, it was not going to be in London. London distorts the picture as certainly as wealth. The world's great metropolitan centres are notoriously fickle in matters of fashion. The *haute couture* houses of Paris and Milan attempt to persuade us to change our appearance four times a year to match the seasons. Alongside sartorial diktats, the well-known central London furniture and interior design stores seek

The smaller ground-floor room had cupboards mysteriously above the fireplace where the flue should be (it proved to be cunningly diverted to the side).

to make us as dissatisfied as possible with everything in our homes. In my life as an architect, I have ripped out more perfectly good kitchens in Kensington to replace them with the latest model than I care to remember. In London, fashion travels fast; it takes a little longer to travel up the Great North, Great West or Dover roads. A house outside London would, accordingly, be more representative of the eras through which it passed.

We wanted a Georgian house because it is the longest surviving house type that we could reasonably expect most people to be familiar with. They know it when they see it, and have been brought up to see the style as the height of dignified English architecture. We turned our eyes to Bath, but its Georgian terraces and grand sweeps there are of a piece. They have been preserved from the day they were built. The story required somewhere that would be more idiosyncratic that had witnessed repeated change. The road of fascination took us 27 miles further west to what was once Britain's second city – Bristol.

To start in Georgian times was to start on exactly the right note. We would provoke a mould-breaking response. No period has become more crystallised in the lexicon of style than the desirable drawing rooms of Jane Austen. However, when I first take people round an ordinary Georgian dwelling, they are surprised by the economy of the rooms, the simplicity and dignity of the design and construction. Once we can establish an enquiring frame of mind about the expected layout of the houses we thought we knew so well, then we are in the right frame of mind to think about the stinking tallow candles and the cesspit at the end of the garden. Furthermore, the Georgian period saw a change in the fundamental forces underlying daily life. Sail and horse-power were about to be replaced by coal and steam. By the latter phase of the Georgian period, timber was replaced by iron, horse-drawn wagons by steam engines, trading merchants by professional capitalists – those who did the work by those who invested and managed. Our house would reflect all this.

The south-facing front elevation of Number 57 at the time of purchase in late spring 2001. Number 59 was under renovation and so was exposing its original brickwork.

It was then but a short step to deciding that the best possible Georgian house would be one built on a greenfield site. This would reduce the influences of previous styles in the area. My first home in Grantham, for example, would have failed this audition. In 1778, Bristol's Kingsdown Parade was a new row of houses sitting incongruously in the middle of a field overlooking the bustling mercantile city. It was a piece of speculative building and typical of the period in that it was completely atypical.

Number 57 Kingsdown Parade is part of a terrace. All the houses in it were built at the same time but are not, unlike those in Bath or London's Bedford Square, all of the same design. As the terrace was built speculatively, the various property developers involved in the project were responsible for some, not all, of the houses. Number 57 was built as a pair with Number 59, though bearing a family resemblance to the houses on either side – giving a sense of order and dignity essential to the classically influenced Georgian mind.

Most houses of this vintage have been meddled with over the centuries, and would not have served our purposes. Number 57 was not listed until 1977, so it is all the more remarkable that it still had all its principal attributes; all the chimney breasts were there along with a wealth of original fireplaces, cornices and mouldings. Even the handsome and very unusual staircase remained untouched. The house had been reroofed in 1973 but, thankfully, in its original M shape with a hidden valley gutter (though the clay tiles employed were, conspicuously, of the wrong type). The house was vacant, in quite good condition and for sale.

We had finally found our house, which was ready to be transported back in time. We had a series of empty rooms inviting us to respond to changes in furniture, lighting, heating and the whims of fashion, but something was missing. It was in the very emptiness of the house that the biggest advantage of a real house, rather than a television studio set, became apparent. A real house would have been occupied by real people, who would, quite literally, have worked out their lives in it.

I need to make a distinction between 'people' and 'real people'. Historians talk endlessly about how 'people' lived their lives – meaning, specifically, the general populace. In the case of Number 57 the 'real people' we would be talking about would be those who actually lived in the house, those known by name, rank and occupation. Researchers can trace all, or nearly all, the families who have lived in the house, using parish records and other sources, while trade directories reveal how they earned their living. Instead of presenting an overview of social history we would have a unique and precise slice of history through the actual lives of real, everyday people. Our house and the people who lived in it would tell us one specific story against which the broader picture could be measured.

My father was an architect. He made me unusually aware of my surroundings. The thrill of spending a year in and around 57 Kingsdown Parade has made me rethink much of what I have absorbed over the years. My father was intensely passionate in his hatred of all things Victorian, teaching me that it was all intrinsically ugly. When I was five or six years old, we would walk around Grantham and he would instruct me that the whole place would be vastly improved if all things Victorian were knocked down the very next day. However, he excused the Victorians their engineering, seeing in it a series of practical responses to industrial need. I have now seen this problem-solving at work in every aspect of the Victorian home, and I have finally grown to respect it. A house built in 1778 has reminded me that everything we accept today as being of today is rooted in a rich and complex past.

It took the stories of ordinary people in what we call Georgian, Regency, Victorian and Edwardian times to stop me thinking about history as simply cut-and-dried eras. What is needed is a more flexible understanding of the relationship between time past, time present and time future. The past can be as real today as we want it to be.

The first-floor landing and staircase, the feature that has dominated the house throughout its history. The north-facing window overlooks the narrow access road at the rear of Number 57.

THE INHABITANTS OF NUMBER 57

What follows is a list of the known owners and occupants of the house. With the exception of John Macey, who owned the house from the early 1960s, what we know about these people are merely the cold, stark facts as found in official documents, such as census returns and parish registers. Their lives, as presented in the television series and this book, are nothing more than informed conjecture. Their real stories, on the other hand, may well have been even more extraordinary than anything we can imagine.

1776

The land on which our house was to be built was, according to the Poor Rates records, owned by a Mr Hopton. We know that the area was mainly given over to smallholdings, and Mr Hopton may well have owned one.

1777–1778

The plot was now owned by Richard Jones, a distiller. We have this information from the Poor Rates records. He no doubt purchased the land with development in mind, as in 1778 he had a pair of houses built on it – one to rent out, Number 57, and one in which he probably lived himself, Number 59.

1779–85

The Poor Rates records tell us that during this period a Mr Wilson occupied the house until 1784, then a Mrs Wasborough, who appears to have stayed for only two years.

1786–1791

During this period Mr John Britton rented the house. We have no hard evidence of there being live-in servants, simply because they were not obliged to be listed or registered at this time. Interestingly, he is listed as John Britten in the Poor Rates files, but from 1791 as John Britton in the Trades Directory. He moved out of the house in 1791 to the more upmarket area of Clifton.

1792–1794

No records of tenancy have been traced.

1795–1831

The Hobbs family moved in. The name of Captain Daniel Hobbs appears in the trades directory for the first year, when, it is assumed, he died as the following year's entry is for Mrs Mary Hobbs. According to the parish burial records, Mrs Hobbs died in 1831. Unfortunately there is no trace of any will left by Mrs Hobbs – this may well have told us about any children or other family she had.

1832–1843

No records of tenancy have been traced and in 1839 the rates evaluation of the house states that it was unoccupied.

1844–1845

The Trades Directory lists a Miss Hazard living at this address, using the property as a 'Ladies' Boarding School'.

1846–1848

No records of tenancy have been traced.

1849–1855

Mr W. P. Tratman is listed in the Trades Directory as residing at the house and as part of Tratman Brothers Merchants. He rented the house from William Fargas, an auctioneer. The census of 1851 informs us that Mr Tratman had a wife named Sarah who, at the age of thirty-nine, was one year older than her husband. The family had a young son and daughter and a live-in servant, twenty-year-old Mary Atherton. On the night that the census was taken the family had two visitors, J. and A. Townsend.

1856–1860

During this period all we know of the house is that it was occupied for just over a year by a Mr W. Grove, a wholesale grocer trading at 43 Baldwin Street in Bristol city centre.

1861–1864

The census of 1861 and Trades Directory for the three years of their residence tell us that three sisters lived at the house. Their names were Harriet, Sophie and Elizabeth Stansbury.

1865–1867

No records of tenancy have been traced.

1868–1878

The Trades Directory informs us that throughout this period Charles Withers owned the house. As he also lived at Number 57, he was the house's first owner occupier. The census of 1871 states that Charles Withers, 'Matchmaker', his wife Mary and their two children Lucy and William were resident, with no recorded live-in servants. The Trades Directory entries do not list Charles Withers as having a particular occupation; however, a William Withers, 'Watchmaker', is listed as trading at St Augustine's Bank in the city. Perhaps the watchmaking establishment belonged to Charles's father – in which case the census taker was either hard of hearing or had terrible handwriting.

1879–1886

Frederick James Alder, an accountant, and his wife Harriet moved in. The census of 1881 also records a servant named Elizabeth Dale, and the Alders' son, Frederick, aged three. For the purposes of the television programme we assumed that Frederick was the first son in a larger Alder family who moved on to the more fashionable part of Bristol known as Tyndalls Park in 1886.

1887–1895

The house stood empty for about a year until a Mr S. W. Dyer moved in for three years. In 1891, another census year, an accountant, Henry Arscott, his wife Anna and children Rowland and Ethel moved in but, again, stayed for only three years. From 1894, according to the Trades Directory, George Amory was resident for two years.

1896–1905

Mrs Annie Edwards, a widow and teacher of music by profession, moved into the house with her two sons Henry and Thomas, who at the time of the 1901 census were both in their early twenties and working as clerks. Mrs Edwards also had a fifteen-year-old daughter named Ethel. The census does not record a live-in servant but does tell us that a lodger lived at the house, Jasper Bussell, a thirty-year-old accountant.

1906–1908

The trades directory records that for one year, 1906, a Mr Tom Davidge lived at the house and for the following two years it stood empty.

1909–1936

Mr Frederick John Nash has an entry in the trade directory until 1915, when his daughter Ada is also recorded, with her profession given as dressmaker. In 1931 Ada was no longer living at the address and from 1932 until 1935 Mrs Nash is the sole entry – presumably her husband had died.

1937–1962

It is known that during this period a couple lived in the house, occasionally taking in lodgers. However, we have been unable to trace them or their descendants, and have had to rely on local records and the memories of surviving neighbours to build up a picture of Number 57. For the purposes of continuity, to keep the human presence in the house, we have introduced a couple we have called Mr and Mrs Evans; they embody what we imagine to be the real inhabitants' experience at a very difficult time.

1963–1990

John Macey bought the house and began rebuilding it. He and his wife Doris must have moved in by 1968, when they are recorded in the electoral register and trades directory. Their son Jim and Suzanne Martin also lived at the address for a number of years.

1991–2001

Two households are recorded during this period, each of whom stayed for around three years: Mark and Valerie Everett and Mr and Mrs Walkey and their daughter. The house had been empty for some time when it was bought for the television project in 2001.

PLAN OF NUMBER 57

Although the television design team did not recreate all the rooms in the house at each stage, they imagined a complete picture of how each room could have been used by each of its successive inhabitants. The page numbers in brackets refer to the first photograph of the room in a chapter, although these rooms and their contents can also be seen on many other photographs in the book.

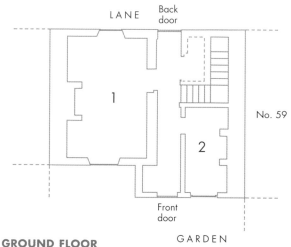

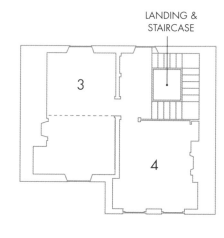

GROUND FLOOR

ROOM 1
1786–1791 Mr John Britton's kitchen
1795–1831 Mrs Mary Hobbs' kitchen
1849–1855 The Tratmans' kitchen (page 74)
1868–1878 The Withers' kitchen
1879–1886 The Alders' kitchen
1896–1905 The Edwards' kitchen (page 106)
1909–1936 The Nashes' kitchen
1937–1962 The Evanses' kitchen/diner (page 154–5)
1963–1990 The Maceys' kitchen/diner (page 173)
2001 Kitchen/diner (page 179)

ROOM 2
This area was used by the television crew.

1786–1791 Mr John Britton's scullery
1795–1831 Mrs Mary Hobbs' scullery
(The first toilet would have been to the side of the front door.)
1849–1855 The Tratmans' scullery and toilet
1868–1878 The Withers' scullery and toilet
1879–1886 The Alders' scullery and toilet
1896–1905 The Edwards' scullery and toilet
1909–1936 The Nashes' scullery and toilet
1937–1962 The Evanses' scullery and toilet
1963–1990 Mr John Macey's workroom
2001 Wall had been knocked down to make a large entrance hall by one of its recent owners, so this is how the house was left.

FIRST FLOOR

ROOM 3
1786–1791 Mr John Britton's drawing room
1795–1831 Mrs Mary Hobbs' drawing room (page 40–1)
1849–1855 The Tratmans' drawing room (page 58–9)
1868–1878 The Withers' drawing room
1879–1886 The Alders' drawing room
1896–1905 The Edwards' drawing room (page 97)
1909–1936 The Nashes' parlour (page 117)
1937–1962 The Evanses' living room (page 142–3)
1963–1990 The Maceys put a partition into this room making one half the house's first bathroom and the other a storage room for a chest freezer.
2001 Living room (page 184–5)

ROOM 4
1786–1791 Mr John Britton's dining room (page 26–7)
1795–1831 Mrs Mary Hobbs' dining room
1849–1855 The Tratmans' dining room
1868–1878 The Withers' dining room
1879–1886 The Alders' dining room (page 86–7)
1896–1905 The Edwards' dining room
1909–1936 The Nashes' dining room
1937–1962 The Evanses used this as a work space
1963–1990 The Maceys' lounge
2001 Home office (page 187)

LANDING &
STAIRCASE

LANDING &
STAIRCASE

SECOND FLOOR

ROOM 5
1786–1791 Mr John Britton's bedroom
1795–1831 Mrs Mary Hobbs' spare bedroom
1849–1855 Mr W.P. and Mrs Sarah Tratman's bedroom
(page 68–9)
1868–1878 Mr Charles and Mrs Mary Withers' bedroom
1879–1886 The Alder children's nursery (page 92–3)
1896–1905 Mrs Annie Edwards' bedroom
1909–1936 Mr and Mrs Frederick Nash's bedroom
1937–1962 Mr and Mrs Evans' bedroom
1963–1990 Mr John and Mrs Doris Macey's bedroom
2001 Master bedroom (page 194–5)

ROOM 6
1786–1791 Mr John Britton's spare bedroom
1795–1831 Mrs Mary Hobbs' bedroom (page 48–9)
1849–1855 The Tratman children's bedroom
1868–1878 Miss Lucy Withers' bedroom
1879–1886 Mr and Mrs Alder's bedroom
1896–1905 Miss Ethel Edwards' bedroom
1909–1936 Miss Ada Nash's bedroom (page 132–3)
1937–1962 The Evanses' spare bedroom
1963–1990 Master Jim Macey's bedroom
2001 Bathroom (page 190–1)

ATTIC FLOOR

ROOM 7
1786–1791 One of Mr John Britton's servants rooms
1795–1831 One of Mrs Mary Hobbs' servants rooms
1849–1855 The Tratmans' spare bedroom
1868–1878 Master William Withers' bedroom
1879–1886 The Alders' spare bedroom
1896–1905 Henry and Thomas Edwards' bedroom
1909–1936 Miss Ada Nash's workroom (page 124–5)
1937–1962 Lodger's bedsit (page 158–9)
(A kitchenette for the bedsit was in the hallway.)
1963–1990 Master Jim Macey's playroom
2001 Child's bedroom

ROOM 8
1786–1791 One of Mr John Britton's servants rooms
1795–1831 One of Mrs Mary Hobbs' servants rooms
1849–1855 The Tratmans' maid Mary's room (page 72)
1868–1878 The Withers' spare bedroom
1879–1886 The Alders' spare bedroom
1896–1905 The Edwards' lodger Jasper Bussell's room
1909–1936 The Nashes' spare bedroom
1937–1962 Unused and empty
1963–1990 The Maceys' attic storage room
2001 Child's bedroom

The final 'room' in the house is the elegant hallway with its landings and staircases. This was the room to change least over the decades and its various incarnations at the time of the Tratmans, Alders, Nashes and Evanses can be seen on pages 62, 184, 126 and 167. It is remarkable how similar it still looked in 2001 (page 199).

Chapter One

A GEORGIAN BEGINNING: *1778–1848*

The city of Bristol in 1779.

Everything in our homes, including their layout and design, has been dictated by two groups of people: first, the architect and contractors, who were responsible for designing and building the house and second, all the people who have lived there. Those who live in a new house will be the first to change the original features if they choose; those who are the latest in a long line of occupants will – unless they intend to gut it – integrate and adapt all the alterations that have gone before. The house at 57 Kingsdown Parade, Bristol is the physical manifestation of over 200 years of ordinary people deciding to change their domestic environment.

The story begins with the very ground on which Number 57 was built. In 1778 Kingsdown was a quiet ridge overlooking the city of Bristol. There were smallholdings providing fresh produce for the daily markets in the city below. John Latimer's *Annals of Bristol* records that Kingsdown was the perfect place for the wealthy and their children to escape the sweaty stench of the city in the summer and enjoy a change of air. A few wealthy Bristol merchants built their summer-houses there in the late seventeenth century. These were not insubstantial, temporary buildings as we think of summer-houses today, but solid country cottages, or sometimes even grand mansions. One still stands, very much altered, 200 metres from Number 57. As the only way to get anywhere was by foot or by some kind of horse-powered transport, even the short distance from central Bristol to Kingsdown could seem a very long way indeed, especially up a steep hill.

Building a new parade of houses on what had been open countryside reflected a country-wide trend. Towards the end of the eighteenth century, Britain was leaving rural life behind. The Industrial Revolution was gathering pace, replacing the age-old agrarian economy with machines and manufacturing. Until now, most people would have lived and worked in the countryside. There are no accurate figures for this period, as the first census was not taken until 1801, but the population of England can be estimated at about seven and a half million. An increasing number of families were migrating to the burgeoning cities, as part of a new urban working class. A new range of products was being made in city centres, and these were creating a commercial attitude based on manufacturing rather than agricultural production or import and export.

Improved transport links – canals and newly surfaced roads – shifted goods more efficiently. Those bound for the export trade were taken to the main ports. London handled anything going anywhere, but Bristol specialised in the triangular slave trade. Purpose-built ships carried manufactured goods such as pots, pans, guns and alcohol to West Africa, where they were used to buy human beings. These souls were then conveyed to the West Indies, and sugar, cotton, mahogany, tobacco, coffee and rum were bought with the proceeds of selling them and carried back to Britain. In 1738, at the peak of the slave trade, the port of Bristol was thriving, handling 42 per cent of all dealings. The city was the second largest in Britain.

Number 57 was built at a time when Britain as a whole was doing well, and the balance of economic power was shifting from traditional landowners to those who were creating their own wealth by their own efforts. These entrepreneurs took ready advantage of the opportunities provided by trade with the Empire and the birth of an industrial economy. Wealth was no longer an exclusive birthright, but there to be gained by all who had the skill, talent and opportunity to grasp the moment. There had always been Old Money; now there was New Money. Beneath the aristocracy lay the ranks of the moderately wealthy, the fastest growing sector of the population. Like the much poorer working classes, they were moving into the cities and becoming more urbanised. They were hungry to show their wealth, their gentility and their taste. The best possible way to spend their money was on what is still the most precious asset most people have, their home, and decorate it lavishly to ape the nobility. Social mobility may have been on the increase, but the upper classes were still seen as the arbiters of taste and style.

So what did the aspiring dandy merchant want for a home? Scions of the aristocracy were parading around Europe on the 'Grand Tour', the highlights of which were the classical sites of ancient Greece and Rome. The trend for classicism was a direct result of the excavations of Herculaneum and Pompeii. These archaeological discoveries, dating from 1748, provided a picture of life in a Roman household. So, back in Britain, a preference evolved for the simplicity and grace of the classical orders. This borrowing of a culture rather than concentrating on developing a vernacular one is typical of Britain as a mongrel nation; its cultural heritage is based on a range of influences from the Romans to the Danes and the Normans, and it remains enthusiastically receptive to foreign ideas today. The newly rich merchant in the late eighteenth century would have wanted to be fashionable, so he would choose the sophisticated language of post-Renaissance classicism.

A fine precedent had been set in 1700 when Bristol city council decided to drain a marsh and fill it in with rubble. On top they built Queen's Square. By firing local clay, dug from beside the river, they made beautiful houses of strong red brick bonded with white-lime mortar.

Brick was not the obvious material for the perfect realisation of the English Baroque home. The seminal buildings from classical antiquity were built from the indigenous material of Greece and Italy: stone. The early Greeks had been quick to realise the problems of building in wood – quite simply, it did not last. So they interpreted timber architectural forms in stone. Tree trunks became columns; the ends of beams became decorative features in cornices above columns. However, the Romans also developed bricks by improving the technology for firing clay. Without brick they could not have constructed the vast arches of their public baths, like that at Caracalla in Rome. So, although stone was the essential language of architectural antiquity, brick had its own pedigree too.

In Renaissance Italy, stone, marble and brick were once again the materials of choice for the founding architectural fathers of the time, from Brunelleschi through Palladio to Michelangelo and Bernini. In England, Gothic cathedrals were built of stone, but it was never the chosen material for domestic application. Medieval houses may have had timber frames but the infill panels were brick; from the thirteenth century onwards, English domestic architecture was, quintessentially, brick.

The brick was the first and most convenient industrialised building product, made in brickworks adjacent to the site and delivered ready for use by the bricklayer. Furthermore, a brick is conveniently hand-sized, being 9 inches in length, 3 inches in height and $4^1/_2$ inches in depth. The length is divisible by the height three times and by the depth twice, which gives many possibilities for the way in which simple bricks can be laid one with another – the so-called 'bond'. Strength, of course, is paramount, and the way in which bricks are laid is intended to give the maximum strength possible.

A brick wall, at least in the Georgian period, was in general 9 inches thick – the length of one brick or the depth of two bricks together. The exposed long face of a brick is the 'stretcher', the exposed short face the 'header'. The traditional English bond pattern of brickwork had alternating layers of stretchers and headers. It worked well and was considered elegant. However, in Flanders another way was developed: each row of bricks was laid with alternating stretchers and headers showing. It was no better than English bond but, by the end of the seventeenth century, Flemish bond became the latest English fashion.

Any Bristolian on his way up had to have this style – no old-fashioned English bond for him. This change in brickwork, in concert with an aesthetic sensibility and other

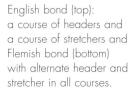

English bond (top):
a course of headers and
a course of stretchers and
Flemish bond (bottom)
with alternate header and
stretcher in all courses.

advances in building, added up to an entire coherent movement in architecture and design. If brickwork could suddenly acquire a new elegance, it could change dramatically what people thought their houses were capable of becoming.

Beauty could be more than skin-deep for the rich, who could afford houses built of brick through and through. On the ridge above Bristol, however, a more economical method was used. The less well-off were happy to build a house out of rubble stone and then merely face it with a single thickness of stylish bricks. (The trick was to use half a cut brick, known as a 'snapped header', to alternate with the stretcher.) When completed, there was no way of telling what was between the outer brickwork and the internal plaster. It seems likely that Number 57 was built in this way. Furthermore, while its brickwork was at some point finished in stucco – a plaster-like covering that could be scored and painted to look like stone – recent renovations to its next-door neighbour Number 59 have revealed the use of the fashionable Flemish bond pattern.

Georgian brickwork could be made to look even better by the careful use of stone in the detailing. For example, the windows could be built with a wedge of stone called a voussoir at the top of the arch, acting as a decorative keystone. Interestingly, it is possible to date Bristolian voussoirs to before or after 1727, the year in which the canal from Bath to Bristol was built, providing a smooth journey for goods, including stone. After that date, voussoirs are things of elegantly tapered beauty. Before, they are rougher and knocked about, having been delivered by horse and cart along uneven, dusty, damaging roads.

If the Kingsdown land had belonged to just one owner, perhaps the parade would have been one grand harmonious terrace the length of the ridge, emulating the splendid terraces and crescents of Bath. As there was a host of smallholdings, however, construction involved a variety of separate building ventures. Number 57 stands on land leased by Richard Jones, a distiller. He put up a pair of matching houses that looked like a single villa; they were an early part of a grander terrace made up of houses of different sizes and designs. With a full Georgian façade, they looked much grander than they actually were – though only at the front. Just as a single thickness of bricks could cover cheap rubble stone, so the back of this pair of houses is distinctly less imposing; the walling material, brick or

FRENCH FANCY

During the first half of the eighteenth century, Beau Nash turned the town of Bath into a gambling and fashion capital. The self-styled King of Bath cut a dash in his cream beaver-skin hat, tight breeches, long embroidered waistcoat and coat. A century later, it was another Beau, Beau Brummell, who was the arbiter of taste. He directed men towards a more sober, well-groomed image. At this time trousers entered a man's wardrobe. Developed from pantaloons – long breeches that gave rise to the American 'pants' – they were in general wear by the 1830s.

Paris was fashion's mecca. For most of the eighteenth century ladies wore tight whalebone stays (later known as corsets) and hooped petticoats under French *sacques* or waisted *robes à la anglaise*, changing outfits up to three times a day. In the mid-1780s, however, Marie Antoinette revolutionised women's dress (before the Revolution took her head) by wearing high-waisted children's chemise dresses and consequently making them all the rage. These thin white muslin gowns, draped like classical statues' attire, were enhanced by handkerchiefs down corsets to puff out bosoms, and cork 'rumps' above bottoms to ensure a straight line from shoulder to floor. It turned into a full-blown neoclassical love affair in the 1800s, and men and women wore hair cropped and tousled *à la Titus*. The most daring women even discarded their underwear, but by the 1820s the waistline was lowering and modesty was covered by corsets and drawers once more.

By the 1840s it was as if it had all been a giddy dream, and the look associated with the young Queen Victoria – tight boned bodices with dropped shoulders and pointed waistbands, voluminous skirts and smooth demure hair – was firmly in place.

Bath's Royal Crescent, designed by John Wood the Younger (1728–81), with its giant ionic columns rising above a plinth. When it was built it was probably the most aspirational addresses in all of contemporary Europe.

stone, is crudely covered over with grey cement render. The public face presented to the world was what mattered.

Georgian symmetry was seen only on the front of the pair of houses, but it was altogether absent inside. Number 57 has two rooms on each of the four floors, linked by a beautiful staircase. Number 59 is divided into a larger number of smaller rooms, and its staircase is positively cramped and mean. It is not known why the interiors of the two houses were constructed so differently; if Mr Jones planned to live in Number 59 himself, perhaps the arrangements simply reflected his personal taste and needs.

A Georgian gentleman would not have been put off by living next door to his landlord, because by the standards of the day the house would conform to his need for grandeur. He could point at it and say, 'I live there,' even though he had only one half. There were truly grand terraces in Clifton, about a mile to the west of Kingsdown Parade; this was a richer area, made so during the eighteenth century by the profitable Hotwells Spa that capitalised on the area's relatively clean and healthy location away from the polluted city centre. People who lived here could happily pretend they owned the whole edifice: a vast stately home rather than just one house in the middle of a grand sweep.

It is not known who built the rather more modest dwellings on Kingsdown Parade. A possible candidate could be the Paty family, who flourished in Bristol's speculative building trade for three generations. In Georgian times, however, all builders in Bristol would use the same yards for their materials. There is no particular reason to think the Patys worked on this house, though their influence as trendsetters is visible throughout Bristol.

The style now known as Georgian embraced a number of simultaneous ideas. The proportions of a Georgian façade follow the classical rules of architectural geometry that can be traced back to the earliest Greek temples. The Parthenon in Athens is a complex essay in optical illusion and the three-dimensional relationships between every element of its composition. The steps, columns, cornice and crowning pediment were all mathematically determined to create, in the eyes of the ancient Greeks and still for us today, near perfect beauty.

The distinctive Georgian fanlight (literally a window in the shape of a fan) over the front door of terraced houses was not just a decorative feature. Without it, the hall would have had no natural light at all because front doors were always solid wood, with no glass. (Here, however, Number 57 benefited from its grand staircase; there are windows on its landings to the rear.) Another new feature was the vertically sliding sash window, its glass panes secured by timber glazing bars; for centuries, much smaller panes had been fixed between strips of expensive lead. The sash window gave the Georgians two things still sought in design today: light and space. Unlike hinged windows, the up-and-down movement of sashes meant that when opened they did not take up precious space within the room, or obstruct the highway outside. Furthermore, they allowed the development of elaborate curtains and window dressings. They were also nearly draught-free. As glass technology improved, the panes got larger and the glazing bars got thinner.

The windows of Number 57 gave light to a kitchen and scullery on the ground floor, and a drawing room and dining room on the first floor. The rooms were designed with a specific purpose in mind, in contrast to previous times when one room may have had a multitude of uses, according to the time of day. For example, when it was time to eat, the old fashion had been to drag a table into the middle of the room. Now, people would move from room to room, depending on the activity. When Number 57 was built, the principal room in the house was the first-floor dining room, where hours were spent eating and drinking. It was fashionable to 'withdraw' from the dining room to a separate room while the servants cleared the table, or when ladies left the gentlemen to their port. There were two bedrooms above these public rooms and two attic rooms above them. At the top the windows would be very small, following the conventions of the time. Upper storey windows would be proportionally smaller than those lower down on the façade.

Number 57 was built to be rented (at this time, about 90 per cent of the population rented rather than owned), and cost £22 per year. As this sum represented the average household income of the day, the landlord, Mr Jones, knew his market was among the new, aspiring middle class. In the growing property market, there were fortunes to be made but, as in most areas of Georgian commercial life (and, indeed, before and since), reward and risk went hand in hand, and speculators could easily come adrift. In a striking example, building work on London's Berkeley Square was halted after the war with the French began in 1793. All the craftsmen went off to fight in the army and navy and, as a result, the developers went bankrupt.

At the time there were no estate agents as we understand the term today. Most people looking for a property to rent would read through newspapers or visit lawyers' offices. Shopkeepers would advertise properties in their premises, hoping that they would make a small commission from the landlord. Today's estate agent 'shops' are a specialisation of this practice. The fine new accommodation at Number 57 scarcely

One of the many beautiful doors in London's Bedford Square built between 1775 and 1780. It incorporates a finely detailed fanlight, two vertical side windows and a surround of man-made Coade stone with alternate textured rustications and a bearded face on the keystone.

John Britton's dining room laid for the main meal of the day with the newly available mass-produced china, glassware and Sheffield-plate cutlery. The wall-mounted mirrored sconces augment light from the candelabrum. The shutters rise from boxes beneath the windows using the same sliding mechanism as double-hung sash windows.

needed advertising, however. In 1760 Felix Farley's *Bristol Journal*, part of the blossoming periodical press, called Kingsdown a 'delightful spot', although he did mention it in the context of having a moan about the developers moving in: 'the public is like to be deprived' of one of the most pleasant promenades of the neighbourhood. 'Kingsdown… is already begun to be dug up and to experience the rude deforming labours of the delving masons.' By 1789, *The Gentleman's Magazine* says the suburb called Kingsdown 'abounds with good houses'.

Rental properties could be fully furnished, part furnished or unfurnished. Arrangements could be made for the house to be redecorated before moving in. There are advertisements by ambitious tradesmen in eighteenth-century Bristol newspapers boasting that they could decorate and furnish a house ready for occupancy within three working days. Alternatively, houses could have been rented with the redecoration carried out by the owner or agent. The new Number 57 would have been freshly painted throughout in the latest colours. In the eighteenth century, the interior design role was undertaken by an upholsterer. He normally covered chairs and made curtains, but he would also fill the house with whatever decorations he considered, with his exquisite taste, were needed. He would provide and fit carpets for those who could afford them, he would put up wallpaper, he would hang curtains, furnish bedsteads, choose furniture, lighting, whatever was needed, plus a complete follow-up service. Intriguingly to us today, this service could follow on to the grave. Having furnished you in life, many upholsterers would provide your coffin and other funeral accoutrements. In fact the great cabinet-maker Thomas Chippendale was an undertaker too, personally attending at the funerals of esteemed clients.

Upholsterers and other tradespeople were listed in local Trades Directories, the *Yellow Pages* of the eighteenth and nineteenth centuries (if rather less well organised and consistent). These directories, which also included information about the history and geography of the area and details of prominent citizens, now provide valuable insights into the structure of communities. Of the fifteen residences then listed in Kingsdown Parade, no fewer than seven of the occupants were 'gentlemen'. At the time, a gentleman was one who lived off independent means, whiling away his time managing a variety of financial interests, none of which, ideally, involved much effort. One of these gentlemen, a bachelor named Mr John Britton, moved into Number 57 in 1786 with his housekeeper and a servant or two. He is the first in a long line of residents of whose tenure there is evidence.

Looking after business in Bristol would hardly take up the whole of Mr Britton's day. He would have combined work with pleasure in coffee houses, discussing politics and reading the newspaper. He may have been listed in the Trades Directory, but he would have been at pains to distance himself from the vulgar realm of commerce. As a gentleman, he was a cut above those 'in trade'. In turn he would look up to the aristocracy, who were at the pinnacle of a society permeated by rules that governed behaviour, style and appearance. It was always the fear of the aspiring middle classes that they would give themselves away. They might be hugely successful capitalists, making a great deal of money, but the *nouveau riche* were all too aware how easy it was to contravene society's rules and betray their humble origins.

Georgian gentlemen at leisure. 'The Backgammon Game', Nathaniel Grogan (1740–1807).

For Mr Britton, having just the right kind of home was of singular importance if he was to maintain his veneer of gentility. He would have had to negotiate the very finely drawn rules of propriety that would dictate, for example, exactly when a room became vulgar with too many pieces of furniture. He also had to contend with a Georgian mindset that said that if your furniture was vulgar, so were you.

Mr Britton would have wanted an environment that he could show off, with interior decor that he could be proud of. He would have invited colleagues to his house to do business and be entertained. He would have seen inside the houses of his 'superiors' when he visited them on matters of business, and, with no design magazines or shops, this was all he would have had to go by. A chance meeting may have taken Mr Britton into some of the best Georgian houses in the land. Number I Royal Crescent in Bath (now a museum and open to the public) was one of the finest private 'terraced' houses and, for the likes of Mr Britton, a showcase of all to which he aspired. He could not afford the solid silver cutlery, fine porcelain or original Chippendale chairs, but within his means he would do his best to emulate the style of the very rich.

Mr Britton's house was his sanctuary against the outside world. As he walked or rode up the hill from Bristol to get home, the streets would have bustled with the grotesques of Georgian life: the beggars and tramps, the pockmarked and the crippled, the footpads and the thieves, a surging tide of humanity washing up against the walls of Georgian buildings that today seem so serene. Elegant sash windows looked out upon a world of vibrant villainy. It was during the Georgian period that people began to surround their houses and gardens with walls. Previously, it was felt that strangers should be allowed to admire your house and garden from close up. Now, as the mood changed and a house

The painted and varnished, sail-cloth floor covering over the broad, plain-edged floorboards.

became more of a refuge, it became more and more common to build a high boundary wall and put some forbidding broken glass on top.

Inside his four walls, Mr Britton would have wanted his dining room, the heart of his house, to be formal, elegant and coordinated. The furnishings of the day tended to be sparse. Mr Britton would not have been worried that people might think he was too poor to afford more furniture. People whose taste mattered would know that simplicity was fashionable and chic. The small dining table, simple chairs and sideboard were all that would fit in the dining room. But, as Mr Britton and his guests knew, they were all of a piece and in the best possible taste. Most surfaces would be easily wiped clean. Chairs were covered in leather or horse-hair, which was woven from horses' tails into a most durable cloth that was easily washable. Indeed, horse-hair cloth is surprisingly shiny and smooth, like the mane of a finely groomed stallion, and is still available today. (After the 1990s fire at Windsor Castle, the architects and interior designers had to search the globe for just the right horse-hair to upholster the replacement royal dining chairs. They were horse-hair before the conflagration, so horse-hair they had to remain.)

The floor would be covered in a piece of ship's canvas (readily available in a port in the days of sail), painted in simple geometric patterns or perhaps in a Roman mosaic design. Carpets were thought to be unhygienic, for few households could afford the endless hours of painstaking cleaning by servants. The canvas floor cloth, a forerunner to linoleum, was varnished so it could be easily wiped clean.

Colours meant a great deal in interior design and had a language all of their own, having, for example, a masculine or feminine character. The dining room in John Britton's time was a male domain and the walls would probably have been painted green – a strong, assertive colour, to reflect this. House painters charged by the square yard or foot of painted surface. They would use cheap and cheerful basic paints for what were called the common areas of the house: the kitchen, the upper stairs, the servants' quarters and so on. These would be treated with distemper, which was water mixed with a colouring material and a binding substance such as glue or size. The formal rooms in the house would be treated with an oil paint, with simple colouring that was blended in the house by the painter himself to achieve the exact colour the client desired, for example, ochre and black would create green.

As a bachelor, Mr Britton was free to indulge in three important pastimes: drinking, eating and gambling. Well-known figures such as the Prince Regent and Prime Minister William Pitt were known as 'three-bottle men' because of the amount of wine they drank, and they were greatly admired for their fortitude. When he needed to shift the excess

WOMEN OF PROPERTY

'It is a truth universally acknowledged that a single man in possession of a good fortune must be in want of a wife.' So the opening lines of *Pride and Prejudice* tell us, written by the shrewd social observer of her time, Jane Austen. She wrote of the preoccupation with marriage, property and intrigue that coloured the lives of an emerging middle class of the late eighteenth and early nineteenth centuries – people self-consciously set apart from the upper and lower classes.

Middle-class men became more politically active during this period, agitating for the vote and a bigger say in national government. While Milton's notion from the previous century that 'woman was made for man' was becoming less well received, women's enfranchisement was absent from the agenda. Men were busy with politics and business, and women were seen as the guardians of domesticity.

The Marriage Act of 1753 made a regularly conducted church wedding the only proof of marriage, and rendered invalid common-law ceremonies, such as a couple jumping over a broomstick together. These traditional unions, while not strictly legal, had been acceptable in the eyes of society. A consequence of the Act was to recognise only those children born within official wedlock as being 'legitimate'. Prior to the Act clergy would often look upon the offspring of cohabiting couples as if their parents were legally married. Common-law marriages were often still preferred by women who owned property in their own right, particularly widows over childbearing age, where a natural reluctance to lose their property rights on taking a new husband could be well understood.

Many people believed that the population of Britain was in decline, fuelling the notion that the country would be unable to compete with the likes of France on the battlefield in terms of cannon-fodder. During the 1780s, the Prince of Wales was patron of the Lying-in Charity for Married Women at their Own Habitations, whose motto was 'Increase of Children a Nation's Strength'. In 1836 the registration of births – as well as marriages and deaths – became compulsory, and when the statistics were analysed it was noted that the birth rate was not in decline as feared.

Marriage was important to a man. It not only brought the comforts of ordered domesticity but also full membership of society, whereas a woman merely became dependent financially and socially upon someone else; a husband rather than a father or guardian. However, marriage brought women some kind of status too. This is why Jane Austen in *Pride and Prejudice* has the youngest of the five daughters of Mr and Mrs Bennet say to her eldest sister, when parading into dinner and pushing to the head of the queue of girls, 'Ah, Jane, I take your place now and you must go lower because I am a married woman.'

liquid, Mr Britton would reach into a special cupboard built for his chamber pot into the sideboard. He would stand in the corner and relieve himself, putting it back into the cupboard for the servants to throw down the privy later. It is doubtful if he would do this with women present, but if the party was men only he would have no inhibition.

Mr Britton's furniture would have been designed, but not made, by one of the great names in cabinet-making. For the first time in the history of furniture-making, craftsmen, such as Thomas Chippendale and George Hepplewhite, produced designs that were to become common throughout the country. In the age before early forms of mass production, cabinet-makers only supplied those who were within easy travelling distance of their local workshops. However, these master craftsmen (now so beloved of the antiques industry) did not make most of their items themselves. They were not even made by other craftsmen in their workshops. They created pattern books of furniture, like Hepplewhite's *The Cabinet-Maker and Upholsterer's Guide*, published in 1788, which were used by local craftsmen throughout the country. As a result, one could boast of 'Hepplewhite' chairs that had never been near the great man but had his unique fashionable touch.

It is remarkable that these same designs were not only being copied all over Britain, but were circulated throughout the known world. A design published in London would be available in Boston, New England, or Kingston, Jamaica or even Rio de Janeiro, within three or four months. By such means, the British increased their global power. They did not have to occupy a country; their presence was already manifest. If they could control something as distinctive as taste in a distant country, they had, in some respects, conquered it already. At a time when the British Empire was about to expand, culturally the British already owned the design of the very table you ate at and the seat you sat on – at least for inhabitants with westernised taste and ambition and the requisite money.

The Romans had been exceptionally good at this stylistic imperialism. Shivering ancient Britons looked across the Channel at an empire with obvious wealth and associated social benefits. Subsequently, the Romans absorbed the natives, and part of this assimilation into empire was thanks to the subtle imposition of taste. A grand Roman house in Verulamium (now St Albans) would have had the same stylistic influences as a similar villa on the outskirts of Rome – and, centuries later this classical style would resurface in the old colonial outpost, demonstrating the continuing cross-fertilisation of cultures.

In its most practical sense, the pattern book was a guide for other craftsmen to use to recreate the ideas of the original designer. This broke new ground and made 'designer' furniture accessible to more people, particularly the middle classes. Mr Britton would have had furniture made of

The Hepplewhite chair was very fashionable and a common sight in the dining rooms of gentleman like John Britton.

mahogany, which took on a wonderfully deep shine, richer than the duller tones of indigenous walnut and oak. Mahogany, a tropical hardwood, had originally come to Britain as a by-product of the slave trade; on their return journey, ships carried vast quantities of the wood for ballast. Once its full beauty after working and polishing had been discovered, craftsmen of all kinds would go to mahogany auctions on Mud Dock in Bristol to buy the very best pieces. It became an essential material for fashionable design.

The staircase in Number 57 is of pine, built before mahogany took over as a fashionable material in the 1790s. It is interesting how, within a very few years of the house being built, tastes were changing and influencing construction. Mr Britton would have enjoyed poring over the pattern books with his craftsmen, planning his new furniture. He could choose an item of furniture from books, and then ask his local cabinet-maker to reproduce it. Hepplewhite created the Prince of Wales's feathers motif and shield-backs for chairs, and designed decorated chairbacks, featuring leaves, drapery, vases and honeysuckle. He also created designs that would have been easy for a less-skilledcraftsman to reproduce.

Other accoutrements of an aristocratic lifestyle were now beginning to be available. For the first time, the middle classes could afford 'silver' cutlery, in the form of Sheffield plate. In the early 1740s, Thomas Boulsover, a Sheffield cutler, was trying to repair the silver and copper handle of a knife. He overheated it, creating a fusion of the two metals that could then be worked as one. He could see that the two different layers did, however, remain distinct. All he had to have was the leap of imagination to make items out of this composite material, with the shiny silver on the outside and the thick heavy copper on the inside. This was the key discovery that led to the creation of Sheffield plate. It was indistinguishable from the real thing, except that it was three or four times cheaper. Mr Britton would have bought as much as he could afford, so that he could bring an end to the earlier barbaric custom of eating an endless series of courses on the same pewter plate with one bone-handled knife and greedy fingers.

The main meal of the day could last up to a mammoth five hours. Visiting Frenchmen apparently thought there was nothing more boring than a dinner party in England. The meal would start at two or three in the afternoon, which handily proved to everyone that the host was a gentleman who did not need to be using daylight for manual labour. Food for Mr Britton's dinner party would be prepared in the kitchen by his housekeeper and servant. In striking contrast to the fitted kitchen with all mod cons of the late twentieth century, this was a bare and strictly functional room, floored with cold flagstones and with no running water. Food was cooked on an open fire; although the kitchen stove was invented in the 1780s, it would not reach middle-class homes for many years. It would be roasted on spits or skewers propped against the

Hepplewhite's published patterned books contained a bewildering array of designs, giving local craftsmen and their customers a great deal of choice.

fire and turned regularly. It was never particularly hot when presented at table, even in the lucky event that it was fully cooked in the first place. Boiling was the simplest and therefore the most common way of cooking food. Large boiling vessels constitute the most widely- used cooking utensils before 1800.

During the dinner it was the host's job to come up with topics of conversation, which also scandalised the French because the English would even discuss politics with women in the room. Mr Britton and his close circle of friends would have drunk deep, and there is little evidence they were careful eaters. There were no napkins, so diners simply lifted the damask tablecloth and wiped their mouths when necessary. Food would have been placed straight on to the table and served by the host or hostess, rather than being put on a sideboard. A typical dinner would have up to three courses, just one of which could include meat, fowl and fish. Perhaps the meal would be embellished by one of the exotic foodstuffs made available by improved trading links – olives from Spain or truffles from France (though possibly Mr Britton would not have stomached reindeer's tongue from Lapland).

The damask table-cloth would be removed when everyone had finished their main courses, then a tempting variety of delicacies would be served for dessert. Many of these could be bought ready-made in Bristol and delivered to the house. The table would look very attractive, with polished plates and glasses laid on the shiny mahogany surface. After all that serious eating, any ladies present would 'withdraw' to the next-door room, and the men would set about some serious drinking (having already consumed what would, by today's standards, be more than enough).

It was popularly thought that excess alcohol, especially port wine, led inexorably to gout – indeed, that misconception is still common. In fact, gout is a kind of arthritis, usually hereditary, where uric acid crystals are formed in the joints, commonly targeting the tiny bones in the feet. There is no doubt, though, that an over-rich diet can exacerbate the condition. It is spectacularly painful, so much so that even the slightest movement is agony. If Mr Britton was afflicted, he would prop his foot on a specially designed gout stool (another pattern-book product from the ingenious cabinet-makers) and beg everyone to keep away.

Had Mr Britton wanted to top up his toping after dinner, he could have gone to the pub. In his time there was a tavern at the end of the street, the Montague Inn.

Opposite: Sheffield plate, invented by the cutler Thomas Boulsover in the 1740s, had the luxury of silver without the expense.

THE EXPANDING PALATE

During this period there were changes in the eating habits of British people of all classes, partly through agricultural and technological advances, and partly through the import of foreign foodstuffs.

Improved transport links allowed fresh fish and oysters to be packed in barrels of sea-water and taken to inland towns, while regional specialities such as cheese, Scottish salmon and 'local-recipe' breads and cakes became available outside their immediate locality. The continental method of growing winter fodder for cattle was adopted, so that animals could be fattened and slaughtered at any time, and fresh meat became available all year round. Furthermore, raw fruit – like any uncooked food traditionally a rather suspect and perhaps dangerous commodity – was now being promoted as a healthy food; hothouses ensured that peaches and grapes were grown throughout the year for the wealthier consumer. The pineapple was an eighteenth-century symbol of hospitality, and as such its motif was used on buildings and bridges; but the real thing was rarely seen, adorning the tables of only the very rich.

Throughout this period there was no shortage of recipe books for the aspiring householder to consult. Traditional dishes were adapted and called something else in order to differentiate between, for example, the labouring classes' 'stew' and the gentleman's 'soup' – even though they used almost identical ingredients.

Many of those who could afford it overindulged in a diet rich in animal fats and alcohol and as a result there was a great deal of ill health. Gout, diabetes and heart problems necessitated respite and the taking of the waters at spa towns, such as Bath.

Busy Bristol Docks, where Mr Britton and his contemporaries would have plied their leisurely trade as gentlemen.

He would go there to meet his friends, whose long-stemmed clay pipes, called 'churchwardens', would line the walls in racks like snooker cues. The Montague was famous Bristol-wide for its fashionable delicacy, turtle soup. This was an example of culinary decadence – yet another way to show off. Like mahogany, which originally had been seen as nothing more than ballast, it was another by-product of the transatlantic trade, the hapless turtle having originally swum in the Caribbean. It was thought that the soup was good for health and aided digestion, allowing Mr Britton to eat even more. He could even have taken it home and had it as a takeaway.

In the pub, a popular topic of conversation was no doubt the declining West Indian sugar trade. Opposition to slavery was growing, and one of the abolitionists' popular campaigns was to boycott sugar and so undermine the slave trade. Meanwhile, Liverpool was starting to dominate the slave trade; by 1803 Bristol would be handling a mere 1 per cent of Britain's slave trade tonnage. In 1833 the slave trade would finally be abolished in the British Empire. The triangular route ceased to bring cheap New World produce to Bristol, which was affected doubly because so many people had invested heavily in the sugar trade.

When Mr Britton had tired of moaning about his sugar interests, he would make his way back home. The street outside would have been dark, with no lamps. He may have felt in his pocket to check he had his 'life preserver' with him, a small pistol or a knife. There was no police force, only watchmen and parish constables. These were not a popular job. Consequently, the men who were attracted or forced into this line of work tended to be old, infirm or common drunkards. The prevalence of crime on Kingsdown Parade in the 1780s was enough to encourage the inhabitants to advertise for some 'able-bodied young men' to act as watchmen on a nightly patrol to reduce highway robberies and crime in general.

Gangs of thieves operated on the outskirts of Bristol. The problem was of sufficient concern for a whole file in the Home Office to be dedicated to a mob called 'The Ruffians' in Kingsdown. People wanted security for their money, particularly when travelling to London. The roads from Bristol to London were plagued by highwaymen who had acquired the knack of escaping justice, which was not surprising as there was little or no policing of the country's main roads. People embarking upon a journey which, today, is taken for granted, were quite literally taking their life into their own hands. Bandits along the insecure route may have threatened 'your money or your life' but in all likelihood would have taken both and then escaped into the anonymity of the largely uncharted English countryside. So, an arrangement came into being that meant you could take a note from your bank in Bristol to a bank in London, rather than take the actual cash: a step forward in the foundation of the banking system as we know it today.

In the 1780s, even property in your own home was not safe. John Britton would have locked away his silver, his best china and even his candles to stop them from being stolen (the housekeeper held the key). He would have protected the house itself with shutters, and a solid lock on a solid door. The majority of crimes were committed in the home by domestic servants stealing from their employers. Clothes were often stolen because they were expensive status-symbols, and easily disposed of through pawnbrokers or lodging-house keepers. Candlesticks and cutlery were particularly attractive items, while food was frequently stolen from the kitchen.

The punishment for being caught was instant dismissal without a reference – which, without the support network of a welfare state, could lead to destitution. Georgian society still teetered on the edge of the medieval abyss. The eighteenth century abounds with positive images – architecture, furniture, art, music, grace and elegance – but to our modern sensibilities it was in many ways a brutal age, symbolised by public hangings and whippings (of children as well as adults), often for what we would regard as petty crimes. Chaos was always stirring just below the surface, like an uneasy monster.

John Britton was upwardly mobile, and in 1791 he moved out of Number 57 to a more prestigious address in Clifton. The next recorded occupants of Number 57 were a naval captain, Daniel Hobbs, and his wife Mary. They took up residence in 1795, but

POPERY AND DISSENT

Thomas Paine, in his 1795 book *The Age of Reason*, stated that Christianity was 'too absurd for belief, too impossible to convince'. But in the late eighteenth century the vast majority of British people were Christian – and Protestant.

The Church of England's fear of 'popery' led to continuing Catholic persecution but, by the late eighteenth century, toleration finally won through. The first Catholic Relief Act came in 1778, allowing priests to take Mass without fear of prosecution. Equality was enshrined in the 1829 Emancipation Act, when Catholics could finally become Members of Parliament.

Catholicism was not the only religion existing outside the Church of England. In 1791 the Methodists, originally a Church society, broke free when the Church failed to support their belief in a more personal relationship with God. But the Evangelical Movement, from 1790, was the biggest rival. Believing in daily family prayer and Bible reading, it counted visionaries such as the slave-trade abolitionist William Wilberforce among its members.

At the turn of the nineteenth century, the Church of England may still have been the official religion, but its services were seen as dull and boring, its clergy demoralised, and its congregations there through duty not desire.

The clerics John Keble and John Newman saw that the Church was in crisis, and aimed to return it to its former glory. Their endeavour, initially called the Oxford Movement in 1833, increased the role of liturgy and ceremony in the Church and insisted on apostolic succession. They published ninety 'Tracts for the Times' – hence their later name, the Tractarians – but their 'middle way' between the Church (Anglicanism) and Catholicism was seen to run ever closer to Rome. They even called themselves the Anglo-Catholics, the name they retain today; and Newman himself eventually converted to Roman Catholicism.

THE QUEST FOR CULTURE

Ladies and gentlemen who aspired to be 'cultured' had many opportunities to enjoy the arts, for both instruction and pure entertainment. Theatres, museums, picture galleries, libraries and assembly rooms were to be found not only in London but the provinces too. During the second half of the eighteenth century, urban areas grew by a staggering 70 per cent, each with a society in need of refinement and diversion.

Provincial towns absorbed and imitated the culture of the capital city. Liverpool had a Drury Lane theatre, while even Richmond in Yorkshire, small by comparison, had its own theatre built in 1788, the Georgian Theatre Royal.

In the summer months London orchestras and theatres toured the country and were no doubt very welcome. Cultural activities in London were generally becoming more professional. The actor David Garrick, for example, was injecting realism into his theatre productions; he insisted on the use of appropriate costumes, dressing as a Moor rather than a military hero when playing Othello – and urged his leading ladies not to wave at their friends in the audience. The provinces, however, were very much the home of the serious amateur.

Local choral societies, orchestras and theatre groups flourished, their performances raising money for local charities and hospitals. There were also many debating and scientific societies, arts and book clubs and subscription libraries, all of which contributed to the interests and tastes of the middle classes.

Pleasure gardens were an important element of entertainment during this period. Bristol had a Vauxhall Pleasure Garden and Newcastle had its own Ranelagh Pleasure Gardens, both London copies. For an entrance fee that depended upon the popularity, or exclusivity, of the venue, one could take tea, listen to music, dance, gossip and observe the latest fashions.

Opposite: Undoubtedly Mrs Hobbs would have consulted Ackermann's Repository of the Arts, the first interior-design magazine.

unfortunately the captain died the following year, though evidently leaving his widow well provided for. With a pension and probably private money of her own, she was able to stay on at the desirable address and devote herself to improving her home. In keeping with her standing in society, Mrs Hobbs would probably have had a housekeeper, a lady's maid or two and a male servant for protection. (Hiring men was subject to a tax of one guinea a head introduced in 1777 to help fund the war in America. It was not lifted until 1837, so domestic staff were normally female.)

During Mrs Hobbs' residence, a new national style came into being, taking its name from the Prince Regent, who in 1811 had to take the place of his ailing father, 'mad' King George III. The Prince was a fashionable trend-setter and a patron of the architect John Nash. Regency design saw interiors becoming informal and intimate, and furniture simple but substantial. The change in design between the Georgian and Regency period was reflected in the first interior design magazine, *Ackermann's Repository of the Arts*, published from 1809 to 1829, which was the precursor of today's plethora of style journals. Ackermann's was democratised design. The rich would always have the top-end items that others could not afford. But now the middle classes could buy more than ever before, especially those items that had been beyond their financial reach only a generation earlier.

Mrs Hobbs would have felt she could move on from Mr Britton's formality, especially in her drawing room, which for her, as a woman, was the all-important room at Number 57. Ladies entertained there, and occupied themselves with genteel pastimes. Furniture was not put back against the wall after use, but remained scattered about, asymmetrically (this was particularly advantageous for smaller houses that lacked sufficient servants to rearrange

REPOSITORY

OF

Arts, Literature, Commerce,
Manufactures, FASHIONS and Politics,

VOL. XI

This Work Approbation

Already honoured by His and Humbly Dedicated by Permission

To His Royal Highness

Prince Regent

R. ACKERMANN

Mrs Hobbs' comfortable drawing room with the table laid for the new social ceremony of taking tea with friends. The bow-grilled cast-iron grate and marble fireplace surround are typical of the Regency period.

the furniture). With informality went simplicity. Regency taste was for more basic geometric forms in furniture; not necessarily heavier, but not the spindly, elegant aesthetic that Mr Britton would have liked. In terms of furniture, the sofa did as much as any single item to transform the appearance of the average drawing room, and epitomised the informal and intimate style of this period. You could sit on it with someone else. It was not pushed back against the wall at the end of the day. It was a relaxed social facilitator. Perhaps it rested on a carpet from Wilton or Kidderminster. The pattern would be unremarkable, but a carpet would make the room immediately more homely.

As the rooms became more intimate, they also became more comfortable. Soft materials replaced leather and horsehair for coverings, and were also used for cushions, curtains and carpeting. By the early nineteenth century, cotton had become the largest single British manufacturing industry. Raw cotton imports from America and the Empire increased five-fold between 1780 and 1800, and thirty-fold during the nineteenth century. As a fabric, it changed British interior design for ever. Cotton was washable, lighter than other fabrics, smelt less, and could be printed on easily. It quickly replaced heavy eighteenth-century wool and linen, and expensive silk.

Matching the cotton revolution, there was a great leap forward in wallpaper technology. Until the 1830s, wallpapers were produced by hand, using traditional block prints. Later there was a tax imposed on it. When this was repealed in 1836, wallpaper became even more accessible. Then machinery was introduced that could produce a continuous strip from wood pulp; by 1839, roller prints could produce an eight-colour pattern in a single operation on to the continuous roll. Wallpaper became dramatically cheaper. Within a generation, it dropped to a farthing (a quarter of an old penny) per yard – one-seventh of its previous price. Meanwhile, paints were also being produced in a greater range of colours; the processes to extract pigment from minerals and chemicals were now becoming cheaper and safer. Yellow paint, for example, now a tremendously popular and bold Regency colour, no longer contained the toxic horses' urine it had in the past.

With fresh fabrics and brighter colours, the drawing room was transformed. It was further enhanced by the Argand oil lamp. In the 1780s, the Swiss inventor Aimé Argand patented a new type of oil lamp that drew air through a hollow tube in the wick, creating a much brighter flame that gave ten to twelve times as much light as a candle. By the time Mrs Hobbs moved to Number 57, Argands were expensive, but within her price range, and they revolutionised the daily cycle. Four or five hours could be added to the day before sleep in winter, rather than an all-embracing darkness bringing the day to its natural end. For Mrs Hobbs, the Argand meant that meal times, for example, could be later and it was possible to spend an evening reading or sewing in a stronger light that did not strain the eyes.

Candles obviously remained in widespread use for many years. Mrs Hobbs would use the most expensive type of candle, made of sweet-smelling beeswax, in rooms where she had guests (a snooty visitor would sniff the air to see what sort of candles her hostess was using). Cheaper candles were made from a waxy substance from the head of a sperm whale: spermaceti. Its smell can only be imagined. Tallow candles, made of

Opposite: The revolutionary Argand lamp, which transformed the domestic round adding four or five hours of light to the day.

Mrs Hobbs' sewing table. Fine needlework and embroidery was a genteel occupation for the daylight hours before turning on the Argand lamp.

animal fat, would have made everything smell of burnt hamburger. Below stairs, or in poorer households, people burnt dips: a strip cut from a rush that was then dipped in animal fat. The Argand might have smelt of oil, but it was a tremendous improvement in domestic illumination.

While the room would have been better lit, heating it was another story. Fireplaces sent most of their heat up the chimney and much of their smoke into the room. Mrs Hobbs' servants would have waged a permanent war on soot in the chilly drawing room. Guests used to huddle about the fireplace in winter as closely as they could, within the realm of good behaviour, naturally. With all this grime about, Mrs Hobbs may have had cotton slip covers on the furniture that she would take off when important guests arrived. It is fortunate that Number 57 still has some of its original fireplaces, which survived the great Victorian purge when they were largely replaced by iron register grates. (What is loosely termed 'a Victorian fireplace' today means a more enclosed fireplace with an iron register or flap that regulates how much heat is held back in the room rather than just racing up the chimney.)

In her elegant yet comfortable drawing room, Mrs Hobbs would enjoy pursuing her various pastimes, alone or in company: perhaps sewing or knitting, for which she would have a collection of patterns, playing the harp, or conversing in French. (Despite the Napoleonic wars, French language and culture was still the height of fashion.) She could have spent much of her time reading, as periodicals and books were now widely accessible, allowing for the sharing of ideas and an increase in the popularity of fiction. Accessibility does not mean books were cheap. In fact, they would have been locked up in the drawing room between readings. It is strange to think that the novelist now so readily associated with the period, Jane Austen, was published anonymously, with only her two posthumously published books coming out under her own name. These were the days when women simply did not write novels. Among newspapers, the *Daily Universal Register* was first published in 1785 and later renamed *The Times*, and the *Observer* was first published in 1791. Mrs Hobbs would have followed the exploits of the Duke of Wellington avidly. The boot was famously named after him, as was a new blue colour. Because of her naval connection, Mrs Hobbs may have bought a small bust of Nelson after Trafalgar. If she was feeling cheeky, she could have had a chamber-pot with Napoleon's portrait in it.

Mrs Hobbs's visitors would have included her neighbours. Perhaps she knew the other widows listed in Trades Directory the second-hand bookseller, or William Oliver the tea dealer – whose commodity was furnishing the latest genteel pastime for the middle classes. The idea of tea as a ritual began in the Georgian period. Tea itself was an exotic, expensive product, although prices were coming down due to a reduction in tea tax after pressure from the tea magnate Richard Twining. Tea sellers would mix up the tea leaves to your specification and give them to you wrapped in a piece of paper. Mrs Hobbs would have had to be careful where she bought her tea. It had to be from someone she trusted such as her neighbour, Mr Oliver. Otherwise she might be sold tea 'cut' with old leaves or coloured with poisonous Prussian Blue or gypsum, or even mixed with molasses and sheep's dung to give the appearance of fresh leaves. A pound of tea cost as much as a maid's monthly wage, so smuggling and adulteration were rife. The tea caddy had to be locked away. Tea was often given to a servant as part of their wages; when this trend ceased, many servants thought it their right to help themselves.

The English started drinking tea 'neat' (or black as we say today). It took several years for the addition of milk and sugar to become fashionable, making the tea ritual thoroughly English. As in most areas, including

The first edition of the *Observer* newspaper published in 1791. Sunday papers had been disapproved of until 1779 with the launch of the *Sunday Monitor*.

The coordinated tea set did not become fashionable until the 1840s. Mrs Hobbs would have used an eclectic combination of cups, bowls, spoons and teapots. The tea caddy was the centrepiece of the ritual and its most important accoutrement. The precious leaves would have been locked away for safe-keeping, the key never leaving Mrs Hobbs' sight.

architectural style and costume, the English have a self-confident knack of making imported rituals and fashions idiosyncratically their own.

Many rituals that turned into 'afternoon tea' were established by 1815. Tea was always brewed in the room and not the kitchen; the servant would bring in a silver kettle and the tea caddy, and then leave the room while the lady of the house would brew the tea. The notion of tea sets of a uniform nature as we know them today did not come into fashion until the 1840s. Mrs Hobbs would have had a tea set of porcelain and silver that would have been an eclectic combination of bowls, cups, spoons and teapots. It was common for fathers to buy their daughters sugar bowls that they would keep with them for life. This shows that some things will always defeat conceptions of the fashionable. If emotional ties are strong enough, people will hang on to nearly anything – and no style trend can change that.

The fashion for tea-drinking prompted the development of the pottery industry. It is impossible to drink near-boiling fluid such as tea from a container made of metal like pewter as it retains the heat, hence the demand for ceramic ware. Pattern books for tea cups were produced by Wedgwood, Royal Doulton and Minton, mimicking the cabinet-makers' means of promotion. Silver-makers copied the porcelain cups and teapots, and silver became all the rage for sugar nippers and milk jugs. There would be teapots, slop bowls for excess tea, and 'mote' spoons that were multipurpose, for measuring and straining, and clearing a blocked spout with their pointed end. Thankfully, as yet, no teabags…

Mrs Hobbs lived at 57 Kingsdown Parade for thirty-six years. Hers would have been an ordered existence up until she died on 17 July 1831 at the age of sixty-eight. This was a good age, as life expectancy for women at the time was only forty years. Death and its associated rituals was accepted in a much more matter-of-fact way than it is today. For religious Georgians, death was part of life, to be confronted and accepted on a day-to-day basis. Infant mortality was extremely high, as was maternal death in childbirth; the most trivial of ailments or injuries could result in premature death. This was a world without antibiotics, antiseptic or anaesthetic.

Mrs Hobbs' funeral would have been quite modest, but serious and respectful. Within twenty-four hours of her death she would have been laid in a lined coffin in her drawing room (the funeral trappings perhaps supplied by her upholsterer). The coffin would have been left open for relatives to pay their final respects. Just as there were rules in Regency life, so there were formalities in death. The house was prepared by reducing light and noise: shutters were closed, curtains drawn, the clocks stopped and a layer of straw was placed on the street outside. Passers-by would recognise the signs and bow their heads and remove their hats in respect. Mrs Hobbs would have specified in her will what she would wear in her coffin, and where she would be buried – probably next to her husband. She may have ordered a piece of her hair to be woven into a ring or bracelet or even framed for someone special. Her possessions would have been left to her relatives or to charity. Often there was a provision for some of the deceased's clothes to be given to a favourite servant, who could either wear the items or sell them on for the money.

The funeral service would take place within a couple of days. The clinical formality of institutional cremation did not yet exist; burials were nearly always in churchyards, or beneath the church itself in crypts or under flagstones, except in times of mass disease. Cemeteries as we know them today were a later Victorian concept. So overcrowded were churchyards that bodies were buried on top of each other often resulting in the most recently deceased's remains protruding from the ground as a timely reminder of the fragility of life.

Mrs Hobbs' last will and testament has not survived. Her legacy to us has perhaps been the opportunity for the twenty-first century to use the fragments of documentary evidence about her to build a portal through which to view her world. Her old home remained unoccupied for a number of years, before being used briefly as a girls' boarding school. Then, at a time of great change in the outside world, towards the end of the 1840s new tenants moved into 57 Kingsdown Parade.

SEARCHING FOR CURES

The Enlightenment philosophy of the eighteenth century advanced by European intellectuals expounded the idea that a better future for mankind could be achieved by embracing advances made by science and technology. Man himself held the key to of controlling nature and thus to his own destiny. Illness was no longer thought of as a punishment meted out to an individual by an unseen divine power and physicians were now spending less time on perfecting their bedside manner and more on considering the nature of disease.

There was a great deal of disease to consider. Diphtheria, polio, measles, scarlet fever, even tonsillitis – all were potentially life-threatening and rife. Perhaps the most feared infection was smallpox, an endemic disease that knew no social or economic boundaries. It could kill anybody, its victims including King Louis XV of France in 1774 and about 3,500 Londoners during 1796 alone. In the Americas whole tribes of indigenous peoples were practically wiped out when sailors and settlers from Europe transported the 'speckled monster'. Survivors of the disease were often seriously disfigured and were left with reduced fertility.

The major breakthrough in the conquering of smallpox came with the publication of Dr Edward Jenner's *An Account of Causes and Effects of the Variolae Vaccinae* in 1798. Using a combination of folk tradition, observation and experimentation, Jenner found that the dairymaids of his home county of Gloucestershire were aware that if they contracted the comparatively mild illness of cowpox they would be immune to smallpox. Jenner extracted cowpox matter from the arm of a dairymaid and 'vaccinated' a young boy who, despite being deliberately exposed to smallpox, remained healthy.

Jenner and his supporters were often ridiculed in the popular press, but within a few decades the vaccination of infants against small pox within four months of birth was made compulsory in Britain. Smallpox was eradicated globally in 1979.

A delicate china teacup would be made using a pattern from a book published by one of the large manufacturers, such as this one from Royal Doulton.

Mrs Hobbs' bedroom
with the new luxury of
a woven carpet from
Wilton or Kidderminster
underfoot. The sparsely
patterned wallpaper
makes for an unassuming
and relaxed room.

Chapter Two

THE RISE OF VICTORIA'S BRITAIN: *1849–1878*

Before the new tenants moved into Number 57, the house had been standing empty and forlorn for a number of years. Around it, the bustling early-Victorian world would have accentuated that emptiness. Bristol had expanded up the hill; streets, squares, terraces and roads had sprung up and engulfed Number 57. The spectacular view, once enjoyed by Mrs Hobbs and her guests from the first-floor drawing room, was now simply row upon row of roofs and chimneypots belonging to the terrace that had been built across the road at the bottom of Number 57's garden.

Half-way through the nineteenth century, Britain's transformation from a predominantly agrarian society was complete. She was now the greatest industrial nation on earth. Huge productivity brought dramatic economic growth, which in turn fuelled a building boom. The census of 1851 records a total population of around 21 million, most of whom lived in towns and cities.

Mr and Mrs William Tratman moved into Number 57 in 1849, renting the house from William Fargas, an auctioneer. At the time of the 1851 census Mr Tratman was thirty-eight years old, and his wife Sarah was thirty-nine. They had two children, a boy and a girl, and a live-in servant, twenty-year-old Mary Atherton. On the night of the census there were also two visitors, the Townsends of Somerset.

The Tratmans' new home was no longer quite as fashionable as it had been, but was still regarded as a good address, an aspirational place to live especially for people in trade. Fittingly, Mr Tratman was a ships' chandler, supplying stores and equipment to the busy merchant fleet in Bristol's docks. He was an enterprising merchant who could provide a ship with anything from ropes and canvas to Navy rum and the indigestible biscuits so loathed by sailors on long voyages. These biscuits or 'hard tack' were baked twice to keep them hard (the name 'biscuit' comes from the French *bisque*, to bake twice). Experienced sailors would tap their biscuits on the table before eating them to try to dislodge the ever-present weevils.

William and other members of his family traded as Tratman Brothers at 77 Broad Quay in the heart of the city's docks. They are listed in the trade directories as 'ships' chandlers, oil dealers, ironmongers and ship smiths', and had a reputation for using quality products to make their sails. There was also a domestic side to their business. As rope merchants, they would supply the cords for sash windows as well as thick hawsers for the Navy. This range of products illustrates a development that had taken hold among Victorian merchants, traders and shopkeepers — they no longer dealt in only one type of commodity. One striking example of this broadening of interests is William Whiteley, founder of the famous eponymous department store in London's Queensway. He started out as a haberdasher, but very quickly grew to provide a huge range of goods and services. His proud boast was that Whiteley's could provide 'anything from a pin to an elephant'. Naturally, this did not endear him to the ranks of competitors, whose livelihood he was threatening; in November 1876, local butchers burnt his effigy in protest.

Bristol's fortunes had fluctuated greatly over the years. For a long time the city had depended heavily on slavery and the sugar trade associated with it. Slavery itself had been abolished in the British Empire in 1833, and with abolition the sugar business had declined. Another important industry, glass-making, had suffered a similar decline. In less than a

hundred years, the number of factories had fallen from fifteen to four. This was due to the imposition of a glass tax, and also the loss of US markets when the American Revolutionary War broke out. This war also had a detrimental effect on Bristol's tobacco trade. Again, within a hundred years, the weight of imports fell from about 4 million pounds to under 2 million.

However, the tobacco trade was to flourish later in the nineteenth century, and by 1900 the Bristol company of W. D. and H. O. Wills was to become the largest producer of tobacco goods in Britain. Indeed, other trades also improved, such as cocoa importing and processing. Some home industries expanded too, including dairy farming and coal-mining. But overall, from the late eighteenth century to 1850, Bristol was moving away from primary industry; the way ahead was the new manufacturing industries such as engineering, printing.

William Tratman represents the entrepreneurial middle class, which was the great new force in mid-Victorian Britain. In the 1850s he was running a business that was thriving. The harbour and its trade were booming and the railways were expanding, with the connection to London completed by the Great Western Railway in 1841. Bristol could now export coal that had been mined all over the country. Other ports, principally Liverpool, were beginning to take the cream of the trade away from Bristol; nevertheless, it was still a significant trading port and manufacturing centre. In 1848 the Bristol Free Port Association reduced its harbour fees, as a result increasing the volume of traffic.

Isambard Kingdom Brunel's Clifton Suspension Bridge, spanning the Avon Gorge. It was begun in 1836 but not completed until 1864. It re-used chains from his defunct Hungerford Bridge over the River Thames in London.

In the 1870s Avonmouth and Portishead docks were opened to accommodate the volume of tonnage transported to and from the city. The docks handled a variety of local products, including Fry's chocolate, Wills' tobacco and Harvey's wine. Tratman Brothers traded into the twentieth century.

Businesses such as the Tratmans' could stay ahead only if they responded quickly to change and innovation. The Bristol-based engineer Isambard Kingdom Brunel exemplified this flexibility through his technological ambition and entrepreneurial zeal. He started his career in 1824, helping his father, Marc Brunel, build pedestrian tunnels under the Thames. These tunnels were later adapted and still provide passage for the East London tube line. Isambard engineered the Great Western line to Bristol, and in 1864 his world-famous suspension bridge over the Severn Gorge at Clifton was finally completed.

The economic energy, imagination and resourcefulness of the time were celebrated in the Great Exhibition of 1851, held in London's Hyde Park. The project was championed by Prince Albert, who had envisaged a great collection of works of art and industry 'for the purposes of exhibition, of competition and of encouragement'. These works were on a global scale. No fewer than 17,000 exhibitors from all over the world paraded their wares in the specially built Crystal Palace; six million people, nearly a third of the country's population, visited it in one summer. This was at a time when transport around the country, despite the railways, was often slow and tiring. The exhibition was always intended to be self-financing, and in fact made a healthy profit – enough to purchase the land south of Hyde Park, where the Albert Hall, Imperial College, the Science Museum and the Natural History Museum were subsequently built. Henry Cole, the Director of the exhibition (who incidentally is credited with inventing the Christmas card), used the remaining profit to establish the Victoria and Albert Museum.

Thomas Cook from Leicester, who invented the package holiday, ran excursions to the Great Exhibition, exploiting the new mobility the railways gave to the masses. There had always been three classes on the railways, from first to third – soft, upholstered luxury to cold, hard-edged austerity. For the exhibition, special cheap day-return tickets were made available, making it possible for Sunday schools, clubs and entire factory workforces to enjoy a day out. Entrance tickets were cheaper after the exhibition had been open for a while, and discounts were available at weekends. The Tratman family, of course, would have found it a social and business necessity to visit the exhibition, and may have been among the four-and-a-half million admissions on 'Shilling-day' tickets. Women were

The vast interior of Paxton's Crystal Palace was six times the size of St Paul's Cathedral. The design ingeniously incorporated Hyde Park's mature trees.

The first Shilling-day — going in.

Four-and-a-half million people took advantage of the Great Exhibition's 'Shilling-day' tickets which cost the equivalent of £2.66 in 2003.

admitted to the exhibition at a concessionary rate, because it was expected that husbands should escort them. However, contemporary prints show women visiting on their own or in groups, unchaperoned.

The Crystal Palace itself was a stunningly innovative structure, pioneering technological processes that would have been impossible twenty years earlier. Six times the size of St Paul's Cathedral, it had been designed by Joseph Paxton, gardener at Chatsworth's, the Duke of Devonshire's stately home. It was built by the Royal Engineers in just nine months, under the direction of Captain Francis Fowke, who went on to design the Albert Hall. He utilised the prefabricated cast-iron and glass technology that Paxton had introduced at Chatsworth's Palm House. The building was so delicate, transparent and apparently flimsy that Captain Fowke arranged for a battalion of his men to march and roll cannonballs around the galleries to prove its stability. Nothing quite like it had been experienced in the world before: a building that seemed to defy natural laws, a space that blurred the edge between inside and out, enclosed by a seemingly gravity-defying structure.

Some idea of how the huge building looked can be gained today from the iron and glass structures at Kew Gardens, which are roughly contemporary. The Crystal Palace itself was taken apart after the exhibition and re-erected in Sydenham in south-east London; it reopened in 1854, and was destroyed by fire in 1936. The park at Sydenham is still known as Crystal Palace, and reminders of the great building remain, including the life-size dinosaur models that were made for the Exhibition.

Needless to say, when it was first built, the Crystal Palace was not popular with all. The aesthetician John Ruskin, who held a confusing mixture of views on art and architecture, commented, 'We suppose ourselves to have invented a new style of architecture... when we have [simply] magnified a conservatory.' Such carping aside, most visitors were enthralled. Inside, it housed a staggering cornucopia of goods. As the exhibition's own *Art Journal* said: 'On entering the building for the first time, the eye is completely dazzled by the rich variety of hues which burst upon it on every side; and it is not until this partial bewilderment has subsided, that we are in a condition to appreciate as it deserves its real magnificence and the harmonious beauty of effect produced by the artistical arrangement of the glowing and varied hues which blaze along its grand and simple lines…'

There was a fabulous array of the exotic and the familiar, the decorative and the functional, from Britain and all over the world – Africa to America, India to Canada, the West Indies to much of Europe, Persia to Russia. Another quote from the *Art Journal* gives a flavour of what was on show:

> We pass from the United States to Sweden, part of Russia, Denmark, a division of the Zollverein, Russian cloths, hats and carpets, Prussian fabrics, Saxony, and the Austrian sculpture court, another division of France with its splendid frontage of articles of vertu and ornamental furniture, its magnificent court for plate, bronzes and china; its tasteful furniture, and carpets, its jewels, including those of the Queen of Spain; its laces, gloves and rich embroideries; Switzerland, China and Tunis…
>
> In the British half are the silks and shawls, lace and embroideries, jewellery and clocks and watches, behind them military arms and models, chemicals, naval architecture, philosophical instruments, civil engineering, musical instruments, anatomical models, glass chandeliers, china, cutlery, and animal and vegetable manufactures, china and pottery… on the opposite side perfumery, toys, fishing materials, wax flowers, stained glass, British, French, Austrian, Belgian, Prussian, Bavarian and American products…

Part of the thrill was mixing with other visitors of every nationality. People could sit down and have a cup of tea under the huge trees that Paxton had ingeniously contained within the vaulted ceiling of the building, and watch the world go by. All levels of society attended; if the Tratmans were very lucky they may even have caught a glimpse of Queen Victoria who, with her family, was a regular visitor, though often going to the Crystal Palace after public closing time to enjoy the show at leisure and in private. The Queen used the exhibition to educate her children about the world and the Empire. She also basked in the fact that her beloved Albert had made it all possible, and had been rewarded with newfound fame and popularity. (Albert's signed season ticket – Number 1, naturally – can be seen, appropriately, in the Victoria and Albert Museum.) The exhibition more than justified Albert's faith in the project; he aptly described it as 'a new starting point from which all nations would be able to direct their further exertions'.

Returning home from London, the Tratmans would have been inspired to direct their further exertions to redesigning Number 57, incorporating as much of the spirit and detail of the exhibition as possible – or rather Mrs Tratman would, helped by Mary the maid. Interior design and decorating was becoming part of the Victorian woman's role in the household. Frances Power Cobbe, an early feminist writer and campaigner, explained it in *The Final Cause of Woman* in 1869:

> A man can build or buy for himself a House, a Mansion, a Castle, a Palace; but it takes a woman to make a Home… the more womanly a woman is, the more she is sure to throw her personality over her home, and transform it, from a mere eating and sleeping place, or an upholsterer's show-room, into a sort of outermost garment of her soul.

This duty to create comfort was placed above all other natural urges. In Jane Austen's *Pride and Prejudice*, when Charlotte Lucas tells Elizabeth Bennet that the dreaded Mr Collins wishes to marry her, she explains, 'I am not romantic, you know. I never was. I ask only a comfortable home.'

The drawing room, as the heart of the family home, would have a special status. Since Mrs Hobbs' time, the role of the room had changed. From being a showcase for display and entertainment, the room became more of a place for the family to gather, to relax, to talk and play and bond together. There was much emphasis on the necessity of stability in society, and the family was seen as the bedrock. A stable family led to a stable society.

The Victorians filled this family retreat to bursting point with a bewildering variety of colours, patterns, textures and materials. Gone was the controlled elegance of the drawing room in Georgian and Regency periods. The physical layout of internal walls of Number 57 remains unaltered to this day, but Mrs Tratman would have considered a full redecoration *de rigueur*. New money brought new taste. Unlike the cachet afforded to antiques today, the Victorian idea was that keeping old things simply meant you could not afford new ones.

It was a time for drapes and curtains. The covering of piano legs was not Victorian prudery, just another excuse to put up small curtains. It was also a time for highly patterned wall and floor coverings, which could lead to some confusion. The huge floral and leaf patterns were designed in perspective but reproduced in two dimensions, which made it difficult to tell what they were

SELF-IMPROVEMENT AND MUSIC HALLS

In the 1840s, many middle-class people were voicing strong moral disapproval of the working classes' apparent predilection for riotous, licentious, drunken and uncontrolled behaviour. Such groups as the Society for the Suppression of Vice and the Temperance Society warned against the very breakdown of society if controlling factors were not put in place. They called for the introduction of more rational and improving recreational opportunities to replace unsuitable amusements such as public houses and fairs.

This call was answered in part by the Free Libraries Act of 1850 funded by the ratepayer. Initially support was rather thin, with only twenty-four libraries provided in the first twenty years of the Act's inception. Free museums and libraries fared better through acts of individual philanthropy, for example by Andrew Carnegie. Wealthy families, especially rich factory owners, provided public parks and concert halls, and day trips were organised by trade unions, churches, chapels and friendly societies. Also mechanics' institutes flourished, as did literary and philosophical societies.

Working men's clubs were established in the 1860s ostensibly to promote a club atmosphere not found in a public house and in order to inject high ideals of improvement and social harmony into the lives of its members. The first flush of members saw themselves as 'New Greeks', rational and vigorous. However, despite these early ideals, by 1870 the main attractions were the exclusion of women and cheap beer.

The music hall was established with the opening of the Canterbury in London's Lambeth in 1852 by Charles Morton, who for the next fifty years would be known as the 'father of the halls'. He also built, among others, the Empire, the Tivoli and the Alhambra, all in the Leicester Square area of London. The Alhambra could seat 3,500 people; for the sum of sixpence ($2\frac{1}{2}$ pence), an evening could be spent watching the singing and dancing. It was from here that acts such as Vesta Tilley, Dan Leno and Blondin later made their names. The music hall attracted not only the working classes but also those of the middle classes who, although they may have found the 'turns' perhaps a little vulgar for their tastes, could nonetheless enjoy the spectacle from the safety of the expensive seats.

The Tratman's overcrowded
and cluttered drawing
room, packed to the
gunwales with furniture,
fabrics and an ostentatious
array of ornaments.

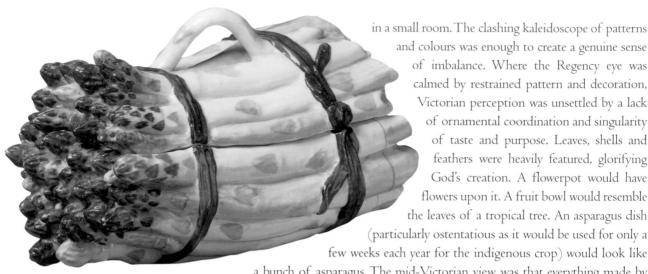

The seldom-used but glaringly obvious asparagus dish was typical of the mid-Victorian desire for ornamentation.

in a small room. The clashing kaleidoscope of patterns and colours was enough to create a genuine sense of imbalance. Where the Regency eye was calmed by restrained pattern and decoration, Victorian perception was unsettled by a lack of ornamental coordination and singularity of taste and purpose. Leaves, shells and feathers were heavily featured, glorifying God's creation. A flowerpot would have flowers upon it. A fruit bowl would resemble the leaves of a tropical tree. An asparagus dish (particularly ostentatious as it would be used for only a few weeks each year for the indigenous crop) would look like a bunch of asparagus. The mid-Victorian view was that everything made by man should aspire to the God-given natural world. This natural realism was also a response to the fact that the lives of city-dwellers were becoming further removed from nature.

Contrary to popular belief, Victorians did not march unfalteringly into their industrial future. In the 1840s, when photography had only just been invented, one of the first things photographers did was to go out into the countryside to try to capture the vanishing land of England. The poet John Clare had written of a rapidly disappearing traditional rural life in *The Shepherd's Calendar*, published in 1827. It is a remarkable poem that showed how a year in the countryside had once moved to more ancient rhythms. The Victorians were well aware of the world they were exchanging for the Age of Steam.

In the 1820s and 1830s steam power was being used in the manufacture of furniture. A steam-powered machine had been invented so that veneers could be cut more thinly, therefore more cheaply, and would adhere to almost any surface. Coiled metal springs were introduced in the 1830s; from the 1840s they were made in huge quantities. These very strong springs could be tied down on to webbing with tough twine and thread so that a rigid frame could be held together in tension. This hi-tech sprung cushion was then covered with a strong, well-woven fabric, achieving amazing curved effects that had never been possible before. Deep buttons held the upholstery in place. A single chair was a marvellous metaphor for the partnership of domestic comfort with restrained engineering.

Mrs Tratman, like all well-trained housewives, would drape a small protective cloth over the back of the expensively upholstered seats to prevent staining from gentlemen's Macassar hair oil (made from ylang-ylang and said to have originally come from the town of Macassar on Celebes in what is now Indonesia). The antimacassar was as redolent of the Victorian interior as the aspidistra, that long-lived but dull green pot plant that resided in many a hall.

This elaborate arrangement of fabrics and furniture would be augmented by a profusion of ornaments, placed on wood surfaces that were covered in layers of shiny lacquer. A small set of shelves called a 'whatnot' was designed to display pieces of Staffordshire pottery, or pressed glass. Pressed glass came about as a result of the

The deep-buttoned chair back used modern engineering techniques to provide the epitome of style and comfort.

mechanisation of glass production, developed in the 1830s. There was no blowing required, and the glass was not 'cut'. Instead, the molten glass was poured into a mould and stamped out, the pressure forcing the glass into all the curves and decorations. Pressed glass could be used for cheap imitation sets of cut glass wineglasses and frivolous ornaments (just as, in John Britton's time, Sheffield plate emulated solid silver).

Among the planters, the transfixed insects on pinboards and stuffed birds (nature in the home again) was the mid-Victorian approach to art: pride of place could well have been given to a statue of *The Greek Slave*. The Tratmans would have been among the many who saw the original statue displayed at the Great Exhibition, where it caused a

Opposite: Number 57's hall with dado, handrail and bannisters all painted in a typical dismal Victorian hue.

sensation. A naked virgin, white as an expression of her purity, represents Christian virtue; she is chained, enslaved by an alien empire, the despicable Ottoman Turks. Sculpted in marble by the American Hiram Powers, it was inspired ultimately by Ancient Greece and was readily reproduced for a modern mass-market. Copies were manufactured in Parian porcelain, a new material introduced during the 1840s. This was a biscuit porcelain that looked like marble. Any life-size or larger sculpture could be modelled in miniature for the home, and to own something like this – under a dome of glass to keep the dust off – would indicate that the Tratmans were in touch with high culture.

Another status symbol for the living room was a gilt-framed overmantel mirror. During the eighteenth century, glass was expensive to manufacture and it was taxed, so mirrors were owned only by the very wealthy. The development of plate glass manufacturing in the 1840s, combined with the repeal of the glass tax in 1845, made mirrors much cheaper. New industrial processes, using new materials and new machines, were transforming domestic interiors. Even humble papier-mâché could take wings with industrialisation. When steam-pressed, the most extraordinary shapes could be made out of moulds, and turned out in great quantities. Papier-mâché was highly versatile: it could be made to look like anything. It could be painted to resemble marble or lacquer work, or gilded, or inlaid with mother-of-pearl. It could be used to make anything from little work boxes, gilded tea trays and painted vases to pieces of furniture. Jennens and Betteridge, a papier-mâché company based in Birmingham, made a cradle and bed to demonstrate their skill.

The home, the family unit, the hearth; all were becoming a refuge in a turbulent world. Mr Tratman would have wanted to escape the bustle of Bristol docks and the sailors' tales of rebellion in Europe, disaster in the Crimea and famine in Ireland, and put his feet up on a footstool embroidered by his dutiful wife or daughter. They would close the curtains to blot out the sights and sounds of the outside world, and light one of the Argand lamps so enjoyed by Mrs Hobbs.

Overall, Mrs Tratman would have assumed the Victorian mantle of 'The Angel of the House', the title of a poem by Coventry Patmore published in 1854, in which the poet waxed lyrical about the perfect Victorian wife. In essence:

> Man must be pleased; but him to please
> Is woman's pleasure…

Endlessly forgiving and patient, always selfless, loving and chaste, the Angel was held up as a paragon to middle-class Victorian women; an aspiration that spread further throughout society because of Queen Victoria's embodiment of domestic bliss. Not all women were lured by the prospect. Florence Nightingale wrote in 1860: 'No man, not even a doctor, ever gives any other definition of what a nurse should be than this – "devoted and obedient". This definition would do just as well for a porter. It might even do for a horse. It would not do for a policeman.' As late as 1931 Virginia Woolf was still moved to write that 'killing the Angel in the House was part of the occupation of a woman writer'.

An early Victorian mantelpiece was incomplete without *The Greek Slave* by American sculptor Hiran Powers, copied from the original displayed at the Great Exhibition.

The 'Angel of the House' fulfilled the Christian calling in the newly discovered pleasures of home education.

Under Mrs Tratman's guidance the children would learn their place in the world – and their duty. She might use educational toys, possibly a Noah's Ark. Any globe or atlas placed Britain at the centre of the world. As for actual lessons, Mrs Tratman would have made her children learn by rote a passage from the Psalms or a natural history book. She would be keen for her son to be educated so he could go into the family business. However, her daughter would be taught to do her sums so she could do the household accounts in the future, and to keep an eye on tradesmen and servants. Similarly Mrs Tratman would practise her needlework and quilting with her daughter, so they could present a harmonious world of virtue when Mr Tratman got home in the evening.

With his flock gathered about him, bathed in the light and warmed by the flickering flames of the essential open fire, he might have read edifying literature to the family. Sir Walter Scott, in his hugely popular medieval novels such as *Ivanhoe*, described a world of chivalry and duty. Charles Dickens on the other hand dealt with contemporary reality in his inimitable way bringing unsavoury truths to the attention of his readers. Whatever the reading matter, it would then be time for the children to go to bed, seeing their way by candlelight. Before getting into bed they would say their prayers under the watchful eye of their mother.

Christianity stood at the centre of the stable Victorian world view. The Victorians masterminded a spectacular boom in church building and restoration, partly funded by people like the Tratmans. There was a huge revival of the Gothic style, which had originally flourished from the twelfth century to the fifteenth, when it was eclipsed by the coming of the Renaissance. Gothic architecture has three defining characteristics: pointed (rather than rounded) arches, flying buttresses (external stone 'props' like ribs that hold up the great medieval cathedrals) and vaulted ceilings like that seen every Christmas on the television broadcast from the chapel of King's College Cambridge. It was during the Renaissance, with its rediscovery of Classical civilisation, that the pejorative term 'Gothic' was coined, to associate that earlier style with the ignorant vandals who overthrew the glory of ancient Rome.

The Gothic revival was popular because once again it represented an idealised medieval past, a time when the rich man was in his castle and the poor man was at the gate. The Gothic style, vigorously promoted by the seminal Victorian architect Augustus Pugin (who with Sir Charles Barry designed the Palace of Westminster), was now considered to be the only truly Christian architectural style. Classical architecture was the pagan style of a pre-Christian Greece and Rome; Gothic was the first and only architecture designed by Christians for Christians. As Pugin wrote: 'In the name of all common

DISSENSION IN THE CHURCH

In 1845, the Anglo-Catholic movement split in two. Some members remained under the High Church wing of Anglicanism, but others – including three of evangelist William Wilberforce's sons – converted to Roman Catholicism.

The Church of England was also challenged by Dissenters from within its own congregations. It felt that its increasing tolerance towards other religions shown in the Emancipation Acts should have made them grateful. In fact it paved the way to constitutional upheaval. By the 1830s the Dissenters – whose strongest voice was Methodist – were a formidable force. They grouped together and rounded on the Church: they did not challenge the Church's ideology, but its legal position as the official religion of England. They wanted the Church to be disestablished from the State (as it was in America), for education to be freed from Anglican control, and most importantly they wanted 'religious equality'.

Although the Dissenters campaigned throughout the nineteenth century for religious reform, the Church of England remained the State religion. The Church argued that it promoted order, and provided the basis for values and laws for an entire society. But it had to change. It undertook a massive building programme, funded by £1.5 million of government money, and established a successful education network. It also commissioned a unique religious census in 1851, chiefly to prove that it was still the church of the majority and therefore entitled to its official position. The results shocked the clergy: fewer than 50 per cent of those who turned out on census Sunday went to Church of England services.

While the middle classes attended church fairly constantly during this period, the five and a quarter million the census had revealed were not attending any form of Sunday service were chiefly working-class city-dwellers. They may have shared common Christian values, but felt the Church did not serve their needs. Only through its Sunday School programme did the Church make any inroads. Methodism had a much greater success rate because its practice was centred chiefly at home, and therefore became an integral part of daily life for its followers.

sense, whilst we profess the creed of Christians, whilst we glory in being Englishmen, let us have an architecture, the arrangement of which will alike remind us of our faith and our country – an architecture whose beauties we may claim as our own, whose symbols have originated in our religions and our customs.'

Of course, the glory of the Gothic style is seen at its best in grand architectural statements, in the new Palace of Westminster and in the great medieval cathedrals, such as Lincoln. But even a relatively humble home like 57 Kingsdown Parade could acknowledge the style in a domestic way. In the Tratmans' bedroom, the main room on the second floor, Mrs Tratman would conduct her toilette at her Gothic-revival dressing table, ornamented with carved tracery inspired by Victorian church interiors. The room would be dominated by the bed itself, big, soft and comfortable. It would probably be a half-tester, which featured a draped headboard and partial 'roof', but not the complete covering afforded by an old four-poster bed. Sometimes the layers of mattresses and covers made a bed so high that steps were needed to climb into it. With the invention of the sprung mattress this mountain was decreasing, but the bedbugs still found places to hide.

Mr Tratman would have used another innovation of the period, the hanging wardrobe, in which clothes could be suspended on coathangers to allow the creases to drop out. Clothes had been previously stored in chests, but the structure of women's dresses now dictated that they be hung up. As gentlemen's suits became more common, a wardrobe was provided for both sexes.

Just as the house as a whole was a haven from the outside world, the Tratmans' bedroom was a sanctuary for the marital relationship. Sex for procreation was considered a fundamental duty, to sustain the Empire and produce another generation of good Christians to maintain it. Clearly, though, there were many marriages with a genuine emotional bond, epitomised by Queen Victoria and Prince Albert. Her diaries reveal her passion for him, which he reciprocated. She adored him, and wrote about seeing him getting up in the morning,

Mrs Tratman's Gothic-revival dressing table is yet another opportunity for flouncey drapery.

A well-furnished Victorian bedchamber would have been unthinkable without the conspicuous convenience of a decorated porcelain chamber pot ostentatiously displayed under the bed.

and seeing him shave. She loved this sense of intimacy. The morning after they got married she describes how he puts her stockings on for her.

While sex could be a pleasure, childbirth was another matter. For most women it was a terrifying and agonising experience, with the ever-present threat of death for both mother and baby. Little was known of hygiene; doctors would often go from the operating theatre or dissecting room straight to delivering a baby without so much as washing their hands. Puerperal fever, a form of blood poisoning contracted in childbirth, was rife, and no respecter of person – rich as well as poor could die. (The renowned Mrs Beeton was one unfortunate victim, dying at only twenty-eight.) Those who could not afford the services of a doctor had to rely on midwives, whose skills were usually as rudimentary as their hygiene and, legend has it, in inverse proportion to their intake of spirits. Matters improved with increasing awareness of hygiene and the introduction of antiseptic. In 1853 Queen Victoria used chloroform during the birth of her eighth child, and popularised the use of anaesthesia.

While the Tratmans could enjoy the comfort and privacy of their well-furnished bedroom, their servant girl Mary had a starkly different kind of haven to retire to at the end of a sixteen-hour working day: a modest garret room on the top floor. Bare boards and painted walls gave little material comfort. This may sound tough to modern sensibilities, but Mary would have appreciated that at least she had a room to herself; plenty of other servants would have to bed down by the fire in the kitchen. Maybe she had a cheap magazine as entertainment, but she would have had little time to read it. She would have been more likely to darn a hole in the heel of her stocking by the light of a strictly rationed candle before sleep defeated her and she nodded off in her chair.

It was Mary's job to keep the entire house shiny and clean. Cleanliness, in all matters domestic, was next to godliness. Every morning, before Mr and Mrs Tratman were even awake, Mary would be hard at work. She would clear out fireplaces using a 'housemaid's box', a tapering wooden receptacle for ashes, and lay a new fire. (Cleaning the flues was a sooty labour saved up for Saturday mornings.) She would carry hot water upstairs for the family's morning wash, and empty the chamber pots. Later, after breakfast, Mrs Tratman would give orders for the day, and the two women would then go about their separate business.

WEDLOCK OR DEADLOCK

Once married, a woman was legally the property of her husband. She had very few rights and was considered legally irresponsible. The husband was the sole owner of the marital home as well as his wife's wealth, whether they were living together or separated, and was liable for any debts his wife might incur. By law, a woman's children belonged to their father; she had no rights over them even on the death of her husband, unless he specifically named her in his will as their guardian.

Divorce was extremely difficult to arrange and only really available to the very rich and the very determined. One method of separation that was open to poorer people, and was still practised in England until about 1887, was that of wife-sales. Thomas Hardy describes this practice in his 1886 novel The Mayor of Casterbridge, set slightly earlier in the century, in which Michael Henchard sells his wife and child to a stranger for five pounds. Although this custom was illegal and considered immoral, it is interesting to note that Hardy portrays Henchard's wife Susan as a more than willing participant in the deal. It was her only way out of a very unhappy situation.

The 1867 Divorce Act benefited men more than it did women. A wife could be divorced for adultery, but for a woman to divorce her husband she had to prove that either an unnatural act such as sodomy or bestiality had occurred, or that bigamy, rape, cruelty or long-term desertion had caused the breakdown of the marriage. Obtaining maintenance and child custody were equally difficult hurdles for a woman.

This Act was a very small step towards later divorce reforms, although it was not without its critics. Outrage was expressed that a government could pursue moral policies that did not derive from Christian dogma. High churchmen such as the Liberal statesman William Gladstone argued that the Act weakened the bond between Church and State since law now diverged from scripture. Nevertheless, this reform enjoyed the support of over half the English bishops, even though the Act was not passed until an amendment was carried allowing clergy to refuse to remarry divorcees in their church, a law that has dominated headlines again in the twenty-first century.

A live-in maid like Mary would have occupied a sparsely furnished attic room. At Number 57 the room still retained the elegantly austere Georgian fireplace.

People like Mary made up the vast majority of society. The struggle to survive predominated. Mary was in no position to refuse all the dirty work imposed on her, because labour was cheap. There was a complex relationship between mistress and servant, each relying on the other. Mrs Tratman would have perceived her lifestyle as privileged and would have tried to put something back to redress the balance between her position and that of people who, through accident of birth, were lower down the social scale.

On top of all her endless cleaning duties, Mary would also cook and get in the shopping. Then there was the laundry. Washing was done by hand, using soap (soda crystals did not come in until the turn of the century). Drying could take days if the weather was wet, and ironing was by flat iron heated on the stove. Perhaps the greatest strain of Mary's job would have come from the fact that whatever she was doing at the time, her other duties were still waiting. The kitchen range needed blackleading, a filthy job requiring the whole thing to be scraped out then repainted with a mixture of turpentine and 'blacklead' (a combination of iron and carbon). Mary might have comforted herself as she scrubbed away with the idea that she might one day put a little bit of money aside, marry and have children of her own. She might see her own family on Sunday if they lived locally. Otherwise she would have scurried about the house on her own, always up against the clock.

On top of everything else, Mary would have to fight floods in the back hall when water poured in under the door from the lane behind the house (at this time it was backed by a track and then fields). With no drains, this was a regular occurrence. De la Beche's survey of Bristol in 1845 found many complaints about the dusty and muddy streets. Backstreets and courts were frequently missed in the thrice-weekly council sweep-up. In De la Beche's report, Evan Roberts of 13 Kingsdown Parade wrote:

> The road at the Back of Kingsdown and St James Parade is almost always floating with water, which sometimes runs into the houses, and when the water dries away it leaves a quantity of filthy mud which in hot weather is very offensive and unhealthy and which is left untouched by the scavengers from year to year, who tell us it is not their work to remove it. We have applied to the commissioners again and again and they say that it ought to be attended to but that they have no money to do it. Many of the residents are proprietors of the houses, some of whom are willing to pay their part towards improving the road, but others are unwilling to cooperate and therefore it remains undone.

The smell – and the risk of cholera – can only be imagined. Epidemics were commonplace; in 1849 Bristol suffered a major outbreak, which killed 444 people. The causes were largely misunderstood. The drawing room was hung with heavy, stifling curtains, seen as protection against disease because it was believed that infection was transmitted through the air in a miasma, a kind of invisible noxious vapour. This was a respectable belief at the time; even Sir Edwin Chadwick the Commissioner of the General Board of Health from 1848 to 1854, subscribed to it.

The sheer power of some of the smells must have made this theory seem true. The Victorians could not see the bacteria, but they could smell what was causing the infection. When the muck was cleared, health improved. They linked this with the disappearance of the smell, rather than the removal of the bacteria. The fundamental problem was the contamination of the water supply. Over in Clifton in 1849 there was a shocking cholera outbreak in Richmond Terrace. Surely these expensive, elegant houses were too clean? In truth, the houses were spotless, but their privies were much like anyone else's, barely improved over a thousand years and leaking into the water supply. A privy was a seat over a pit in the ground. This hole would simply fill up until the smell made it time for the 'nightsoil men' to come and take the accumulated sewage away. Seepage was inevitably continuous. We know from the deeds of Number 57 that there was a well and pump to the 'rear of said premise'. Near the privy…

Sir Edwin Chadwick's Public Health Act of 1848, through a complex system of local regulations and committees, instructed all Bristol householders to get rid of their

Number 57's kitchen has remained in the same room throughout the life of the house. The Victorians inherited the Georgian dresser but were grateful for the newfound cleanliness of an ingenious cast-iron range.

DEVELOPMENTS IN DENTAL HEALTH

Dental surgery began to be regulated in the nineteenth century. The first examinations to assess the competence of those wishing to practise were held in England in 1858. Historically, having the right tools for the job (simply a sturdy pair of pliers) and the ability to swiftly engage them with a jerk and twist to remove the offending tooth was all that was needed. Barbers, blacksmiths, farriers, watchmakers and cobblers had traditionally carried out such operations. Women often worked in this line. No doubt some of these were widows who were carrying on their late husbands' trade.

Tooth decay and disease, with the resulting pain, was not confined to any particular social group. However, those with the ability to pay for treatments were able to have troublesome teeth filled with molten lead or an amalgam of mercury and silver scrapings which, unless very carefully applied could lead to poisoning.

One way of replacing lost teeth was to acquire someone else's. The poor could sell theirs for a little cash, and battlefield casualties of the Napoleonic and American Civil wars were stripped of their teeth for transplanting into the mouths of those who could afford such luxuries. Indeed, these 'second-hand' teeth were preferred to dentures made from bone, ivory, mother of pearl or silver. False teeth were also fashioned from Wedgwood porcelain paste and later from an ingenious combination of vulcanite and celluloid, which, being highly flammable, put smokers at great risk of setting fire to their dentures.

Until the beginning of the nineteenth century toothbrushes were a rare commodity, and those that did exist did so in the form of a small paintbrush. William Addis, a manufacturer of household brushes, felt that a brush would be much more effective if the handle was held sideways. By the middle of the century, today's familiar toothbrush shape was in production, with a smooth tapered handle made from cattle shin-bones and bristles from the necks of cold-climate pigs. Toothpaste during this period was made from soap with chalk added as an abrasive. The Colgate company first began mass-producing toothpaste that smelt and tasted pleasant in 1873.

overflowing privies and replace them with proper water closets. In Bristol the water supply was put in by private contractors. Bristol Waterworks was founded in 1844, but the enterprise soon turned out to be uneconomic. These early water closets were simply using too much water, principally because their cisterns were inefficient and flushed nearly all the time. Also, fastidious users would leave the chain pulled down or the lever pulled up (whichever system operated the flush) to make sure the pan was really clean. To prevent the unnecessary wastage of water, legislation was introduced locally to regulate the system. There is little evidence to suggest Mr and Mrs Tratman would have gone so far as to get fully connected to mains water, so Mary probably swilled the waste matter down the pan with a bucket of well water.

A true pioneer in sanitary matters was Dr William Budd, who researched the water-borne nature of typhoid. He worked with Bristol Waterworks to disinfect drains, sewers, clothing, bedding and corpses, and set up depots where Bristolians could get free disinfectant. When cholera returned in 1854 and 1866, the death rate in Bristol was a fourteenth of that elsewhere. Compared with a rate of twenty-eight per thousand in 1850, the general mortality rate in Bristol was twenty-two per thousand in 1869. In October of that year *The Times* said 'the plain lesson of Bristol' was that other towns should be made to follow her example. Dr Budd had done his work thoroughly.

In the mid 1850s the Tratmans moved up the hill to a better life, even further away from the poor and the noise and dirt of the city. They wanted the villas and semi-detached houses of Redland, about half a mile away to the north. These were aesthetically much closer to the Victorian ideal of generous amounts of both materials and space than the relatively modest Georgian house on Kingsdown Parade.

The next occupant of Number 57 is recorded as a Mr W. Grove, who was a grocer. After several years, he was followed by the three Stansbury sisters, middle-aged spinsters who had recently arrived from Calcutta in India. According to the 1861 census, Harriet was fifty-four and Sophie was fifty-two. Elizabeth, the youngest at forty-seven, was born in Britain, which suggests that their mother had come back to this country for the birth; it was the custom to then go back out again to India. Their father would have had one of the top three professions in India; a military man, tax collector or merchant.

The Stansburys probably seemed rather strange in their own land. There would be something about their dress, which, while being undoubtedly British, showed the influence of their time in India. They would have seen the original paisley patterns in India that were to become one of the great fashionable Victorian styles. Soon, Britain would be exporting paisley back to the land of its birth apparently more cheaply than it could be produced there. (This concept of reversed export was later vilified by Gandhi, who pointed out the insanity of exporting raw cotton from India to Lancashire to be woven in Indian patterns, only to be returned, via an arduous sea passage, to be sold at a profit back to those from whom the raw material had originated. He stressed the importance of home-weaving as a means of breaking the imperial stranglehold on produce.)

Spinsters generally lived a quiet life, and often had little status. Society's ideal was an abundant family: in 1851 there were half-a-million 'redundant' women in Britain, who could not find a husband. There was even a suggestion that these 'excess' women should be sent abroad to populate the Empire but, as the example of the Stansbury sisters returning from India makes clear, there was no guarantee of a husband overseas either. In 1857 the country was profoundly shocked at the bloody excesses of the Indian Mutiny, and this may have been the reason the Stansburys returned to Britain. They could well have found it hard to penetrate polite society, even in a cosmopolitan port like Bristol. An effective way of making friends as well as keeping busy would have been to throw themselves into charitable work. Perhaps they brought back with them

CRINOLINES AND THREE-PIECE SUITS

By the mid nineteenth century, ladies were wearing five horsehair petticoats under their billowing skirts. So in 1856 a single hooped petticoat called the crinoline – after the French for hair, *crin* – was introduced. It was hardly practical and, despite its size, was seen by some as indecent. If the wind caught it, a flash of ankle (or more) could be seen – the fashion for scarlet flannel drawers and striped stockings gave the onlooker more than they bargained for. However, the crinoline passed out of favour in 1868.

The Industrial Revolution transformed clothes. Isaac Meritt Singer invented the first sewing machine scaled for home use and it was in common use in England by the 1860s. Dresses became frothy and frilly, adorned by garish waterfalls of flounced fabric supported by 'rumps'. Women's hair was equally frothy, which led to bonnets being worn forward to allow for big hairstyles behind.

For men, while colours remained sombre, their clothes became much more comfortable, and in the 1860s the prototype three-piece lounge suit was regularly seen. Up to this point, the fabric of a man's waistcoat, coat and trousers had not particularly matched. The jacket's cut changed to include shoulder padding and a longer-waisted style which is still seen today. The suit was worn increasingly with a straight narrow tie, developed from the 1840s 'Byron', named after Lord Byron.

Following the Crimean War, sideburns grew to full whiskers in various styles such as bushy mutton-chops or combed 'Piccadilly weepers'. Smoking for men became popular; women found the smell unbearable, so men would change into quilted smoking jackets and pill-box hats to indulge their habit.

The Bristol Waterworks led the way in providing houses throughout the city with fresh cholera-free water. At Number 57 this came through one tap in the kitchen – over a life-threatening lead-lined sink.

household goods with an Indian flavour, as well as photographic records, which lent them an exotic appeal.

If they were short of money, then the only realistic job for them would have been as a governess, like the heroine of Charlotte Brontë's *Jane Eyre*. It was too early for the other alternatives – working in a shop, teaching or nursing. However, these options were open to the daughter of the next recorded residents of Number 57. In 1868 the Withers family moved in. They had been the landlords of the Stansbury sisters, having bought the property on 24 January 1859 for £437 10s, without needing a mortgage. They were thus Number 57's first owner-occupiers. Charles and Mary Withers were both forty-one; their children were Lucy, aged seventeen, and William, twelve.

By the time of the 1871 census, both father and son were watchmakers, but there is no trade listed in the directory. They probably had their own watchmaking and clockmaking business at 10 St Augustine's Back, a quay on the River Frome, half a mile away. This was behind St Augustine's Parade, which had a long tradition of this type of manufacturing. The company may have survived until the end of the century. Clockmaking was increasingly becoming a matter of clock assembly, with the parts manufactured elsewhere.

Clocks, of course, meant that the whole world could become systematised. In 1841, when Brunel's first train had arrived from London, the time in Bristol was eleven minutes behind the time in the capital. That, of course, was no way to run a railway, so the citizens of Bristol sorted out the anomaly in the 1850s by adopting Greenwich Mean Time – although it took Parliament another thirty years before they made GMT the national standard.

Although the Withers family would have been comparatively poorer than the Tratmans, technical innovations had made domestic goods even more colourful and abundant than during that earlier period. Wallpapers and fabrics had more resilient dyes, so the curtains could be opened and more light allowed in without risk of fading. In 1856 William Perkins was experimenting with coal tar, a mining by-product, and created a purple dye that he called mauve. Instead of purple being the prerogative of the Roman Emperors, anyone could now have anything in mauve and, shortly after that, another derivative, magenta. The Victorians would always use what they could make. Acid yellows, startling blues, spots and stripes – together they must have been a bilious treat for the eye. There could be more drapes, more coverings and more pictures on the wall, all for less money. The Withers family could frame an engraving from the *Illustrated London News*, which was founded in 1842 and had a huge circulation. Naturally, if there was room for another mirror, one would go up. All this lightness and brightness would be further set off by improvements in lighting, with lamps now using paraffin or kerosene to give a cleaner, whiter light.

The Tratmans may have been the first family in Number 57 not to have a live-in servant; they probably had a daily help. It would therefore be sensible for the daughter of the house, Lucy, who was twenty in 1871, to learn all the domestic arts – as a potential 'Angel of the House'. She and her family would now be benefiting from a range of technical innovations that had improved their hygiene and quality of life. In the kitchen they would have had the luxury of being able to turn on a tap and have fresh clean water come out it, now that it was piped throughout the city. Cooking was done on the new closed range, where the hot air from the fire now passed through flues in the brickwork around the ovens and under the hotplate before going up the chimney. This was more efficient than the old fireplace, but required a lot of fiddling around with dampers to control the flues. Glazed pottery kitchenware was now common, along with glassware and enamel items, which were much easier to keep clean.

On the sanitary front, Lucy would have known to wash her hands after going to the water closet – indoors for the first time, on the ground floor – and before preparing food. Her bible would have been *Mrs Beeton's Book of Household Management*. This was written by Isabella Beeton in serial form and then published in 1861 when she was just twenty-five.

The Industrial Revolution not only provided the house with mass-produced decoration but also started the trend towards labour-saving kitchen utensils.

These days we probably think of this volume as a cookery book — indeed, she invented the twenty-minutes-a-pound rule we use for cooking meat today (only possible in her time through the recent invention of the kitchen clock) — but in fact it was a huge compendium that tackled every issue the dutiful homemaker could wish to know: how to deal with servants, how to fix an unruly grate, childcare... Mrs Beeton summed it up:

> As the commander of an army, or the leader of any enterprise, so is it with the mistress of a house. Her spirit will be seen through the whole establishment; and just in proportion as she performs her duties intelligently and thoroughly, so will her domestics follow in her path. Of all these acquirements, which more particularly belong to the feminine character, there are none which take a higher rank, in our estimation, than such as enter into the knowledge of household duties; for on these perpetual depend the happiness, comfort, and well-being of a family.

While Mrs Beeton covered cookery, hygiene, servants and much else, Charles Eastlake's *Hints on Household Taste*, published in 1868, gave sound advice on all elements of interior design. Among his topics he included floor coverings, wallpaper, the design of furniture, hardware, crockery, table service and colour combinations.

FOOD PROCESSING

The process of coating tin with steel had recently been perfected, enabling the first sizeable meat-canning factory to be opened in London by the Admiralty in 1865. Food preserved in this fashion allowed troops and sailors to be fed wherever they were in the world and thus lessened the risk of mutiny because of empty stomachs.

Canning also allowed meat, treacle and other foodstuffs to be imported into Britain from colonies such as Australia, making for a more varied diet.

The invention of margarine provided a cheaper substitute for butter, which during the winter months of low milk yield became an expensive item — so much so that Emperor Louis Napoleon III of France offered a substantial reward for the person who could produce a satisfactory substitute. The prize was claimed by Hippolyte Mège-Mouriès, who had successfully made artificial butter using margaric acid, a fatty acid component that forms in droplets with a pearly sheen; it was duly named 'margarites' from the Greek word for pearl, leading to 'margarine'.

Convenience for the cook during this period also came in the shape of dried yeast, custard powder, concentrated egg power, cans of condensed milk and bottled sauces.

Middle-class householders could probably not afford more than one resident cook, who would have appreciated the time saving brought by such convenience foods.

All classes benefited from the development of the roller-mill process that produced refined white flour without wheatgerm, and thus a softer, more digestible loaf. Until this time the texture of bread had been rather coarse, and its colour could be grey and unappetising. The first of these roller mills was opened in Glasgow in 1871 and within three decades windmills and watermills were mostly redundant.

One major problem during this period was the practice of adulterating food. Legislation was required in 1860, 1872 and 1875 enabling local authorities to inspect and prosecute offenders. In 1875 Eliza Acton, the doyenne of food preparation, commented that British bread had the reputation abroad of being made from less than genuine ingredients. Sand was added to sugar, fine earth added to cocoa powder, chalk to flour, and dust to pepper. Tea continued to be adulterated too, with, among other things, hedgerow leaves such as sloe added. This resulted in the more reputable companies such as Liptons and Brooke Bond only selling tea in sealed bags.

Meanwhile, the drawing room would have seen the introduction of the sewing machine, a very welcome technological advance. The Singer machine made its debut in Britain at the Great Exhibition. Lucy would have bought hers on hire purchase, using it to make her clothes and curtains and drapes. There could be no advertisement more suitable than this to some prospective beau. She could also snare him at the other social machine, the pianoforte. Now more affordable because models could be machine-made around an iron frame, a small cottage upright, ornately decorated, would be perfect for the drawing room. Piano-playing had long been seen as a useful social ritual, particularly for a female showing off her accomplishments and (in a low-cut dress) her body, encouraging a gentleman to turn the music pages for her... altogether a promising stage for romance and courtship.

Lucy would have been an attractive catch. If, however, her beau was a bit slow on the uptake she was nowhere near as socially constrained as previous generations of women. She could get on a bus and go to the city centre to meet friends. (Getting on a train was far more fraught. What if the train pulled out and only she and a young man were in the single compartment? People in these situations literally did not know what to do.) Lucy could legitimately go to art galleries or museums unescorted, or get a job in a shop. She could join choral societies, where she might meet a suitable man. She could have gone to the park or the music hall with her young man, but it would not be long before he would be brought home to meet Mr and Mrs Withers in the drawing room.

In 1871, 30 per cent of women over twenty were still unwed, and Lucy would have no intention of being in that class for long. The Angel would want a house of her own.

There were signs that Lucy's house of the future was likely to differ greatly from her parents' in style. For decades, more and more goods in greater and greater variety had been manufactured and pressed on to a receptive public. Never had there been such an abundance of *things* to decorate your home, embellish it from top to bottom – the Tratman family and the Withers gladly enjoyed the exuberance and technological breakthroughs. Inevitably, though, there were the beginnings of a backlash. People started to ask, 'Do we need it all? Do we need to fill our homes with all these objects?' A shift in thought began to percolate throughout society. A new design philosophy would make its mark on the next phase of Number 57's history.

An occasional table beckoned yet another object for the energetic Victorians to dust.

Chapter Three

LATE VICTORIAN LIFE: *1879–1908*

When the next residents of Number 57 arrived, in 1879, the house had been standing for just over a hundred years — nearly half-way through its recorded history. Throughout late Georgian times, the Regency, and the early and mid-Victorian period, it had seen great changes in Bristol's fortunes, which ebbed and flowed according to the dictates of trade and the ramifications of politics and war. The country as a whole was past its mid-century high point when it could claim to be the leader of the industrial world, but it was still immensely rich, and continued to add colonies to its Empire. However, other countries were expanding their power bases, especially the young and vigorous United States and a revitalised Germany.

By this time, Kingsdown Parade itself had slipped somewhat down the social scale. Two-thirds of the houses were still occupied by single families, like the Alders who had just moved into Number 57, but the other third were now given over to multi-occupancy — only those in straitened circumstances need to subdivide the premises to pay the rent. The better-off, more fashionable households were moving, or had already moved, to a newly developed suburb of Bristol called Cotham. Nevertheless, Kingsdown Parade was still a decent place to live, its inhabitants embodying none of the extremes of wealth and poverty evident in Britain at the time. It is estimated that a third of the nation's population of 30 million lived in poverty, despite mass migration (three million people emigrated to the colonies between 1853 and 1880 to escape destitution). In stark contrast, in 1873, 7,000 individuals owned 80 per cent of the land.

The Alder family was very much of the middle class, which was expanding on the back of advances in commerce and manufacturing, and incorporated a diverse range of

THE POSITION OF CATHOLICS AND JEWS

By 1860, there were 750,000 Irish-born people living in England's cities. While most were Catholic, their faith centred on home worship and pilgrimage rather than Mass, and they had their own customs. English priests had to accommodate these differences and this huge increase in practising Catholics; consequently priests' numbers quadrupled to 3,300 during the second half of the nineteenth century.

Irish Catholic neighbourhoods emerged with their own schools and churches. Being Catholic was patriotic (as was being Methodist to English settlers in America) and, when loyalty to Ireland faded, Catholicism was in place to bind the community together.

With increased tolerance, Mass could be openly celebrated, and pictures of His Holiness the Pope were in every Catholic home and school. The priest, as the Pope's servant, was available around the clock to administer last rites or tend the sick, living humbly and celibately so as to

dedicate himself to his work. This dedication ensured a strong working-class following.

Another influx of immigrants transformed a religion present in England since 1066: Judaism. The Jews had had a perilous time in England — they were expelled in 1290 and readmitted only under Cromwell — but they achieved partial emancipation over a century before the Catholics. By 1880 many were anglicised, living in wealthy suburbs such as St John's Wood in London, with a network of united synagogues and a chief rabbi, a Jewish college and a weekly newspaper (the *Jewish Chronicle*). But in 1881 their numbers tripled, as a million Russian immigrants fleeing persecution poured into London's East End. This poor, Yiddish-speaking workforce was blamed for overcrowding and unemployment, leading to anti-semitism and anti-alien immigration leagues. This was all at a time when Christian missionary work was reaching its peak abroad.

occupations, incomes and lifestyles. Frederick Alder, then in his thirties, lived with his wife Harriet and their children. He is described in the trades directory simply as an 'accountant'. There is no way of knowing whether he was a clerk in a big company or a trained professional, although the latter is a reasonable supposition. The great professions began to be organised and institutionalised at the beginning of the nineteenth century: the Institution of Civil Engineers was established in 1818, the British Medical Association in 1832 and the Royal Institute of British Architects in 1834. Between 1850 and 1880 the number of people in the professions trebled. Accordingly, it is quite probable that Mr Alder, who could afford a perfectly respectable home for his family, was what today we would call a chartered accountant.

By the late eighteenth century the first-floor landing outside the drawing room was more functionally decorated but it still maintained the charming seat beneath the north-facing window that it had had earlier in the century.

While prices generally fluctuated, Mr Alder's salary would probably have remained stable or even increased. When prices fell – between 1875 and 1900 there was a 40 per cent drop, due to the flood of foreign imports from the Empire – the Victorian pound in his pocket would have gone further and he would have felt progressively better off. By 1881, Mr Alder was obviously prospering because, as the census reveals, he now had a live-in servant, Elizabeth Dale, aged twenty-one. By this time, just 50 per cent of households had a live-in servant.

Number 57 had experienced only one major physical change since the days of John Britton: the water closet was now indoors, though still flushed by a bucket of water. Otherwise, the house was organised in the same way as it always had been. The kitchen, hallway and scullery were on the ground floor. The two public rooms, the drawing room and dining room, were on the first floor; above them were the two bedrooms for the family; and on the top floor were the two small garret rooms (one of which was presumably used by Elizabeth Dale). All these rooms, regardless of their style and function, were linked together by the grand staircase that continued to lend dignity and authority to the house.

Like the Tratman and Withers families, the Alders would have wanted to make their home a haven from the challenging, competitive and rapidly industrialising world outside. In perennially middle-class fashion, they would have considered the appropriate interior decoration and furnishings of the home an important indicator of social status. They would have liked to show off their knowledge of contemporary interior design trends, and decorate their home in the latest style.

During this period, the drawing room would have been a feminine space, heavily ornamented with classical decorative styles, an impressive fireplace and densely embroidered furnishings. The dining room, the smaller room, was the most formal room in the house; a hundred years after John Britton's robust and rather austere masculine style, it still retained a certain masculinity, its walls once more coloured green. It was where the Alders entertained their guests and had their family meals. This room was also an ideal setting for what was to rapidly become an integral part of the annual round: the Christmas celebrations.

Late-Victorian Christmas in the dining room at Number 57. The Christmas tree, introduced to Britain by Queen Victoria's German husband Prince Albert, was obligatory in a middle-class home.

The 150 million cards sent over Christmas in 1885 would have adorned mantelpieces across the country.

The new rituals of Christmas were introduced to Britain by Queen Victoria and her German husband Albert. The centrepiece was the decorated Christmas tree, essential for any aspirational family. Industrial innovations meant that lametta, glass balls and tinsel were cheaply available. People also took great pride in the expanding British Empire and there was a popular trend to hang the Union Jack and flags from all nations of the Empire alongside the tinsel. Then there were the Christmas cards. The idea of sending a card to one's friends and loved ones during the festive season had originated with traders giving out cards to customers to wish them a Happy New Year, and soon blossomed into a hugely profitable commercial industry. In 1885 a staggering 150 million cards were sent out.

Year-round, the style of the dining room was still Gothic revival, which had become popular decades earlier and still denoted, ironically, 'Modernism'. By this time, it was treated less seriously and had become a playful decorative vocabulary with which everyone was familiar and could, accordingly, be applied to any aspect of domestic decoration. This second-generation Gothic saw the mass-production of curved and ornamented furniture – chairs, tables, fireplaces, mirrors, overmantels – as well as stained glass, fabric and wallpaper. Gothic wallpaper eschewed the vegetable excesses of mid-Victoriana, in favour of clear, flat and linear patterns. Gothic colours such as courtly rust-reds, greens and blues were used. Pugin's encaustic tiles, carpet and wallpaper for the Palace of Westminster are perfect examples of this. (In April 2000, the Accommodation and Works Committee of the House of Commons was keen to ensure that, although the manufacturers of their favourite wallpaper were relocating, there would be no interruption to the supply of the classic design.)

As we have seen, industrial mass production had made it possible for the average middle-class Victorian household to be stuffed with all manner of decoration and elaboration not just Gothic. But behind all this, there was little, if any, consistent aesthetic approach. Cynical industrialists could make fortunes, with new machinery turning out more and more goods that were often shoddy and without any real style or taste. Voices were raised throughout society questioning the wisdom of this apparently unbridled materialism. Linked to this was a profound unease at rampant, intensive industrialisation, which was despoiling the countryside and making traditional skills and crafts redundant. A new design movement, the most significant of the late nineteenth century, began to emerge, inspired by the

Pugin's elaborate Gothic-revival interior of the Palace of Westminster. It remains a contradictory backdrop for contemporary democracy.

CROSS-CULTURE INFECTION

Industrialisation both raised and depressed living standards, depending on one's position in society. The better-off sections of the population could enjoy the fruits of mechanised ingenuity, while being able to distance themselves from the filth and pollution engendered by such processes. Certainly it was a fact that industrial towns were breeding-grounds for the diseases of poverty, dirt and overcrowding, and working people bore the brunt.

However, the middle and upper classes were equally vulnerable to the dangers of infectious diseases. While there was mass immunisation against smallpox, the old enemies of diphtheria, polio, scarlet fever, measles and chickenpox still stalked the land, and recognised no class boundaries. Prince Albert himself had succumbed to typhoid in 1861, probably a victim of the insanitary conditions of the cesspools of Windsor Castle.

One of the most feared afflictions though, that affected all levels of society, was tuberculosis, also known as 'consumption' because sufferers appeared to be quite literally consumed, losing weight as the illness progressed. Tuberculosis was characterised by fever, night sweats and the coughing up of blood. It was the century's worst killer and there was simply no cure available, although fresh air and a healthy diet were recommended – more accessible of course to wealthier people. However, only the very rich could take advantage of the newly opened sanatoria on the Continent.

The designer and socialist William Morris (1834–1896).

natural world and seeing beauty in handmade products. It cleared the fog of design chaos and uncertainty and paved the way for the birth of twentieth-century Modernism. At its core was the designer and devout socialist William Morris.

Morris was born in Walthamstow in 1834, the son of doting parents who bought him a pony on which he pretended he was a knight in shining armour – a common fantasy of a century in love with the Middle Ages (or rather, a rose-tinted view of those distant mythical times of romance and chivalry). When he encountered the works of Pugin, Morris read them with enthusiasm. He followed two of the ideas contained in Pugin's *The True Principles of Pointed or Christian Architecture* (1841) all his life. 'The two great rules for design are these,' Pugin wrote. 'First, that there should be no features about a building which are not necessary for convenience, construction or propriety; second, that all ornament should consist of the essential construction of the building.' Morris's interpretation was that the mass production of the Industrial Revolution had soured, almost beyond redemption, the essential aesthetic purity of all design. He focused tightly on the singular integrity of genuine medieval craftsmanship, admiring the old craft guilds and their use of natural and indigenous materials.

Morris formed his own company – Morris, Marshall, Faulkner & Co. – in 1861. He worked alongside a group of architects, craftsmen and designers including the painters Dante Gabriel Rossetti and Edward Burne-Jones (who had been a college friend of Morris) and the architect Philip Webb. They advertised themselves as 'Fine Art Workmen in Painting, Carving, Furniture and the Metals'. The company produced murals, wood-carvings, stained-glass windows, metalwork, furniture and embroideries with the artisan-craftsman conceiving, designing and actually making his own work from conception to completion. In 1883 a number of leading Arts and Crafts designers, artists, architects and craftsmen were brought together as equals in the Art Workers' Guild.

Morris & Co. (the name of the company from 1875) eschewed imported timber such as mahogany; they preferred oak, ash and elm. Their furniture was built by hand, showing the way in which it was made, demonstrating its integrity. There were to be no nails, screws or glue, just mortise and tenon joints, dowels, wedges, broad exposed hinges, everything to show the eventual owner the means and method of construction. Often the seat backs, for example, would be pierced with a simple motif to show that the object was made of solid wood rather than surfaced with a veneer.

Morris coined the aphorism, 'Have nothing in your house that you do not know to be useful, or believe to be beautiful.' It was the kernel of his view of the world, as he took a stand against accelerating industrialisation and dehumanisation. Was it all to end, he asked, 'in a counting house on the top of a cinder heap, with the pleasure of the eyes having gone from the world'? But in the long term his approach proved to be inconsistent with his socialist principles and yearning for rustic brotherhood and fellowship. In his day, just as in ours, people did not care where anything came from as long as it looked right. The Victorians wanted their cheap cottons and plush upholstery, just as today many people want their designer trainers, caring little that their manufacture had been possible only with slave labour and energy-intensive mechanical processes.

An Arts and Crafts chair was simple, handmade and medieval in style. Here lay the irony at the heart of all Morris's work. Such an item, representing the dignity of simple labour, could never make its way into the hands of simple labourers themselves. Instead, his pieces only reached the elite and moneyed upper classes, because the materials and the whole artisan process was so extraordinarily expensive.

The style, over time, filtered down to the less well-off. Some of Morris's acolytes were to make the items cheaper, and thus more accessible, over the years. While Morris was alive, however, his company stuck to their principles and produced, for example, block-printed wallpapers. One of his most famous designs was the 'Willow Bough' pattern, with the foliage apparently growing diagonally from the bottom of the wall to the top. It expressed living nature, in its linear and two-dimensional simplicity. Morris's imitators used machines, and artistic subtleties were, of course, lost; furthermore, the rich hues derived from Morris's natural dyes could not be reproduced by chemicals.

However, there was plenty of cunning deployed to make the imitation look as much as possible like the real thing. Competitors designed a way of minutely pitting the surface of a machine-made metal object to make it look as it had been beaten by hand (just as today some items are artificially aged in the manufacturing process). It was probably these copies that a family like the Alders would have been able to afford.

In fact, as long as the Alders were willing (like nearly all Victorians) to compromise, they could easily dress their house in an Arts and Crafts style. Morris would have favoured neat plain floorboards following his principle of showing, not disguising, simple things performing their function. However, as long as the noble boards could be seen around the edge of the room, a rug in the middle was completely in order. Number 57's old pine floorboards may have looked a little ignoble and shabby, but the Arts and Crafts look could be faked by covering these with a parquet-effect linoleum. The Alders could have completed the effect by laying an Axminster carpet in the centre of the room rather than an expensive hand-knotted Morris original.

The refreshingly simple 'Willow Bough' pattern by William Morris is still available on fabric and wallpaper today.

(Linoleum, made from hessian, cork-dust and linseed oil, had been invented in England in 1863 by Frederick Walton, but a Scottish flooring manufacturer called Michael Nairn perfected the art of patterning the material. 'Kirkcaldy floorcloth' was laid on Tsar Alexander II of Russia's yacht in 1880.)

The principles of Arts and Crafts simplicity could have been applied to great effect in one of Number 57's rooms that now had a novel use. In the later Victorian middle-class household, the new cult of the child ('baby worship', Queen Victoria called it) was beginning to dominate. For centuries, children had been treated rather like mini-adults from the age of about three. Now, the idea that children should be given a distinct space became widely accepted, and was part of a new wave of thinking that individuality should be cultivated and respected. Children deserved a room – a nursery – all of their own. In Number 57, this was adapted from what had been the main bedroom on the second floor. When the Tratmans lived in Number 57 in the 1840s, the room was typical of the early Victorian era – cluttered, with heavy, elaborate furnishings, and decorated with rich, vibrant, strong colours. But it was now transformed to make a modern nursery, designed according to all the most up-to-date notions of health, hygiene and education.

Now that the Victorians had begun to learn about the true nature of infection and transmission of disease, there was a new enthusiasm for hygiene in the home. Developing technologies had transformed the metalwork industry, and for the first time new metal beds were being made of tubular iron that were light and easy to move. They were seen as more hygienic than traditional wooden beds, being easy to wipe down and clean. They would also have had light, sprung mattresses rather than old stuffed ones that harboured bedbugs and germs.

Other items of furniture would be plain and simple, again easy to keep free of dust and dirt. On the floor, there was more wipe-clean linoleum. Flat glazed tiles were used for fire-surrounds and splashbacks, and were readily cleaned with a damp cloth. Moreover, they were more than just utilitarian. They could be decorated with

The Alders' nursery at Number 57. For the first time children became the objects of consumerism, owning a host of educational toys. The new tubular iron metal bed with light sprung mattress was easy to clean and so considered more hygienic.

'Nursery Rhymes' by Walter Crane. Even nursery decorations like these could include educational messages.

motifs and stories that would both educate and entertain. A number of small tiles could make up a single strong narrative using bold colours and naïve, simple images: the perfect aesthetically pleasing and educational interior design for the nursery. There was quite a vogue for these from the 1870s that continues in the decorative borders still popular in the twenty-first century.

Similar designs could also feature on wallpaper. Previously this had been a hidden curse in the home, unhygienic and even dangerous. As far back as 1839, Pye Henry Chavasse had warned in *Advice to a Mother* that 'four children in one family have just lost their lives due to sucking green paper-hangings', the green colour having been derived from a mixture of arsenic and copper. Now the new washable and non-toxic sanitary wallpaper had a protective layer that provided a barrier against germs lurking in the old plasterwork. Like nursery tiles, it too could provide an aesthetically pleasing surface – either painted in clear, light colours, surmounted perhaps by a simple colourful frieze, or with an intrinsic design to appeal to children. It could show animals, or boats, or even illustrations from a familiar story book. The eminent artist Walter Crane, who was President of the Arts and Crafts Exhibition Society, also designed themed wallpapers, with 'Nursery Rhymes', 'The House that Jack Built' and 'Sleeping Beauty' for Jeffrey & Co. among his works.

The nursery was the ideal setting for another idea that had gained currency in this period: home education for children. New techniques in colour printing and paper manufacture meant that children's books were cheaper and more readily available. The well-read household could amass a varied library of educational material for its children – and books for entertainment too. Adding to the fun, for the first time toys became big business. As well as its more sober achievements, the Industrial Revolution led to a commercial boom in toy manufacturing not only in Britain but also, and particularly, in Germany. A large number of the toys found in the Alders' second-floor nursery would have been imported and many were cheap, ephemeral items such as automatons, dolls and tin soldiers – the precursor of most of what is still found in a child's room today.

Mrs Alder would have used all these goods at her disposal to amuse and educate her young children. She was seen as the heart of the home; just as the cult of the child had grown, so had the cult of motherhood, with Victoria herself seen as the prime example of domestic devotion and duty. Mrs Alder would stay at home attending to all the needs of her family, while Mr Alder went out to work to earn the money. He must have continued to prosper, because in 1886 the family moved from Kingsdown Parade to a more fashionable Bristol address in Tyndalls Park.

Number 57 was then occupied over the next nine years by a number of families: the Dyers, the Arscotts and the Amorys. Sadly, history does not leave any trace of them except their names. Meanwhile, the 1890s saw a surge in the building of new suburban houses. These were adorned with fashionable, mass-produced decorative details: brickwork, stone, stucco, stained glass and roof tiles. Old Georgian terraces like Kingsdown Parade, however, were still seen as desirable; they could be adapted to incorporate modern ideas of comfort and hygiene. Number 57 obviously appealed to the next long-term resident, Mrs Annie Edwards, who arrived in 1896.

Mrs Edwards was a widow of forty-two. There is no record of Mr Edwards. A man's life expectancy at the time was about forty to forty-four (four years less than a woman's), so there is every chance Mrs Edwards had moved into Number 57 upon her husband's death. Possibly she found herself short of money, and had to move out of better accommodation. She certainly could not afford a live-in servant, and probably employed a daily cook to help her in the kitchen.

Mrs Edwards worked as a 'professor of music', a courtesy title meaning that she was a music teacher. She would give private lessons in her house to students who wanted to learn the piano, or perhaps the violin, which had recently become all the rage for young women. (In late-Victorian society, it would be deemed more appropriate for a girl to learn musical skills from one of

New colour-printing techniques meant that books specifically for children became cheaper and more readily available.

her own sex rather than be in close proximity with a man.) So where once an elegant harp graced Mrs Hobbs's Regency drawing room, Mrs Edwards was using her musical expertise to make her living and maintain her independence.

Mrs Edwards' two sons were living with her: Henry, a wholesale stationer's clerk aged twenty-three, and Thomas, a newspaper clerk aged twenty. Both would have brought money into the family. (To be a clerk was to be a member of one of the defining Victorian professions. In 1861 there had been only 92,000 clerks, nearly all men. By 1896 they numbered 370,000 men and 19,000 women.) Mrs Edwards' daughter Ethel, aged fifteen, completed the family.

Mrs Edwards was not rich, even with two extra incomes coming into the house. Had she had enough to get by, she would not have taken in a lodger, because this would have given the neighbours a painful insight into her financial affairs. As Jerome K. Jerome put it in *Idle Thoughts of an Idle Fellow* in 1886: 'Being poor is a mere trifle. It is being known to be poor that is the sting.' If she wanted to have a few luxuries, however, she would have to swallow her pride. The lodger's name was Jasper Bussell, a thirty-year-old accountant of customs. He would have become an integral part of the family.

There were naturally changes to the ways in which the Alders had used the rooms in Number 57. The nursery of course would be redundant, reverting once more to the main bedroom, used by Mrs Edwards. This was simply decorated and furnished with a bed, dressing table and washing area. The attic rooms were no longer set aside for servant accommodation, and provided separate private bedrooms for the grown-up children and the lodger. Without a live-in servant, the house became a more informal space for all the family to enjoy together. The drawing room on the first floor lost its earlier formality, and became a space that everybody could gather in to relax and enjoy as a family.

MUSIC TO THE EARS

Music and music-making in Britain have hardly ever been comparable to that on the Continent, although during the late nineteenth century there was enough on offer to satisfy most tastes. Many middle-class homes had a piano, and sheet music was relatively cheap; belonging to a choir was a popular pastime. The cult of the brass band started during this period and largely thanks to bands formed by miners and factory workers, such as those employed by Wills cigarette manufacturers in Bristol, who not only gave regular concerts but also played as their colleagues boarded the train for the annual outing.

Opera, once the reserve of the aristocracy, was becoming popular among the middle-classes. The only opera house in Britain during this period was the Royal Opera House, in London's Covent Garden. Increasingly seats were being purchased by the upper-middle class, rather than aristocrats who frequented the House only during the London season.

Gilbert and Sullivan's light operas were popular, due to their combination of rhythm, easy-going harmony, sense of fun and very topical librettos. During a period of just twenty years, Gilbert and Sullivan had a staggering ten major 'hits', from *The Pirates of Penzance* in 1880 to *The Grand Duke* in 1896. Sir Arthur Sullivan also wrote music for 'grand' opera such as *Ivanhoe*, first performed in 1891, which enjoyed a run of 160 nights.

Sullivan's work was considered to be typically English in its concept, as was another favourite composer of the period, Edward Elgar. Elgar composed his very popular *Enigma Variations*, a musical picture of his friends, between 1889 and 1899. This brought him success not only at home but also abroad.

It was this room where the influence of the Arts and Crafts movement was most keenly felt. The walls were divided horizontally into three, in true Arts and Crafts style. The wall beneath the dado rail was painted a green; above the dado was William Morris wallpaper and then, beneath the ceiling, a stencilled frieze. The hearth was still very much the focal point of the room, although the fireplace was no longer made of marble but was carved out of wood in line with Arts and Crafts thinking. Blue-and-white tiles would form the surround, a popular Arts and Crafts touch (though now mass-produced and within Mrs Edwards' price range). An essential element of the Arts and Crafts design philosophy was to bring the feeling of nature into the home and Morris's wallpaper and furniture drew its ornamental inspiration from simplified interpretation of natural forms. Mrs Edwards would have loved to fill her drawing room with flowers and pictures inspired by the natural world.

However, unlike the ideal Arts and Crafts drawing room that would be uncluttered and simple, containing only those things that were either 'useful' or 'beautiful', Annie Edwards would no doubt have maintained the Victorian tradition of displaying as many objects as possible. There was certainly no diminution in the

As the nineteenth century became the twentieth, the Victorian drawing room maintained its clutter but also acknowledged the Arts and Crafts movement.

Mrs Edwards' drawing room lacked the consistency and stylistic commitment of earlier periods – a sign of changing times as Queen Victoria's reign neared its end.

A PENNY NEWSPAPER FOR ONE HALFPENNY.

Daily Mail.

THE BUSY MAN'S DAILY JOURNAL.

NO. I.   [REGISTERED AS A NEWSPAPER.]   LONDON, MONDAY, MAY 4, 1896.   [BEYOND 50 MILES FROM LONDON ONE PENNY: MAY BE CHARGED FOR THIS PAPER]   ONE HALFPENNY.

BUSINESS NOTICES.

The Offices of the "Daily Mail" are "DAILY MAIL" BUILDINGS, CARMELITE-STREET, LONDON, E.C.

BIRTHS.

MARRIAGES.

DEATHS.

PERSONAL.

TRACKED BY A TATTOO.

THE WAR IN EGYPT.

HOTEL CECIL.

CHATTO AND WINDUS'S NEW NOVELS.

THE ILLUSTRATED CARPENTER AND BUILDER
THE WEEKLY PAPER for ALL THE BUILDING INDUSTRIES. 1D.

SWAN SONNENSCHEIN & CO.

HISTORY OF THE PARIS COMMUNE

ALLOTMENTS AND SMALL HOLDINGS

WILLY BURMESTER'S VIOLIN RECITAL.

MLLE. CLOTILDE KLEEBERG'S EVENING CONCERT. ST. JAMES'S HALL.

HERR FRITZ MASKAEN'S

MISS MURIEL ELLIOT'S PIANOFORTE RECITAL.

BOW BELLS. THE BEST FAMILY MAGAZINE. 1D.

REYNOLDS'S NEWSPAPER. THE LARGEST, CHEAPEST, AND BEST.

GORDON TANNER'S VIOLIN RECITAL. ST. JAMES'S HALL.

MADAME GRIMALDI

RICHTER CONCERTS, ST. JAMES'S HALL.

EMIL SAUER FIRST RECITAL.

THE CYCLE MANUFACTURERS' TUBE COMPANY, LIMITED.

mass of consumables being produced. An ever-increasing selection of products were available from far-flung corners of the globe. Britain had become without doubt a stylistically diverse country.

Mrs Edwards would have been inundated with a unprecedented degree of choice in furnishings for her home. Hundreds of magazines and newspapers were launched with the aim, among others, to guide consumers through this ever-increasing choice. The *Daily Mail* was founded in 1896, the first newspaper aimed specifically at women – despite Lord Salisbury's cutting comment that it was written 'by office boys for office boys'. It was such a success that within a few weeks of its launch it was selling 200,000 copies a day, and remained the aspirational newspaper for the middle classes – the voice of middle England.

Art in the Home and *Woman's World* were among the new magazines that gave ladies advice on how best to decorate their homes. They also aimed to educate and open up an artistic way of thinking to a wider group of people. For the first time good taste and artistic judgement were no longer the preserve of the experts and the aristocracy. Morris's approach to design and manufacture stemmed from his philosophy about a balanced and equitable society. For him, art of quality, in all its manifestations from furniture to pure art, should be available to all.

The Pre-Raphaelites embodied the ideals of the Arts and Crafts movement in fine art. 'Pre-Raphaelite' is a nebulous term that supposes that the artists were reaching back to the time before the painter Raphael, as if the latter had single-handedly perverted the course of art away from the 'honesty' of the early Renaissance. However, as a phrase, 'Pre-Raphaelite' is rather lacking in substantive meaning.

The group advocated realism: freshly observed nature transferred to the canvas. Their pictures were dominated by dewy-eyed responses to medieval themes, prime examples being *The Light of the World* by William Holman Hunt and the works of Morris's business colleagues Edward Burne-Jones and Dante Gabriel Rossetti. The two movements shared members and ideas with each other. If an Arts and Crafts designer had wanted a picture on the wall, it would have been a Pre-Raphaelite one.

In stark contrast to Arts and Crafts values and egalitarianism was the decadent and elitist Aesthetic Movement, which proclaimed and even lived the philosophy: 'Art for Art's Sake'. It had avowedly different aspirations from Arts and Crafts medievalism and pious functionality, but is more properly termed a style than a movement because it had no social purpose or moral underpinning. Indeed, it was quite the opposite. Leading lights of Aestheticism – such as the artists Aubrey

Opposite: The first edition of the *Daily Mail* on 4 May 1896 shows the preoccupations of the English middle classes of the time.

Below: Aubrey Beardsley's illustration for Oscar Wilde's play Salome epitomised the sensuous and erotic aspirations of the Aesthetic Movement.

Not an Arab prince's palace but Lord Leighton's entrance hall in London's Holland Park.

Beardsley and Lord Frederic Leighton and the poet and dramatist Oscar Wilde — were practising a liberating cult dedicated to pure beauty. Beardsley's semi-pornographic illustrations for Wilde's play *Salome* in 1894 showed how unconnected Beardsley's art was to the real world. The black-and-white pictures contrast sensual and shocking images with an artistic approach that draws on the curvilinear forms of Art Nouveau, but is, in other ways, utterly non-derivative.

Lord Leighton lived at 12 Holland Park Road in London, a house that had been designed for him by George Aitchison, an expert in interior design, who was Professor of Architecture at the Royal Academy when Leighton was its President. It was a vehicle for Leighton to live out an extreme life of artistic decadence and luxury: Aestheticism in three dimensions. As the foremost portrait painter of his age, Leighton was a wealthy man and used his wealth to create a luxurious sensual home for himself. The interior was ruthlessly eclectic, with no attempt at homogeneity; to the Aesthetics, beauty was supreme. There was an Arab hall focused around a shallow interior pool reminiscent of the Alhambra Palace. The walls were covered in genuine antique Arab tiles from Syria which Leighton himself bought on his travels and had transported to London at great cost. However, in an adjoining part of the hall, the centrepiece was a statue of Narcissus, the Greek mythological youth who, appropriately for the Aesthetics, fell in love with his own reflection; here he was reflected in a golden 'pool' on the ceiling.

Leighton led a life of such dedication to Aestheticism, in behaviour, dress and every aspect of his life that his large house had only one bedroom. He did not wish to encourage guests to stay; the right sort of Aesthete was more than welcome at his dinner parties and soirées but an overnight visitor would interfere with the delicate balance of his beautiful life.

Alongside the Arab influence and the Classical statue of Narcissus, Leighton and a wider group of discerning interior decorators were embracing the Orient and in particular Japan. Japan had deliberately isolated itself against foreign influence up until the middle of the nineteenth century. In 1853 the Americans more or less forced Japan to trade with the West, fearing that such a rich market might go unplundered. The items that began to flow out of Japan showed that the centuries of isolation had meant that the country's craftsmen had remained pure to their design principles. Japan's art had remained medieval, in a Japanese sense — it was still made using the same techniques by the same sort of artisans. Japanese items were geometric, light, simple and unobtrusive. There could be no greater contrast to the leaden early Victoriana, and they were received rapturously, especially by the Aesthete.

The American painter James McNeill Whistler, best known for his *Portrait of the Artist's Mother*, lived in London and painted exquisite landscapes and riverscapes that were highly influenced by Japanese prints. Edward Godwin, architect turned Aesthete designer, was another enthusiast. Originally from Bristol, Godwin had designed the Town Hall in Northampton, which has been described as an 'Anglo-Franco-Italian Gothic Revival essay'. No wonder he was receptive to yet another style. He delighted in Japanese design's strong feeling for nature and was so enamoured of it that he decorated the interior of his house in Bristol in the Japanese austere style. The interior was painted yellow, cream and grey, and Godwin's collection of blue-and-white Japanese vases was displayed on straw matting. Even today, such a rigorous devotion to a single design idea would be thought bold, innovative and possibly obsessional. How his neighbours reacted is sadly not recorded. All this was a decade before Godwin designed a Japanese-influenced interior in 1877 in the house of a shipping magnate, conceived with the whole purpose, of being the perfect place to display the owner's collection of blue-and-white porcelain.

Godwin's furniture designs were similarly serene and sharply fashionable. His British take on a Japanese sideboard was described in his own words as 'a grouping of solid wood and void'. Oscar Wilde sang the praises of some furniture Godwin designed for him: 'each chair is a sonnet in ivory: the table is a masterpiece in pearl.' If Mrs Edwards had been asked to name a material she associated with Japan and Aestheticism, she would undoubtedly have picked bamboo. Godwin designed items that were put together in Britain but made of bamboo grown in the Far East. There was something rather flimsy, impermanent and un-British — or at least un-Victorian — about bamboo, which made it the perfect material to set Aesthetic design apart from the rest.

Godwin also stained his furniture black so that it would resemble Japanese lacquerwork. The deception meant that his 'ebonised' items would therefore be within Mrs Edwards's price range. Such goods were

WOOL AND WAISTS

Oscar Wilde once wrote, 'In matters of grave importance, style, not sincerity, is the vital thing.' His style as a leading Aesthete – clean-shaven with long hair, in silk knee-breeches and a loose-fitting velvet jacket – was as much a part of him as his rapier wit. London's department store Liberty's opened in 1875, and became the chief fashion source for the Aesthetic Movement.

Wool as a clothing material was increasingly popular, particularly in intellectual circles. Dr Jaeger, a Stuttgart zoologist, claimed that 'cool' wool should be worn from the skin outwards. The distinguished playwright George Bernard Shaw agreed; from the 1880s, when he bought his first wool suit from Jaeger, he never wore any other material, an obsession described at the time as 'eccentric healthy-mindedness'.

In 1880 the bustle reappeared as the new look for women as dictated by Paris. It took a few years for English ladies to fully accept it; English actesses such as Lillie Langtry led the way – in 1881, the year of her stage debut, she brought seventeen trunks of the latest Paris fashions back to London. But increasingly the frivolous tiers of lace and ribbons disappeared and by 1890 the trendsetters finally listened to the reformers and Aesthetes and dropped the bustle in favour of floor-length A-line skirts and blouses. This change came from across the Atlantic, where Charles Dana Gibson's illustrations depicted the sporty-looking 'Gibson Girl'.

The thirty years leading up to the twentieth century saw a phenomenal rise in sporting activity. Male sporting garments, including the scarlet blazer, were acceptable day wear, with less formal hats such as the bowler gradually replacing the 'topper'. In the 1890s, when cycling was the latest craze, women finally took to wearing 'Bloomers', first introduced in the 1850s by American reformer Amelia Bloomer and which led to music hall wags talking about women now 'wearing the trousers'.

Women still wore corsets but in 1900 their shape significantly changed. The new flat-fronted corsets gave the body an S-bend shape. Padded hair, plumed hats, slimline dresses and high-heels emphasised height, but the corset gave them a fashionable Art Nouveau curve.

For Mrs Edwards Japanese prints framed in mock bamboo – available from the newly built Liberty's store in London – were a token Aesthetic gesture.

available in Arthur Lazenby Liberty's famous half-timbered store in London's Regent Street, which opened at the height of Japanese mania in 1875. He created a retail atmosphere which, given that it was open to the public was, nevertheless, a quasi-Aesthetic environment – as, to a certain extent, it remains today. In 1887, *Woman's World* wrote that there was hardly a drawing room in the land that did not have a Japanese item in it.

Someone like Mrs Edwards would have happily mixed Arts and Crafts, Aestheticism and Gothic in one room, as there was a great desire to display the new trends, but little contemporary understanding of the thinking behind each design movement.

Mrs Edwards would have been the first occupant of Number 57 who would have felt that she could do a little of her own home decorating. Previously, being caught holding a paint brush only telegraphed to the neighbours that one could not afford sufficient servants. The crucial difference was that undertaking design work in the home was now fashionable. Mrs Edwards could add her own finishing touches to her sitting room; following the Aesthetes by stencilling a sunflower or peacock feather motif on to the frieze, or dyeing some muslin curtains a forceful yellow. Some projects were more substantial. *Amateur Work Illustrated* was published from 1881 to 1891 and included handy hints on constructing a sundial, pigeon house, violin and even a do-it-yourself piano.

Away from these more artistic realms, the kitchen at Number 57 had experienced little physical change throughout the nineteenth century. Originally situated on the ground floor to allow for easy delivery of coal and fresh foods, its primary design feature had always been function over form. In Georgian times, the owner of the house would rarely have entered the room. Throughout the Victorian period, the lady of the house or her daughter would have entered the kitchen only to confect a Mrs Beeton recipe on the cast-iron range or to access the fresh piped water. Nevertheless, the kitchen was still a place dominated by servants. By 1900, not only had technology moved on but so had thinking about what was acceptable in the home, and Mrs Edwards would have been the first occupant of Number 57 to spend significant time in the kitchen.

The increasing awareness of hygiene naturally spread to the kitchen. Light-coloured walls meant that dirt could show up and be removed. This continued interest in cleanliness also started a trend for plain kitchen tiles that could easily be wiped. New developments in the production of ceramics meant that Mrs Edwards would have replaced the lead-lined sink with a ceramic one. In terms of design, the kitchen

was many years away from neat rows of matching units, so food preparation would have been carried out on a large wooden table as it had been for over a hundred years. Mrs Edwards also still kept the dresser that had been in Number 57 since the house was first built.

One enormous difference in the kitchen was the new gas cooker. It was no longer necessary for underpaid and overworked servants to carry fuel, light kitchen fires, remove ash and fight a losing battle against grime. Alongside the novelty of the gas cooker came the ice chest, where butter, meat and eggs could be kept cool. Instead of having to

A sign of things to come. Alongside items influenced by the Arts and Crafts and Aesthetic Movements, Number 57's mantelpiece also boasts an Art Nouveau vase.

By the end of the nineteenth century Number 57 still just had a single tap. However, the lead-lined sink has now been replaced with a ceramic one.

purchase fresh meats on a daily basis from the hawkers on Kingsdown Parade or in the markets of Bristol, Annie Edwards would buy ice brought into Bristol Docks from Canada and put it into the top of the chest to keep meat cool for a few days.

The canning of food had been around for some time, but mostly only as supplies for daring young Victorians on expeditions to inhospitable places. Now more and more canned goods were seen in the kitchen, promising exotic, cheap and easy meals. There was salmon all the way from America, ox-tongue, lobster, and even a complete rabbit in a can. The producers advertised these canned products as 'fresh', which was a little cavalier with meaning, but as some of these items would never otherwise have made it to the British dining table, the consumers were hardly going to quibble. Seasonal foods were now available all year round, a fundamental change to the national diet. Food could even be stored in the cupboard in case there were unexpected guests, an hitherto undreamed-of convenience. There were accessories to main foods, too – relishes had long been popular. No doubt Colman's Mustard, Worcestershire sauce and tomato ketchup were permanent fixtures in the Edwards' family kitchen, helping them to liven up meat that was a few days old.

By the end of Victoria's reign electricity was finding its way in to some homes, if not Number 57. Originally the wires were threaded through old gas pipes, which made handy, readily available conduits. However, few householders saw the potential of this new source of power; it was not seen as revolutionary, but merely as a cleaner alternative to gas, principally for lighting purposes. Advances in plumbing and drainage bypassed Number 57 in a similar way to electricity. However, elsewhere sanitary conveniences became masterpieces of china, brass, copper and steel. Water closets, taps, and washbasins were made by the greatest ceramicists of the day, like Royal Doulton. An up-to-the-minute, turn-of-the-century bathroom was a triumph of plumbing, with endless hot water from a gas-powered geyser. There would have even been early showers, normally a walk-in contraption of many jets and nozzles all of which celebrated the fact that, at last, people could be clean.

Cast-iron baths replaced the older tin versions, their enormous weight borne on ball-and-claw feet, the design copied from eighteenth century classical chairs. This made the bath not so much an object in which to bathe but more of a French throne. The happy bather could sit in it using Pears soap – which was now a leading contender in the bright, brash new world of advertising.

None other than the Pre-Raphaelite painter John Everett Millais had his painting *Bubbles* used as the basis for a Pears soap advertisement, which would have given the product immense social cachet and would have made it feel like a privilege to wallow in wonderful hot water using a simple bar of soap endorsed by a style leader. (In 1884 *Punch* parodied the practice of writing testimonials to manufacturers praising their products in the hope that the words would be printed on the packet and the author richly rewarded. The cartoon showed an unkempt individual penning the opening words, 'I used your soap two years ago, and since then I've used no other.')

Images designed to beguile and persuade now proliferated, becoming familiar parts of the landscape. When Ethel Edwards rode down the hill on her bicycle – itself a hugely popular liberating vehicle for women and men alike – into the centre of Bristol she would have seen posters advertising Bovril, the concentrated beef extract. One Victorian poster by W. H. Caffyn may not have the same appeal to modern eyes: it showed a tearful bull eyeing a pot and saying, 'Oh, my poor brother.' Bovril was

MAKING A MEAL

Life in a late-Victorian household would be easily recognisable to most people today. For the middle-class family it usually meant that the man of the house would spend his working days away in the office. To accommodate his absence, breakfast was taken earlier and dinner later, with a light lunch for those who remained at home. To bridge the gap between lunch and a late dinner, afternoon tea was introduced. Delicate sandwiches, dainty small cakes and maybe a large fruit cake would be served, perhaps on the best china when friends of the lady of the house came to visit.

If lunch was light and tea was a delicate affair, breakfast and dinner were certainly not. In the 1891 edition of *Mrs Beeton's Book of Household Management* a selection of heavy meat pies are recommended for the first meal of the day. She also suggests serving hot fish dishes, such as kedgeree or mackerel. Sausages, chops, kidneys, bacon and eggs were also considered suitable as well as toasted bread and muffins, butter and preserves, all washed down with tea or coffee.

During this period, dinner for the middle-class family was a lavish affair when guests were invited, but usually quite frugal when dining *en famille*. A new way of serving was introduced around this time, copied from the French, whereby separate courses were offered to each guest in turn by staff. Soup would be served, and when finished would be cleared away before the next course was brought out, breaking the tradition of serving most of the food at the same time. This new way of serving dinner was more labour-intensive and necessitated the need for more plates, cutlery and glassware.

For the first time the dining table was dominated by labelled goods, many of which are still household names today.

nationally advertised and declared to be a health product beyond compare; it tasted the same whenever, wherever and from whomever you bought it. It was even endorsed in theatre programmes by the Prince of Wales's mistress, Lillie Langtry.

None of this coherent marketing would have been possible until the end of the nineteenth century. National advertising was now possible because improved transport could get products to every part of the British Isles. New media, including the brash and breezy *Daily Mail*, meant that advertising campaigns could be undertaken and brand names could be forced upon the nation's consciousness. Economies of scale could be implemented as never before. Small producers, used to selling their goods to a few small shopkeepers, were left standing. The small shopkeepers, once the consumers' only connection to suppliers of all sorts of fresh goods, were rapidly becoming the men who sold packets of packaged goods while the manufacturers spoke directly to customers.

But although there were many new inventions in late-Victorian times, social values were slower to change, and there remained a huge divide between the roles of men and women. Women still did not have the vote and men would not be seen anywhere near the kitchen.

When Queen Victoria died in 1901, she had been on the throne for sixty-three years. She had ruled one-fifth of the land-mass of the globe, with one-quarter of humanity living within her boundaries. Only the oldest of her subjects could remember any other monarch. She gave her name to a period that was distinctive for being the most stylistically eclectic episode in British history, helped by ever-increasing access to cheap, manufactured goods. Late-Victorian society also saw the most dramatic technological changes. It is hard to comprehend the impact that the telephone, the motor car, light bulb, camera and even the bicycle must have had on a society where infant mortality and cholera were still common.

The era was about to end. The next generation of residents at Number 57 were to have a very different world come knocking on their door.

With the growth of branding, national advertising became important.

THE WOMAN'S ROLE

Queen Victoria, her husband Prince Albert and their nine children were the very model of a nineteenth-century middle-class family. Despite the fact she was Queen and Empress, Victoria was seen to be the epitome of everything a woman should be: domestic, decorative, retiring, a support for her husband and a civilising influence upon her children. This image prevailed long after Albert's death in 1861 and continued even when rumours of strained relationships with her offspring threatened to taint it.

The Industrial Revolution had provided working-class women with increased opportunities for working outside the home, particularly in the numerous factories that were springing up all over Britain.

On the other hand, middle-class women found they had less to do. Their husbands left home each day to work in the office and servants looked after the house. Therefore women, in need of a role to play, took their lead from Queen Victoria, the paragon of motherhood. The average family rose in size from 4.7 children in the 1850s to 6.2 in the 1870s.

For those who could afford it, this was the era of the coach-built perambulator, the cosy middle-class nursery and the trained nanny. In September 1892 London's Norland Institute started the first classes in 'Training for Ladies as Children's Nurses' with the aim of producing educated and enlightened nannies for the children of the upper and middle classes. The students themselves were required to be of genteel birth and were aged between eighteen and thirty. Similarly in 1901, under direct Royal patronage the Princess Christian Nursing College was opened in Manchester providing employment for gentlewomen who needed to earn their own living.

Furthermore, a mother was no longer pressured into breastfeeding her children, thanks to advances in technology. The second half of the nineteenth century saw the development of more hygienic feeding bottles and the availability of substitute breast milk, such as tins of evaporated and condensed milk that could be watered down. During the 1880s and 1890s 'humanised milk substitutes' made from dried cow's milk were manufactured by Nestlé, Horlicks and Cow and Gate. A mother could feed her baby without exhausting herself in the process.

Chapter Four

A NEW CENTURY: *1909–1936*

Edward VII was a new king for a new century. But there was no sudden change throughout the country from 'Victorian' to 'Edwardian'. Most people went on living in the same old way, in the same old dwellings – whether cottage or mansion or, indeed, 57 Kingsdown Parade – with the same old décor and accoutrements. Edward himself was certainly not interested in changing society radically. His enduring image is of a stout English country gentleman, much given to the pursuit of pleasure, whether at table, on the racecourse or in the bedroom. In striking contrast to the domestic propriety of his parents, his appetite for huge meals, fast horses and faster women became legendary.

Yet for all his hedonism and lack of intellectual leaning, Edward did have a serious side, expressed in his interest in European politics. Through his marriage to Alexandra of Denmark, and through his brothers and sisters, he was connected to most of the royal houses in Europe. He used his influence to promote peace between nations, and was instrumental in creating the entente cordiale between Britain and France; as a result, he became known as the 'uncle of Europe'.

Other European developments, however, in the sphere of art and design, would not have appealed to Edward's innate conservatism. Here he was representative of most of his subjects, who would have found manifestations of the new 'Modernism' alien and unsettling. It is perhaps not too unfair a stereotype to say that English taste tends to stick with the traditional, the familiar. While there are always innovative individuals at the cutting edge, the majority of people are quite happy with a gradual evolution of style and taste. They could cope with the arrival of that alarming vehicle, the automobile, but only if they could hark back to an earlier age and call it a 'horseless carriage'. They could watch moving pictures in a cinema only if the venue resembled an old-style music hall, complete with redundant curtain in front of the screen. They could contemplate installing a gasolier, the new and powerful way of lighting a room with gas, only if it looked like an old-fashioned candelabra.

While Edward's name would be used to describe certain elements of style, perhaps the strongest, most poignant resonance of the word 'Edwardian' is of that long 'summer' before the catastrophe of the First World War.

When Edward came to the throne, Britain was embroiled in another war, in South Africa. Since 1899 it had been fighting the Boers, settlers of Dutch descent, essentially for control of the diamonds and gold of the Transvaal. Employing highly effective guerrilla techniques, the Boers had caught the British out more than once, and inflicted humiliating defeats. There were questions asked about the condition of Britain's troops. When the nation's sons answered the call to arms from the crammed Victorian slums, they were found to be malnourished, suffering from rickets and a full six inches shorter than their officers. After the war, the Committee for Physical Deterioration criticised working-class housewives for domestic incompetence. The burden of evidence before them, however, suggested it was more likely to be due to poor housing and chronic poverty. The implications of these findings were far-reaching in terms of national life. The seeds of the welfare state were being sown.

After the early Boer victories, British forces eventually prevailed and the nation rejoiced. Enthusiastic patriots could have had no inkling that this dispute would sound the last trumpet-blast of Empire. While the nation fretted that it could not produce enough fit young men to police its far-flung colonies, the world as a whole was changing.

Crucially, Britain's industrial supremacy, unchallenged in the middle of the nineteenth century, was by the beginning of the twentieth significantly eroded. Germany, France and the United States had caught up with, and in some areas outstripped, the old 'workshop of the world', especially in steel production. Britain's industrialists, again echoing that national distaste for innovation, were slow to appreciate new developments and lacked the foresight and dynamism of their competitors.

The world was changing at an accelerating pace, bringing in new ideas that challenged security and complacency. In 1900 Sigmund Freud published *The Interpretation of Dreams*, claiming that people might not be fully in control of their own minds. In 1905 Albert Einstein published three dramatic works of theoretical physics, one being his 'Special Theory of Relativity'. The call for Irish home rule was rumbling, suffragettes were being arrested, the Germans were building Dreadnoughts…

On the Continent, especially in Germany and France, the intellectual, psychological and aesthetic orthodoxies were being challenged and overthrown. The new order, Modernism, was a world view that rejected every single aspect of the old order and evangelised the new, without making any critical value judgements on its worth. New was good; all old attitudes, behaviour and symbolism were, without question, bad – and, worse than that, they were impediments to a new age of rational certainty.

The classic British response was to recoil from these challenges, and take refuge in the familiar. In insular defiance, British architecture retreated towards a reconstructed version of its grandiose past, to the overblown classical style of late Empire. One monument to this is Selfridges' store on London's Oxford Street, which was designed by Daniel Burnham of Chicago in 1907–9. John Nash's refined Regent Street was demolished at the beginning of the century

THE GROWTH OF HEALTH CARE

In 1902 the coronation of Edward VII was postponed because he was suffering from acute appendicitis and needed urgent surgery. Although historically a life-threatening procedure, an appendectomy was performed on the king with great success, due in great measure to advances in surgical procedures during the latter years of the nineteenth century. The impact of germ theory, resulting in a better understanding of antiseptic regimes and the use of dressings soaked in phenol, eliminated to a great extent post-operative infection. The increased use of non-corrosive stainless steel instruments made sterilisation easier, and the use of protective gowns, masks and gloves diminished cross-infection. Developments in general and local anaesthetics were making their routine administration safer.

At the beginning of the twentieth century hospitals were beginning to be seen less as refuges for the sick poor and more as centres of specialised medical care. Medical technology had advanced, X-ray machines had been installed, laboratory tests and post-mortems had become routine, nursing standards had raised and there was a standard ambulance service. Costs had also grown.

As chancellor of the exchequer, David Lloyd George introduced the National Insurance scheme in 1911, to try to meet the health needs of the working classes and the poor. This compulsory scheme was paid for by contributions from workers, employers and government. However, the scheme only covered the contributor, not his family, although a small maternity grant was paid.

The sheer number of casualties during the Great War necessitated the wholesale construction of a centralised medical facility that was beyond anyone's wildest expectations. Not only were thousands of buildings requisitioned but medical, nursing and administrative staff were organised and mobilised on an unprecedented scale. As daunting as this was, it was seen that perhaps a large coordinated system of healthcare could be the way forward for medicine in Britain. This was even more pertinent when in 1929 the abolition of the Poor Law workhouses left suitable infirmary buildings empty.

Shopping at the beginning of the twentieth century was a fashionable, American-influenced activity. Gordon Selfridge opened his palace of consumerism in 1909, designed by fellow American, Chicago architect Daniel Burnham.

to be replaced by Reginald Blomfield's quadrant of arches, colonnades and decorated columns.

After the First World War, Britain's architects found the courage to tackle, albeit timidly, the emerging Modernism. They adopted stripped-down classicism, a style found elsewhere in Europe; in Paris, Vienna and Berlin, among other cities, the establishment simply could not bring themselves to throw out all the contents of their architectural wardrobe. The layout and proportions of the buildings were still classical, but the columns were flattened and all ornamentation removed, in an approximation of the new look. This style reached its peak in England in the 1930s, when Grey Wornum designed the headquarters of the Royal Institute of British Architects in London's Portland Place. Simply proportioned classical windows were flanked by bare Portland stone, and accompanied by two freestanding columns surmounted by strange figures. Some of the decoration was provided by the sculptor and typographer Eric Gill, who brought an idiosyncratic tone of uncertain Modernism firmly rooted in craft and history. Inside, there was some acknowledgement of modernity, but this was a building pulling in several directions. Although it is imaginative and skilful, and beautifully executed, it is still an architecture firmly rooted in the past.

The domestic response was similar. In the years before the First World War, the reaction had been to let some parts of modernity in, but not others. Hygiene was obviously important, because it could affect the human resources of the Empire. Mrs Peel, a popular domestic commentator who was soon to become editor of the women's pages in the *Daily Mail*, wrote in 1902 that 'it is more important for a house to be sanitary than to be beautiful… keep the house dust-free for therein the microbe is most likely to abound'. In 1904 Walter Shaw Sparrow wrote in *The British Home Today* that since new wallpapers were so cheap and plentiful, 'no spring cleaning is considered complete without a change of pattern or colour'. Sometimes changing interior decor was not judged to be enough for a healthy lifestyle – perhaps a change of house was required. Cities tended to be low-lying and filthy, so house advertisements for middle-class homes emphasised how high they were above sea level (just as in an earlier century Kingsdown Parade was praised for its altitude).

The Ideal Home exhibition, first put on by the *Daily Mail* in 1908 and still thriving nearly a century later, provides a vivid barometer of these attitudes. The newspaper was keen to show itself to the world, and particularly its women readers. A puff for the forthcoming 1912 exhibition neatly summarised the strategy: 'All the World and her husband flocked to the [1908 and 1910] Exhibitions and will do so again.' There had been exhibitions since the Great Exhibition of 1851, of course, and the Building Trades Exhibition had been going since 1895; all that the *Daily Mail* picked up on was the mood of the times. Its exhibition eventually became the annual event that continues today, with the whole show acting as a kind of in-the-round advice manual. From the start, rooms were recreated on design themes, and manufacturers had stands to promote their newest lines. Then, as now, people probably went home clutching cheap kitchen gadgets that they would never be able to use with the dexterity of the salesman.

The exhibition saw the beginnings of the notion of 'housekeeping' for the middle classes, whose domestic life had long centred on a building occupied by a family and their servants. Now one woman, Mother, took on the role of keeper of the house, assisted perhaps by one daily 'help'. Factories were already attracting labour away from service, and in any case household incomes could fluctuate with the nation's changing fortunes. The exhibition proposed solutions to these problems by presenting ways in which one woman might do everything herself. There were vacuum cleaners, more washable surfaces, a lack of fussy decoration and an accompanying passion for lighter and paler colours – everything to make life simpler and more straightforward.

The *Daily Mail* ran a story in 1912, possibly full of journalistic licence, that claimed a young couple had got engaged at the exhibition when the man realised the woman was a domestic little creature and 'maybe it was time they set up an Ideal Home of their own'.

Lessons in hygiene and dubious tales of romance are not all we can learn from the Ideal Home Exhibition. It also reflects the needs and aspirations of ordinary people, which would manifest themselves throughout the land.

September 1929 1/net   SPECIAL LIGHTING & HEATING NUMBER

In the early twentieth century homemaking became an enjoyable hobby, aided by a range of new magazines, including *Ideal Home*.

FOOD AND SHOPPING

Throughout this period the majority of shops on any high street would have been small and owned by independent traders, who usually specialised in one type of commodity – meat being supplied by the butcher, fish by the fishmonger, vegetables by the greengrocer and so on. Although shops such as Sainsbury's and Lipton's, selling a range of goods, were established in the second half of the of the nineteenth century (1869 and 1871 respectively), and had many branches, it would be not until the 1950s that the British public embraced the American idea of supermarkets where every commodity was available under one roof.

Motorised transport enabled goods to be delivered to shops more quickly than before, and commercial food production, canning and freezing, offered customers more choice. As a consequence competition grew between traders, and promotion and advertising products became important influences on customer choice. Brand identification, eye-catching logos and friendly characters the consumer could admire or identify with were all employed.

The British diet was still rather stodgy. Raw fresh fruit and salad were still viewed with some suspicion, and the more exotic varieties such as pineapples and bananas generally remained too expensive for most consumers.

Above: The twentieth-century fashion for 'Tudorbethan' homes was even stretched to multi-storey living, as seen here in north London.

Opposite: The Edwardians may have had a fresh approach to design, but their choice in ornaments still had Victorian enthusiasm.

In 1910, one of the main features of the exhibition was the homely Tudor Village, offering a slice of 'Merrie England' and an atmosphere of peace and quiet. Only firms that had been in business for over a hundred years were allowed to run the shops, which were staffed by people in Tudor dress. In 1912 there was a separate show at Earl's Court called 'Shakespeare's England', which also centred on a recreated Tudor lifestyle. Such whimsy in design might be excusable had it just been a passing diversion, but it was because of these early exhibitions that mock-Tudor, or 'Tudorbethan', became the dominant English house shown in the Ideal Home Exhibition until 1939. Furthermore, they were built all over the country. The winner of the 1912 exhibition design competition was an eleven-roomed half-timbered detached house, which was taken down and later rebuilt in Kent and offered for sale. Inside, all was mass-produced Tudorbethan reproduction furniture (although the house had kitchen and bathroom fittings). Outside, all was stable and majestic, redolent of the Tudor fleet known as 'the wooden walls of England'. Tudorbethan made reference to other historical styles, using bays, porches, gables and dormers to break up the building mass, and make each house distinctive.

Number 57 Kingsdown Parade was soon to become a physical example of this retrograde trend. Mrs Edwards, the music teacher, had continued to live in the house until 1905, after which a tenant called Tom Davidge took possession. His details are sadly lost to history, and after he left there is no record of anyone being in the house until 1909, when the Nash family moved in. Frederick Nash was a gentleman's tailor; he and his wife Mary lived with two of their grown-up daughters, Lillian and Ada. The younger, Lillian, helped her mother in the house, while Ada, at the age of twenty-eight, could have been learning to be a dressmaker in 1909, because she was listed as such in a 1915 Trades Directory.

By this time, Kingsdown Parade was not as upmarket as it had been. In 1901, nine houses out of a total of seventy-eight were surviving on their 'own means' rather than by a trade or by renting rooms to lodgers, and these last few gentry had completely disappeared by 1910. The street was now populated mainly by artisans and craftsmen — such as the Nashes.

The new residents of Number 57 would have fallen in with the prevailing British popular styles of their times — not that there was much scope for them to know about what was going on in the wider world, even if they had had much spare cash to afford it. They may well have chosen a neo-Regency look for their parlour, as the main living room was now called. Mrs Hobbs of the early nineteenth century would not have felt too out of place had she been brought forward a hundred years by a time machine.

The Nashes could create the Regency look by painting the walls in paler colours, and using heavily decorative wallpapers as friezes. One of these, Lincrusta, had been developed as far back as 1877 by Frederick Walton, whose father had invented linoleum. Using practically the same raw materials, Walton made a heavily embossed washable wall covering that could take any fashionable design. In 1887 Thomas Palmer manufactured a paper with a cotton and pulp base that could be embossed while wet. This was much lighter and cheaper than Lincrusta, and became another Edwardian mainstay, Anaglypta. These wallpapers could have a powerful and dominant effect on a room.

The fireplace and the Anaglypta frieze from the nineteenth-century remain but the Nashes' Edwardian drawing room is comparatively uncluttered and simple, harking back to the Regency of Mrs Hobbs' days at Number 57.

While the Nashes may not have been able to afford many neo-Regency items, there was another Edwardian feature that they would have striven to include in their house: the 'cosy corner'. In fact, they would have had room for two of them, one on the first-floor landing, and another in the parlour.

The corner, or nook, was designed to create areas of peace, perhaps behind a simple screen. In this way a room could double its functions. A nook could, for example, become the quiet study area in an otherwise busy parlour. As for size, the period guide *Furniture and Decoration* said that a nook was 'sometimes merely a seat, at other times, a miniature boudoir'. The Nashes' first-floor landing nook could have been little more than a comfortable cushion on the window-sill. The parlour version would have been grander, with books ranged in an arched alcove, favourite ornaments gathered on shelves and an armchair for sitting in to read or listen to the gramophone. Portable folding cosy corners were offered for sale, with Maples, the London furniture store, offering in their 1910 catalogue a neo-Adam-style cosy corner complete and ready for installation.

The Nashes would have been imposing their Edwardian look on a lot of what had gone before. The hall would still have featured plenty of Victorian details: the stair carpet and the rug, an aspidistra (the thickly leaved pot plant emblematic of the Victorian era), cheap prints cut from magazines framed on the walls, and an elephant's foot umbrella-stand redolent of India. It would still have been lit by an oil lamp.

The parlour had a similar quality. Most of the more substantial decorative pieces remained stuck in a previous era. The fireplace was mainly Arts and Crafts, as were the mirror and mantel. There may have been a gramophone, but even this modern entertainment centre would have throwbacks to an earlier style, in the shape of little classical columns surrounding the base. Nevertheless, the gramophone represented a revolution. While music had been played in the house throughout its history, this was the first time that people could enjoy recorded music in their own home.

Meanwhile, out there in the wider world, the quickening pace of life had given birth to a design style of daring line, asymmetry and colour. This was Art Nouveau. If the Nashes had wanted to have anything in this style before the First World War, they would probably have only been able to afford small, portable items – a clock, perhaps, or a freestanding ashtray. One exception to this might have been their choice of Lincrusta, which did come in striking Art Nouveau designs at no greater expense.

Art Nouveau favoured the curving and flowing lines of plant stems and foliage, suggestive of growth, evolution and natural progression to complement the forces of man-made modernity – in marked contrast to

Opposite: As the world continued to accelerate, every middle-class home would have harboured a quiet 'cosy corner'.

Below: Mechanically reproduced music emitted through a tulip-shaped horn must have been a remarkable mystery of the changing modern world for the Edwardians.

French architect Viollet-le-Duc's mid-nineteenth century reconstruction of the French city of Carcassonne to its original medieval splendour added an extra dose of romanticism.

the regular, cyclical revivals of classical and Gothic styles. Unlike eastern European countries that looked to their folk cultures and art to express themselves in this period, the French and the Americans particularly used nature as their symbol for progress and modernity. The look was epitomised in the image of a dream maiden or *femme-fleur*, her long wavy hair intertwined with exotic plants.

There had been intimations of this style in earlier decades. In the 1850s, the French architect Viollet-le-Duc had been given the job of restoring the old walled city of Carcassonne and other medieval buildings. He opted to make the original towers and crenellations more pointy and dramatic than they had ever actually been. Slightly more restrained but showing the same tendency, Blackfriars railway bridge and the Holborn viaduct, both built in London in the 1860s, turned usually mundane and practical structures into fairytale set pieces, complete with capitals, winged lions and rampant dragons.

In Britain, Continental Art Nouveau was an obvious successor to the Arts and Crafts Movement that so charmed the previous inhabitants of Number 57. It took a German to put Arts and Crafts architecture into a wider continental context. Hermann Muthesius had been the attaché for the Imperial German Emperor in London from 1896 to 1906. He had identified other Arts and Crafts pioneers – Philip Webb (William Morris's architect) and C. F. A. Voysey – as designers of buildings and housing estates right at the forefront of British domestic architecture. Muthesius's book, *The English House*, exported these ideas to the Continent. His later influence on the Bauhaus movement, as will become clear, connected the old notions of 'fitness for purpose' via 'form follows function' to full-blooded Modernism in the 1920s.

Art Nouveau had an early headquarters, a Paris shop and gallery called *La Maison de l'Art Nouveau*, run by art dealer Siegfried Bing, which opened in 1895. Liberty's of London, opened twenty years earlier to sell Japanese items, brought Art Nouveau to London. The Edwardians felt there was something unbridled, untameable and suspect in designs that could be so asymmetrically luxuriant and have such creative tension flowing through them. When twenty-five examples of mainly French Art Nouveau were donated to the Victoria and Albert Museum after the Paris Exposition of 1900, there were moves made in secret to prohibit them from being shown. Disparaging references were made to the 'squirm', the fluidity of line that showed how far Art Nouveau was ahead of traditional designs and motifs.

Many art historians claim that Art Nouveau is an architectural and design movement. It is not. A true movement must be underpinned by intellectual rigour; Art Nouveau is essentially a decorative style. A swift glance through the names and nationalities and dates of the leading proponents of Art Nouveau immediately suggests that these were far-flung individual innovators, not a coherent group of radicals. This is a far more likely explanation than pretending some Americans, Scots,

French and Spanish seriously comprise a movement. Louis Comfort Tiffany created lamps, windows, furniture and vases in New York from the 1870s to the 1900s. The Glasgow Four, a group of artists and designers trained at the Glasgow School of Art and centred on Charles Rennie Mackintosh, practised their style in buildings, furniture and interior design, in the 1890s. Hector Guimard designed the entrances to the métro stations of Paris from 1899 to 1913. Antoni Gaudí, the staunch Catalan architect, was working on the Sagrada Familia, his 'melting cathedral' in Barcelona, when he was knocked down by a tram in 1926 (the cathedral remains under construction). This disconnected group of distinguished talents does not make a movement.

Back at Number 57, there was not a squirm to be seen – at least not downstairs. However, something was stirring in the attic. Ada Nash, twenty-nine in 1910, would have had her dressmaking workroom under the pitched roof of the house, in what was once a Mary's cheerless room. For the first time in its history, the house was being used as a place of work. The Industrial Revolution had taken work out of the home and concentrated it in purpose-built factories, but artisans and craftsmen were always able to buck that trend.

Dancing, a design for the entrance of *La Maison de L'Art Nouveau* in Paris, by Sir Frank Brangwyn.

Ada's job brought her into contact with rich women in the neighbourhood, who had a far greater sense of what was happening beyond the Bristolian horizon. Mr and Mrs Nash could clutter their parlour and jumble their styles as much as they wished. Up in her workroom, Ada could impose a little of her sense of the modern: uncluttered surfaces, simple wallpaper with Art Nouveau detailing, a new and adventurous Venetian blind and a drawing board and chair. This grew to be commonplace, but was used by very few women in this era. However, just like Miss Lucy Whithers in the late 1870s, she was using a Singer sewing machine. Lucy had used hers to snare young men with her seamstress's skills. Ada was using her machine in a very different way, to potentially set herself up as a completely independent woman.

Perhaps Ada would have had a smart black bookcase to hold magazines that showed the busy world not just outside Bristol but in America and beyond, not only in terms of fashion but every other form of modernity. But soon every publication would be full of war and rumours of war.

King George V had been on the throne for only four years after the death of his father, Edward VII, in 1910 when the cataclysm of the First World War befell the world. The huge casualties in Flanders and elsewhere changed life irrevocably. Many women of Ada's generation lost husbands or fiancés; possibly Ada herself never married because her

A pitched-roofed attic room made a perfect workroom for seamstress Ada Nash.

Overleaf: By the beginning of the twentieth century, the window seat that once looked over fields looked over other people's back gardens. Nevertheless, it was still a pleasant place for quiet reflection.

beau went off to the trenches and never came back. With so many men away, women took on a greater proportion of work than ever before; Ada might have employed her sewing skills in making uniforms, while many of her contemporaries worked in munitions factories or made other war materials.

When the war ended, there was much talk (if not much action) of providing 'homes fit for heroes'; the returning men would not only get their jobs back but there would be a concerted effort to build new houses. Women would be encouraged back to the domestic front. The chief sphere of operations would necessarily be the kitchen, a fresh, clean and hygienic place. New enamelled metal furniture, with wipe-clean surfaces, was now being turned out by the presses that had once made munitions. So modernity, largely rejected at the front door before the war, was once again trying to get in by means of the kitchen.

When the Ideal Home Exhibition returned after a gap of seven years in 1920, it positively revelled in its desire to march, servant-free if necessary, into the future. It started with a competition to design the 'Ideal Worker's Home'. This picked up on many of the recommendations of the Design and Industries Association, which had been founded in 1915 to promote better design. By now their espousal of hygiene meant they could put on a 'Chamber of Horrors' at the exhibition with approved examples and their horrible alternatives presented side by side. One sign described 'a depraved china milk-jug with a hollow handle which fills with milk. The handle can never by properly cleaned and acts as a poison centre. A virtuous, sensible milk jug will keep it company.'

Although the 'Ideal Worker's Home' competition was not open to the public, many *Daily Mail* readers wrote in asking for 'light and airy' houses with 'attractive exteriors', and also labour-saving devices. This need was partly met by a competition for an 'Ideal Labour-Saving Home', grouping appliances together for efficiency, determining optimum heights of work surfaces, rounding off corners, eschewing dust-collecting mouldings, and damp-proofing a house heated by a coal fire and lit by electric light.

WOMEN'S RIGHTS

The 1918 Representation Act gave British women, for the first time in political and legal history, the opportunity to participate in the democratic process. After years of campaigning women became voters. Undeniably a landmark in the process of equality, it was only the beginning. A further twenty-one pieces of legislation over the ensuing ten years would be necessary for the changes demanded by the women's suffrage movement to be reflected in the democratic process on anything like an equal footing. While Britain could boast that from 1918 the majority of its adult population were enfranchised, males were able to vote from the age of twenty-one, but women could only vote from the age of thirty. It would not be until 1928 that equality in that sphere would be achieved.

In 1919 the Sex Disqualification Removal Act allowed women to pursue careers in the civil service and the judiciary. They could now also practise as chartered accountants, veterinary surgeons, solicitors, barristers, bankers and magistrates and be called for jury service. As well as these legal reforms, technological advances and better educational opportunities may well have contributed to wider employment opportunities for women as much as their enfranchisement. Nevertheless, employers could, and regularly did, choose to ignore the Act and dismiss female employees once they married.

Economic power still remained in the hands of men. Despite the widespread employment of women during the First World War (1914–1918) they were still primarily seen as wives and mothers rather than workers, and the suffrage ideal of equal pay was ignored. Female civil servants earned 25 per cent less than their male colleagues, and female teachers 20 per cent less than theirs. Working-class women could expect to receive only half the average male wage for jobs in light industry and agriculture and for domestic work.

The 1923 Matrimonial Act enabled women to divorce husbands on the grounds of adultery, a right enjoyed only by men so far; 1925 saw the introduction of the Guardianship of Infants Act, giving both parents equal right to apply for custody of their children. Both Acts demonstrated an increasing recognition of equality in the home, as well as in the workplace and the ballot box.

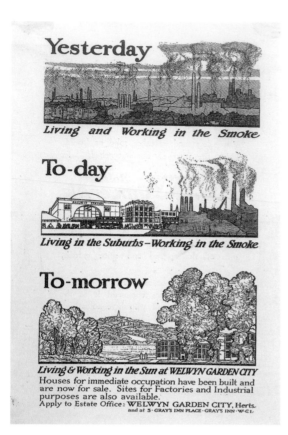

The Garden City movement made extravagant promises that remain unfulfilled today.

Production-line techniques influenced kitchen design. A display at the exhibition showed how a kitchen could be organised with the refrigerator, hob and sink in a triangle. The making of a cup of tea would then require only seventy steps to be taken rather than 320.

In 1921 there was no Exhibition, as the *Daily Mail* village was being built on a plot of land at Welwyn, the first Garden City, in Hertfordshire. The following year coaches took visitors out there to view four-bedroomed houses with the new rational kitchens at their very centre. Meanwhile, Number 57 was not even connected to the electricity supply. It still used gas for light and cooking. It was during this period that the house becomes detached from the main thrust of domestic history. The slow change was not unique to Kingsdown Parade – or Bristol for that matter. There was still little regularity in electrical supply because an appliance could work in one street and not in the next, where the voltage might be different. People tended to stick with what they knew.

After the horrors of war, there was a returning appetite for fun and frivolity. Not for nothing was the succeeding decade known as the Roaring Twenties. Such a demand was served by a new and flashy design

THE SPORTING LIFE

When it was realised that a great many First World War conscripts were either too small or too unwell to serve in the army, efforts were made to encourage better health across the nation through participation in sport.

Football was essentially a working-class man's game, and many of today's successful clubs had their roots in the industrial north, such as Manchester United which was initially formed by the Lancashire and Yorkshire Railway Company. Liverpool, Aston Villa and Birmingham City football clubs sprang from church congregations. The beginning of the twentieth century also saw a steep rise in spectator numbers; 120,000 people watched the cup final of 1913, compared to a crowd of only 17,000 just thirty years before.

Other sports grew in popularity during this period too. The English Rugby Football Union was able to record a satisfying win over its Welsh opponents at the first international game played at its newly opened ground at Twickenham, in 1910. Cricket was popular both internationally and locally.

In 1908 London hosted the fourth modern Olympic Games and treated spectators of all classes to a showcase of track and field athletics, swimming, fencing and gymnastics.

If football was the game of the working classes, tennis was the choice of the middle class. The heady mix of athletic activity together with the opportunity to wear some daring, predominantly white clothes and to enjoy the social events associated with the tennis club were attractive to dashing young men and women. The ailing All England Croquet Club at Wimbledon laid down several grass courts at the end of the nineteenth century and never looked back. The game put individuals into the limelight and one of the first glamorous stars of the game was a handsome young American named William Tatem Tilden II, who was Wimbledon champion three times during the 1920s.

style: Art Deco. Modernism, the movement underlying it, was far more complex. To understand Art Deco, it is important to see how Modernism was growing in the 1920s, although the effects of Modernism itself would only directly impinge on Number 57 decades later.

Modernism was a movement. It was not a style. In the early part of the century, while Britain was in its Edwardian doze, Europe had been discovering a whole visual language. It fed off, and gave life to, the modern world of flight, the automobile and ocean-going liners: 1903 had seen man taking to powered flight for the first time, the first Rolls Royce Silver Ghost rolled out in 1907, and the liner *Mauretania* smashed the record for the fastest crossing of the Atlantic in April 1909. Modernity embraced speed, change and the energy of the machine.

It is often said that the First World War was one fought by man against the machine – the machine in this case being the machine-gun. In the post-war years modernity and machines, properly deployed, were seen as a way of solving all the social problems of living, in a clean, rational and completely contemporary way. The Swiss architect Le Corbusier wrote in 1923, 'A house is a machine for living in,' and machines could help build those houses. The production lines that had made war materials could now produce the steel girders that made the clear, undecorated open spaces of modernist buildings a reality. Then, as the German architect Walter Gropius of the Bauhaus School in Wiemar, Germany, had said in 1920: 'The artist possesses the ability to breathe soul into the lifeless product of the machine.' Gropius was balancing this with the notion that designers could and should 'reunite all artistic disciplines – sculpture, painting, design and handicraft – into a new architecture'. In this he echoed the old Arts and Crafts ideas Muthesius had espoused in *The English House*.

Modernism, though, began to develop into a new understanding of the relationship between art and technology. The belief grew that the old divisive barriers of aesthetics, technology and society could be broken down. The new purity of thought would

THE CHURCH AT HOME AND ABROAD

By the time the twentieth century dawned, there were English missionaries across the Empire, evangelically converting the world to Christianity. Many missions were set up in England throughout the nineteenth century, and lay people from all walks of life enrolled. These early missionaries were ill-prepared, having received no theological training and arriving at their posts not speaking the language or understanding the culture. They held a steadfast belief that they were servants of God and it was their duty to spread the word, but many died from local diseases.

They worked to establish local churches with indigenous pastors, but by 1900 there had been a decisive change in thinking. The informal, collaborative imperialism of the past gave way to colonial control, and the government realised that missionaries were their most effective tool as the 'preparer of the white man's advent'. Consequently the men who became missionaries were more suited to govern than preach. But the Church abroad continued to grow, and the missionary achievement was colossal in terms of converts. In the inter-war years it doubled its members in India and quadrupled them in Africa. Today there are over 70 million Anglicans worldwide.

In England, however, the Great War made the Church realise that it had been marginalised. Men at the front line preferred concerts to sermons; on their return many felt that formal Christian worship did not meet their needs. The Church knew it must change to survive: it rewrote its hymn music, started to update the *Book of Common Prayer*, and embraced technology – the first church service was broadcast in 1924.

The Church's position was still being weakened by splinter groups, and it made several attempts to create a unified church with an appeal to 'all Christian people'. Free Churches – increasingly popular and open to various Dissenting members such as Methodists and Baptists – operated their own unification scheme from their modern, liberal suburban churches, but did not seek alliance with Anglicans. The Anglo-Catholics sought reconciliation with Rome, but nothing came of talks; unification of the Church was still a dream.

improve conditions for every member of society. Like most youngsters, this meant that Modernism could have little truck with the old; summarising later in 1933, Wells Coates, designer of the liner-like Isokon building in London's Hampstead, said, 'We cannot burden ourselves with permanent tangible possessions as well as our real new possessions of freedom, travel, new experience – in short, what we call "life".' Modernists wholeheartedly abandoned the past.

One early figure had attempted to straddle the divide between the traditional and the modern. Scottish Art Nouveau designer and architect Charles Rennie Mackintosh, last mentioned as one of the Glasgow Four, had been both forward- and backward-looking in his designs. Rooted in a humane Arts and Crafts sensitivity to the artisan's skills, Mackintosh's Art Nouveau designs were cleaner and more rational and presaged Modernism. Perhaps it was a Scottish unfussiness or austerity that enabled him to mix the plain whiteness of his spaces with an understanding of medieval and rural vernacular. The result was a successful blend of the best of the old with a rational and calm approach to the new. His masterpiece in this style, Hill House in Helensburgh, Scotland, was built for publisher Walter Blackie, early in the century in 1903.

Wells Coates was commissioned by Isokon's owners Jack and Molly Pritchard to build the 1933 Modernist Isokon Building in Hampstead. Progressive-minded residents included the German architect Marcel Breuer and Agatha Christie.

Charles Rennie Mackintosh's Art Nouveau Hill House on the outskirts of Glasgow is seen as the architect's masterpiece.

England's – not Scotland's – reaction to the rise of Modernism on the Continent was once more to shy away. For all Gropius's intentions to 'breathe soul' into open modernist structures, the movement's abandonment of nostalgia could never sit easily with the Tudorbethan British public. Ordinary people like Ada needed their Modernism through a filter. They chose Art Deco.

Art Deco had its birth through an exhibition in Paris, the *Exposition Internationale des Arts Décoratifs et Industriels Modernes* in 1925. Possibly feeling the need for some manifesto to put Art Nouveau firmly into the history books, the Exposition produced a twelve-volume illustrated catalogue-cum-encyclopedia of Art Deco objects and styles. Art Deco wallowed in its foreignness: a little Egyptian motif here (the discovery of Tutankhamun's tomb in 1922 was a global media event), a smattering of Aztec and other Central American art there. Gone were the pre-war curling plant motifs. Here were chevrons, pyramids, stylised waves, flowers and palm trees. Materials included chromium and early plastics. In the United States they were busy showing the Old World how they sought adventure through streamlining, aerodynamics and speed. William van Alen's Chrysler Building in New York was a rocket ready to shoot into the stratosphere of science fiction.

Art Deco may have had an encyclopedia, but it did not have a stringent philosophy and did not seek to change the world. It sought only to lift and entertain. It was a style of surface decoration, and the surface of things was all it addressed. It was summed up in the 1950s by Nikolaus Pevsner, possibly Britain's most widely respected twentieth-century architectural critic, as 'sham splendour', which neatly contrasts its aspirational nature with its ultimate superficiality. (Pevsner was never a fan: he called the startling Art Deco Hoover factory on Western Avenue in London 'perhaps the most offensive of the modernistic atrocities along this road of typical by-pass factories'.)

But at the time, the world wanted some fun, and Art Deco fitted the bill – white with garish orange, emerald and jade green. Hollywood movie scenes were set in glamorous Art Deco interiors. The cinemas themselves were Art Deco palaces, particularly the Odeon chain, which was opening two cinemas a week by the mid-1930s. There were nearly 5,000 picture palaces in Britain by 1939, giving a touch of elegance and swank to every high street. The cinema exported the style all over the globe, creating the world's first universal 'look'.

Ada Nash would have gone to the picture palaces in Bristol as many as three times a week, and her smoking requisites (a streamlined chrome-plated lighter and a

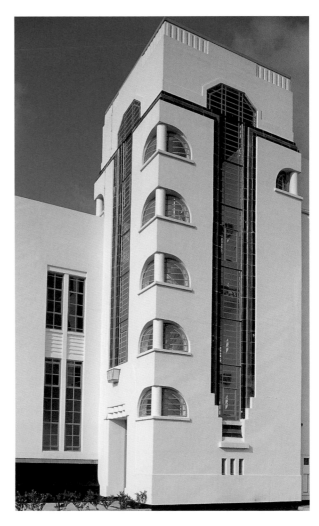

The Art Deco Hoover building in west London.

Ada Nash's bedroom shows us that she was a thoroughly modern girl with her radio, cloche hat, shift dress and a suitcase fit for a cabin on an ocean-going liner.

packet of 'moderne' cigarettes) spoke of her desire to join the cast of the latest thriller on the silver screen. Whereas her family could not have afforded to change any of the interiors of Number 57, she would have had many portable items like her smoking accessories that expressed her interest and taste. Some of these personal objects would be found in her bedroom.

Ada's Art Deco dressing table set of hand mirror, compact and hairbrush could have been made from materials often associated with the style: enamel, ivory, ebony or shagreen, a leather with a rough granulated surface. This made original items very expensive, but Ada may have bought imitations. Plastic, a new – and at this time miraculous – material provided a perfectly respectable way of copying original designs, with none of the opprobrium later attached to it. Whatever the set cost, her budget would have dictated that it rested on an old Victorian dressing table without a shred of modernity. She may have used make-up tips from *Vogue*. A British version had been published since 1916 when wartime convoy restrictions meant it could not be imported from the United States. The magazine had a classic Art Deco typeface and the best in chic new illustrations.

Above: As a dressmaker, Ada kept up to date by reading the newly available fashion and style magazines.

Opposite: At least at her dressing table Ada Nash could afford the luxury of Art Deco accessories.

Top: The wireless made entertainment and information from an exernal source available in any room in the house.

Bottom: A view of the White Garden, part of Gertrude Jekyll's famous creation at Sissingurst in Kent.

By this time, Ada was rather too mature to be a flapper, as the Bright Young Things of the 1920s were called, but she could still listen to dance music from the infant BBC on her battery-powered radio. These were clumsy things, requiring a high-tension battery that had to be removed and charged at the corner shop. In the 1930s, radios were often made of Bakelite, a brittle new plastic reinforced with fine sawdust. Originally used because the end product resembled wood, Bakelite could also be made in the bright colours of the jazz age. Ada had a semi-portable Bakelite radio. Had she been able to afford a state-of-the-art model she would have a Pye radio that featured a stylised sunrise cut into the loudspeaker grille. This was a very common Art Deco motif, also used in suburban fanlights and for garden gates. Whatever the decorative frills, the wireless itself was the first chance for many people to own a piece of modern technology – one, furthermore, that brought the outside world directly into their homes. It made a huge impact on people's lives.

Advances in industrial chemistry brought in new materials. On her bed, which by now would have an interior-sprung mattress, Ada could place her new 'satin' pillows, which were cheaply spun from man-made fibres rather than pure silk. The lustre and sheen of the fabric put the purchaser in mind of the shimmering depth of focus of the black-and-white films of the era. One of Britain's finest Art Deco houses was built on the profits from satin. In 1904 the Courtauld family bought the British rights to 'artificial silk' and, with the fortune it generated, bought and rebuilt Eltham Palace in south London in the 1930s. Although externally the new building is in the Classical-revival style called 'Wrenaissance', internally it is Art Deco at its best. The aluminium-leafed ceilings, ocean liner-style veneered walls and built-in furniture of the new building were joined to a lovingly restored medieval Great Hall. It is a romantic coupling that speaks of an Hollywood-inspired, satin-swathed fantasy, like *Citizen Kane*'s mansion of juxtaposed and reconstructed European treasures in California. (This fictional castle was based on William Randolph Hearst's 'San Simeon', built in the 1920s by the newspaper magnate and his architect Julia Morgan, north of Los Angeles.)

In harsh contrast, Number 57's development had slowed down dramatically. The days of the Georgian upholsterers who would redecorate and refurnish an entire house in three days were long gone. One area, though, had seen a transformation during the early years of the twentieth century. The garden in Number 57 was no longer needed to grow food as had been necessary during the Great War. It was now an extension of the house, almost another room.

Gertrude Jekyll, an artist and gardener, had pioneered a subtle new relationship between house and garden from the 1880s. She rejected the Victorian bedding system, and replaced it with a casual and profuse look that echoed the country cottage garden. A terrace, a pond, plants in pots, perhaps an orientally inspired pergola covered with wisteria, as well as a plain oak or elm seat, would have aided the sense of a room outside.

After 1918, the garden acquired a new significance. The notion grew that a little piece of personal countryside could be a buffer against the upsets of the world. It is curious that the word 'suburbia' has such a pejorative connotation today. Then, suburbia meant that a successful blend of town and country had been found, all on the one plot. The fact that these houses, and their gardens, stretched in serried ranks for miles and miles worried their owners not a jot. Be it in a garden city or a sprawl of speculative building, the Englishman had finally found his little castle.

Frederick probably died in 1931, as his wife was listed as the head of the household from 1932. The last record of her in the house was in 1935, when she was eighty-four.

In the late 1920s, as Mr and Mrs Nash enjoyed their retirement pottering about in the garden, and Ada caught a few rays of sunshine, Number 57 must have been a reassuring place that none of them would have swapped for the dynamics of Modernism – all dazzling white concrete and crisp lines. The truth was, though, that the house was slipping further and further from the realities of domestic design in Britain. Within thirty years, this slumber would bring Number 57 to the very brink of destruction.

But before Number 57 was to reach its very lowest point, the whole world was to face destruction. The 'war to end all wars' turned out to be nothing of the sort: it spawned a second global devastation.

FOLLOWING FASHION

To be fashionable still meant you bought your clothes from *belle époque* Paris. Marie Antoinette's dressmaker Rose Bertin and Empress Eugénie's costumier Charles Frederick Worth did much to raise the status of dressmaker to 'designer', but it was Paul Poiret who started Parisian haute couture in 1903. By 1907 he had introduced a slimmer, sleeker line for women, culminating in the tight, straight, floor-length hobble skirts of 1911, and he was the first to abandon the corset for the brassière. For those who could not afford French fashions direct, the American magazines *Vogue* and *Harper's Bazaar* were on hand to help, and copycat ready-to-wear dresses were available in department stores.

The Great War had a significant influence on women's fashion; skirts were raised by several inches and flared for ease of movement, and from 1916 women wore trousers in factories (although they did not catch on as a major fashion statement until the 1960s). After the war, women felt emancipated by their war work and the vote, and the 1920s style reflected this new-found independence. 'Coco' Chanel was largely responsible for the look, with her liberating knee-length jersey dresses and neat and practical cloche hats. Young women danced the Charleston, cropped their hair, smoked cigarettes and sported bright lipstick, wearing short drop-waisted sleeveless dresses, earning themselves the derogatory name 'flappers' from the older generation.

Men's clothing did not change dramatically, but in the 1920s a general trend towards informality became apparent. Collars were no longer stiff and winged, and the tweed sports jacket became popular, along with 'Oxford Bags' – wide trousers up to 24 inches at the hem.

The popularity of sport for all also led to new outfits for tennis, shooting, golf and swimming.

Chapter Five

WAR AND DECLINE: *1937–1962*

The port of Bristol was a natural target for enemy attack during the Second World War. The surrounding area was heavily bombed, and much of the city was laid waste. Kingsdown Parade was not spared. Numbers 10 and 16 were hit, as were many other houses in neighbouring streets. Another casualty was Mr John Britton's old turtle soup emporium, the Montague, at the end of Kingsdown Parade. Number 57 itself managed to escape unscathed – at least from direct action. Like most dwellings throughout the country, it would have suffered from lack of materials and manpower for day-to-day maintenance, as well as rationed fuel, during the long dark years when most resources were directed to all-out war effort.

Victory in 1945 brought jubilation, but no immediate improvement to the quality of life. Indeed, in many ways life became even more impoverished for people who had endured so much hardship already. Britain was effectively bankrupted by the war, and the post-war years were to be devoted to endless toil to earn money abroad, with little money to spare at home. Worldwide, food and fuel were scarce. Food rationing in Britain, which had begun in 1940, was not completely phased out until 1954. In 1946 even bread was rationed, which it had not been at the very height of war. Coal, the primary means of domestic heating, would remain rationed until 1958. The year after the war, miserable conditions were made even worse by the coldest winter in living memory.

The best coal was kept for industry and the railways, so what coal there was for domestic use was poor quality; in Number 57 the sitting-room fire would probably have

Opposite (top): With newsprint in short supply the nation relied upon the radio for information about the successes and failures of the Second World War, transmitted to them in the brave tones of Winston Churchill's voice.

Opposite (bottom): No lawn or carefully tended shrubbery was exempt from the need to grow food.

FAIRER FOOD

Throughout history, the way in which food was acquired, cooked and consumed in a wealthy household was very different to that in a poor household. One of the most striking features of the twentieth century is the narrowing of that difference. Economic factors and freely available information about food in the form of advertisements and, from 1927, radio programmes helped to raise awareness and aspirations for ordinary people across the country.

During the Second World War the central part played by civilians was recognised by the coalition government and manifested as a policy of inclusiveness and 'fairness'. This led to a system of rationing of goods, notably food. In theory, no matter how much or how little money a citizen had, each had a right to buy a designated amount of food, which was the same for everyone.

Food rationing was introduced in Britain in January 1940, and every man, woman and child was issued with a book of coupons setting out their entitlements. Basic commodities such as sugar, tea, cheese and meat were rationed on an 'amount per person' basis, while other foodstuffs such as cereals, pulses, tinned and dried goods could be purchased on a points system. Some important items such as milk and eggs were rationed on a needs basis, with expectant mothers, children and invalids given priority; these people also received free or subsidised orange juice and cod-liver oil.

Bread was not rationed until after the war, in July 1946. However, much of the Ministry of Foods' preoccupation was with the subject of wheat and bread, as so much flour was being imported from the United States and was taking up valuable shipping space. In March 1941 a National Flour was introduced for use for the duration of the war. This looked very much like the 85 per cent wholemeal flour that can be bought today, but with added calcium carbonate. Loaves made from this flour were not popular, though, as they were often badly baked.

Nonetheless, the government was keen that bread was used well and issued leaflets warning of the perils of wastage, with such titles as 'Bread into Battle'. Indeed, with the ploughing up of Great Windsor Park and the moat surrounding the Tower of London for growing wheat, bread was very much seen to be part of the frontline war effort.

smoked and given out little real heat. Still, it gave a heart to the room, after a fashion. The occupants would sit close to the fire, listening to the wireless. It had been the main source of information during the war, when newspapers had shrunk to a few flimsy sheets to save paper and wood pulp. By the end of the war, there were 10.8 million wireless sets in use. Wirelesses were beginning to be 'rectified' so they could run off the mains rather than the two batteries of Ada Nash's day. A sizeable Bakelite model was a piece of furniture in its own right, a secondary focus to the room after the fire.

After old Mrs Nash left Number 57 in 1935, the next residents were Mr and Mrs Evans, who arrived in 1937. Their quarter-century tenure would take them through the Second World War and its aftermath, to a time when the house reached its nadir. The middle of the twentieth century saw a long way from the desirable gentleman's residence of its early days: shabby and run-down. During the war, the spindles from the staircase and the window shutters had to be sawn up for firewood. Such sacrifice and thrift were emblematic of the domestic war effort. With resources in such short supply, people had to 'Make Do and Mend', use their ingenuity and make the most of very little. Clothes would be refashioned and made over, darned and darned again, while home-grown vegetables ('Dig for Victory') supplemented the ration.

When it came to interior decorating, there was little material to work with. Wallpaper production was halted, so wartime walls were painted in any available colour. Not that many people would have had much energy or resources for such home improvements. After working long hours in munitions factories or in other essential war work, followed by chores on the domestic front, they may well have preferred to slump into a familiar armchair in an unchanging living room, and listen to Churchill's rousing speeches on the wireless.

At this time the living room in Number 57 would have been dominated by a heavy, cumbersome three-piece suite with rounded arms, upholstered in an uninspiring brown and dating from the years before the war. The wispy fire would be smoking away in a 1930s fireplace. An Art Deco mirror may have hung above the mantel, surmounted by some of those flying ducks so beloved of kitsch interiors today, with the old Lincrusta Adam-style wallpaper still running as a frieze above the picture rail. The room was still lit by gas (with an oil lamp for close work);

The principal room in the house, now, for the first time, called the living room, was as comfortable as it could be made during the austerity of war. Out-of-scale 1930s furniture is cheek by jowl with the tiled Modernist fireplace surround.

there was as yet no electricity in Number 57. By 1946, 86 per cent of British homes were wired up, so our house was becoming a real exception.

While new furniture and fabrics were largely unavailable during the war, there were exceptions in the shape of well-made and practical 'Utility' items that were designed under the auspices of the Board of Trade. These items were available on a rationing-style points system to either newly-weds or people who had been bombed out of their homes. (The number of the latter varied from year to year, but there was a steady annual rate of half a million wartime marriages.) Gordon Russell, a pre-war furniture designer and prime mover at the Board of Trade, had grown up in Chipping Camden, one of the Arts and Crafts artisan communities. He knew that the Utility furniture should be neither baroque nor cheap. He fell back on his training, producing machine-made Arts and Crafts style furniture to simple, standardised and well-thought-out designs.

Plywood was used in Utility furniture as it was cheap and strong. Sometimes the board edges, showing the multiple layers of ply, were not neatly covered as they would previously have been. Instead the different coloured bands were seen by their designers as honest decorative features in their own right. As it was not decorated, Utility was, almost unwittingly, Modernist.

Utility products were stamped with the 'CC41' logo (originally standing for 'Civilian Clothing 1941', the year the Utility label was introduced). It was used until 1951, on all kinds of necessities as well as clothes and furniture. Not only were Utility items a boon in straitened times, they were patriotic too. Attitudes would change, though, after the war; many people thought of Utility as 'government issue', and wanted to cast such items aside. However, the furniture was cheap and easy to pick up for those of a different mind – and indeed graces more than a few rooms to this day. Much later, in the 1960s, Terence Conran's whole Habitat 'look' mirrored the philosophy of Utility. Cheap, practical furniture was matched with crockery, textiles and other household goods. A whole house could be furnished from one shop, and every item came with an implied social seal of approval – Conran equalled good design.

Utility was at least a growth in design culture while the war was in progress, when everything might have become stagnant. A second green shoot was the creation of the Council of Industrial Design (later to be renamed the Design Council) by the Board of Trade in 1944, to 'promote by all practical means the improvement of design in the products of British industry'. It was rapidly being realised that industry would not only have to provide for post-war Britain, but it would have to export currency-earning goods abroad. The cancellation of the United States' wartime policy of almost unlimited aid,

Utility furniture with the 'CC41' logo surreptitiously introduced wartime Britain to the simplicity of Modernism.

'Lease Lend', immediately plunged Britain into even deeper debt. To show British industry was back in business, there was an exhibition in 1946 at the Victoria and Albert Museum of new goods and products called 'Britain Can Make It'. The name was a play on the old wartime propaganda slogan 'Britain Can Take It', but when the 1.5 million visitors to the show realised how much of the output was intended for export, and that most people could not afford the items they saw anyway, the show was dubbed 'Britain Can't Have It'.

Abroad, a third green shoot of new design was appearing. In France, fashion designer Christian Dior unleashed his 'New Look' on the catwalk. Emphasising the bust and hips again, with a pinched waist and flowing skirt, his 'hourglass' style could not have been a bigger contrast to the more fitted and drab fabric-saving wartime fashions. Dior's look sent a thrill through global womanhood, and was denounced worldwide for its extravagant waste of material. The French government were keen to place France back at the centre of haute couture, so they encouraged Dior as much as they could, and it was not long before there was a Utility copy of the new style of dress. The flow of Dior's skirt is often associated with a new informality in Modernist design. One of Modernism's fundamentals was its pursuit of the straight and functional line. The sweep of the New Look asked if that line could not only be simple, but also exciting. This more fluid line began to appear in 1950s contemporary design.

Just after the war, dresses of whatever design were hardly a priority of the government, whose collective mind was concentrated on the problem of housing. In 1944 half-a-million homes were considered uninhabitable because of war damage. In Bristol alone 30,000 people needed rehousing. Nationally in 1948 there were 177,000 more marriages than new homes built, which meant that nearly half of newlyweds had to live with their parents. Alternatives were few. The departing American Forces had left behind 3,000 Nissen huts, which were pressed into domestic use, and councils requisitioned many empty houses. Single-storey prefabricated homes were built by the thousand, with accommodation consisting of a living room, two bedrooms, kitchen, bathroom and WC. These so-called 'prefabs' were made in aircraft factories and used aeronautical engineering techniques. The Modernist

FROM COUTURE TO CARNABY STREET

The silver screen increasingly influenced ladies' fashion in the 1930s, which saw a return to elegant bias-cut dresses. Men sported trilbies and 'toothbrush' moustaches as they emulated Laurence Olivier. During the war, with clothes rationed, women resorted to using their hair – curled and piled-up – to imitate stars such as Garbo and Dietrich. Designers created simple outfits under the 'Utility' label; the only luxury was nylon stockings brought over by the American GIs.

In 1947 a distinctive post-war style emerged. Christian Dior launched the 'New Look' in Paris, with soft shoulders, small waists and full calf-length skirts holding sway for eight years.

By this time, a new market had emerged that the couture houses did not cater for. The 'teenagers' found their style on Carnaby Street. In 1955 Mary Quant opened her boutique Bazaar, creating sharp and sassy clothes with hemlines rising throughout the 1960s: the 'mini' was born. Op and Pop Art-inspired dresses were teamed with tights, white boots, geometric Vidal Sassoon hairstyles and black kohl makeup as modelled by the androgynous Twiggy.

In 1957 John Stephen started his Carnaby Street crusade to add colour to a man's wardrobe, with red slacks, frilly shirts and striped coats. But it was the Beatles who led men into the 'Peacock Revolution' – their Pierre Cardin collarless suits influenced a whole generation – and other designers, among them Hardy Amies and Emilio Pucci, soon left women's couture for men's.

In the 1950s film continued to inspire fashion, with James Dean and Marlon Brando showing what a white T-shirt and pair of blue jeans (made from riveted denim, formerly used for nineteenth-century workmen's overalls) could do. By the 1960s they were staple wear for the youth generation, remaining the design classic of the twentieth century.

The inevitable housing shortage after the wartime blitz energised underworked aircraft factories into producing pre-fabricated homes. For those used to the austerity of war a 'pre-fab' was a palace indeed.

dream of machines and aeroplanes had come down to earth in a practical and unpretentious way. There was no posing polemic here, just a practical engineering solution to a pressing problem that happened to be utterly in tune with the aspirations of pre-war Modernism. Some of these dwellings, designed to last for ten years, are still standing and serving their fond owners well.

Rebuilding Britain was going to take a very long time. In the late 1940s the reasons for this slow progress were many and problematic. At the war's end there was an acute shortage of labour; hundreds of thousands of service personnel had been killed, conscription was still in operation, demobbing took time and some workers were only slowly being returned to the regular labour market from wartime jobs. Building materials were also scarce. There were shortages of timber, because so much of it had been used to repair bombed buildings temporarily. Bricks were a rarity because it took so much valuable energy from coal to fire them but there were few alternatives.

There was, however, no shortage of young and able minds to address the problem. Britain was about to experience the effect of the combined energies of a unique and interesting generation of architects, town planners and social scientists; men like Hugh Casson, Peter Moro, Basil Spence and Ralph Tubbs.

Their design education had been interrupted by the war. Before it, they had only had a brief opportunity to absorb the principles of continental Modernism at their schools of architecture. They had also rubbed shoulders with some of the European architectural greats fleeing German persecution, who passed through this country on their way to the United States. During a short stay, Walter Gropius, head of the Bauhaus, in partnership with English architect Maxwell Fry, had designed Impingham Village College near Cambridge in 1936. Marcel Breuer, who had worked with Gropius at the Bauhaus, designed the restaurant for Wells Coates' Isokon building in Hampstead in 1935 (he lived there with Gropius). He also designed Isokon furniture which was manufactured in Bristol. Erno Goldfinger and Erich Mendelsohn were other refugees who brought fresh thinking and idealism to a war-weary Britain. Le Corbusier, possibly the most important Modernist architect of them all, had passed through Britain giving lectures in the early 1930s. The young Britons were inspired, but their teachers were perhaps a little confused. When Gropius was visiting the Birmingham College of Arts and Crafts, he was asked if he could supply a copy of the Bauhaus timetable, perhaps as a way of obtaining a similar creative result. Gropius could only reply that the Bauhaus was not about its timetable, it was about 'the atmosphere'.

Thus educated, the young architects were snatched away for the duration of the war mainly by the Royal Engineers. They were not yet fully trained as architects, but the Sappers taught them, through the war, how to get organised, confidently use the great responsibility placed on their shoulders, solve practical building problems and get structures erected as quickly and efficiently as possible. They did this with Modernism always in mind. It could be said that they stormed ashore on D-Day with a copy of Le Corbusier's *Vers une Architecture* ('Towards a New Architecture') in their knapsacks. These were the men, now equipped with a first-class vision and training to match, who were to rebuild Britain.

They were a heroic, raffish breed. Their priority profession merited the use of a car. It might be an old RAF model with roundels still on the doors, but it reflected their perceived status. Well-paid and stylishly dressed in bow ties and sports jackets, they mixed with the intelligentsia and the creative elite. When Basil Spence rebuilt Coventry Cathedral from 1954 to 1962, he could call upon all his artistic friends. Graham Sutherland designed the altar hanging, John Piper did the stained glass, Jacob Epstein sculpted the main statue that hangs outside.

WOMEN AT WAR AND PEACE

During the Second World War, the changing status of women was reflected in such propaganda films as *The Gentle Sex* (1942) and *Millions Like Us* (1943). Women were seen doing their bit on the home front, in war work every bit as challenging as men's: driving lorries, toiling in armaments factories, staffing ack-ack guns. Many women found economic – and social – independence for the first time, and were not willing to give it up after the war. However, there was great pressure from both government and society as a whole for women to go back to the home, as this would free up jobs for the thousands of young men returning from the front line.

Not surprisingly, the basic relationship between men and women did not change, and the family continued to be regarded as a fundamental institution in society; a woman's role as home-maker, child-bearer and child-rearer continued to be stressed as did a man's role as the family's bread-winner.

Nevertheless, some things had already begun to change. It is estimated that at the beginning of the century a quarter of all married women had a baby every year, but by 1930 the number had halved. Women had already become increasingly practised at using contraception before the war; it is thought that three-quarters of sexually active women were using contraception of some form or another. By the late 1930s birth control had become respectable, even though the Roman Catholic Church voiced its opposition. Advice could be sought from maternity welfare centres and family planning clinics, particularly so after 1938, when the very strict abortion laws were relaxed slightly. However, this did not stop the trade in 'back-street' abortions; it is estimated that up to 300 a day were performed during the post-war years and it was not until the introduction of the contraceptive pill in 1961 that this number began to reduce.

Smaller families meant an improvement in living standards with fewer mouths to feed and fewer bodies to clothe. Moreover, it was also easier for women to work outside the home environment, and during the 1950s double the number of women were in paid employment than before the Second World War, a significant advance.

Some of the architects were card-carrying members of the Communist Party, and took up the challenge of social housing with relish. They joined ranks with the Young Turks of strategic urban planning, which had been recognised as an academic discipline since 1914 with the founding of the Royal Town Planning Institute. The planners were given not just an economic but also a social responsibility – factories were important, but just as important were the houses and schools and hospitals of the new welfare state. The government had proved that it could win a war using centralised direction, so why not continue in peace time? The welfare state had been debated and designed while the war was still on. The Beveridge Report, published in 1942, pledged to rid the country of the 'five giants': 'Want, Ignorance, Disease, Squalor and Idleness'.

Housing policy was also being shaped while the prospective inhabitants were still in uniform. In 1944 a booklet, brimming with pictures of possible post-war housing and called *Planning Our New Homes*, was published by the Scottish Housing Advisory Committee. Its frontispiece read 'Men and Women in the Forces, by sending in their ideas on post-war homes, helped make this book. They would welcome a chance of reading it. If you hand a copy in at a Post Office it will go to them.'

The ideas, then, were already there. So were the people to mould them. The labour to build them, and the materials needed to do so, were not. Winston Churchill summoned the young architects and planners and asked them what possible answer there could be. 'The solution is concrete,' they replied. Concrete was cheap, and an entire wall, complete with windows, could be precast in a factory. Building tower blocks with concrete required fewer skilled men than traditional bricklaying. Cement could be shipped over from America. Lift technology was improving, meaning all could live easily high in the sky. Furthermore, there was a precedent for the plan, because system building was successfully working in Scandinavia.

THE NATIONAL HEALTH

It could be argued that the Second World War was good for medicine. The impetus to find alternatives to the unsatisfactory harsh chemical antiseptics for wounds sustained by both military and civilian casualties resulted in a renewed interest in Alexander Fleming's 1920s work on penicillin. In 1940 a team of young Oxford scientists started experimenting using Fleming's theory, with increasing success. By 1943 penicillin was being mass-produced, enabling large-scale testing on wounded troops in North Africa, and by the following year it was in common use for all Allied servicemen. The overall success of penicillin cannot be overstated with regard to the fight against previously dangerous conditions such as tetanus, anthrax, syphilis and pneumonia.

It had long been held that the pre-war hospital service was in urgent need of an overhaul. The mix of voluntary and public sectors was unable to cope with the ever-increasing demands of advances in medicine and patient numbers. In a sense, a solution came to light when in 1939 the Ministry of Health commandeered all hospitals in order to be ready to deal with war casualties.

This new way of dealing with the nation's health, albeit at a time of dire emergency, was taken into consideration in the Beveridge Report of 1942, which was to form the basis of the welfare state in Britain. William Beveridge concluded that one of the threats to society, disease, could be tackled by introducing a comprehensive health service. A bill was introduced to Parliament in April 1946, and the National Health Service was born on 5 July 1948: available to all, free at the point of service, without payment, means-testing or insurance.

In the post-war housing famine the miracle material that was concrete enabled the British government to satisfy the demands of the electorate by building fast and building high.

Faced with this rosy picture, Churchill immediately gave his imprimatur to a high-rise concept that has dominated our cities ever since. Housing authorities received bigger grants from the government the higher the blocks were built. The more storeys, the more homes – but still on the same footprint. Land in cities was, even then, in short supply, so the answer to inner-city housing was, quite simply, to build high and the higher the better. Those on the topmost floors cared little. Here was plenty of fresh air, that age-old desirable commodity that had determined Number 57's construction on the hills above Bristol 170 years earlier.

The manufacture of G-plan furniture made ultra-modern pieces available to those on a limited budget.

Modernist thinking underlay the more desirable middle-class homes, as can be clearly seen at Leslie Goodall's 'Long Wall' house in Weybridge, Surrey. Built in 1963, it sums up the entire sweep of Modernism in domestic design. The living spaces are all on one floor, with a vast picture window reducing the differentiation between the inside and outside of the building. A spiral concrete open staircase rises into a small gallery giving out on to the room below. The fireplace is a simple hole in the wall. The log store next to it is another. Concrete columns divide the different areas of the main space into kitchen, dining and relaxing areas. These spaces are informal and egalitarian; there is no longer a need to hide the servants. This is a building for living in. The outside appearance is secondary but, in a typically English way, remains soft, pragmatic and picturesque.

Pre-cast reinforced concrete terraces from the 'Hartcliffe' housing estate on the outskirts of Bristol. The idealistic intentions of the creators never came to fruition.

The ribbon estates of two-storey houses that spread outwards from some of Britain's cities, such as Bristol, drew on the same philosophy, even if they were not quite so rigorously executed. They were a little more open-plan than the speculatively built homes of the 1930s and were constructed from reinforced concrete without any insulation. Unfortunately this encouraged widespread condensation on wall surfaces, not just windows. The houses themselves were simple living spaces with plain surfaces and doors. There was no panelling, no fuss of any kind. The house was easy to clean. Fitted kitchens topped with wipe-clean Formica (a compressed laminate of paper and resin) and complete with aluminium sinks were sold by the English Joinery Manufacturers' Association. This association worked in an unprecedented union with the makers of ovens, refrigerators and washing machines to create an innovative hygienic standard.

The estates themselves did not resemble the serried ranks of Victorian speculative building. Instead, the planners attempted to draw upon the experience of Ebenezer Howard's Garden City movement earlier in the century; the first of these garden cities, Letchworth, had been built in 1903. Now, the New Towns Act of 1946 gave the go-ahead to a number of new, centrally planned urban areas, including Stevenage and Harlow. Further enlightened Acts were passed to protect green belts, national parks and access to the countryside and to control the distribution of industry. Everyone was entitled to a functional house.

As for the reality, an estate of mixed high- and low-rise housing was proposed in Bristol in 1947 in the old area of Dundry Slopes, four miles south of Kingsdown Parade. Preliminary work was started in 1949, when the estate was given the name 'Hartcliffe', derived from an old Saxon place-name. By such means it was hoped the estate would gain its own identity. By 1952, the residents began to arrive. They all had to wear Wellington boots for many years to come, and all have long memories of the early times. Tony Brisbane, who arrived in November 1954, remembers: 'We had no footpaths, no pavements. All we had was one road through the estate and a little bit of concrete at the front door, then a sea of mud.' Fred Bond described Hartcliffe as 'a wilderness. For seven years we were publess. If a man wanted a drink he had to walk nearly two miles.' Colin Griffin recalls, 'They said it would have the latest facilities, but when we got there it was quite demoralising. There were no schools or shops or churches. We had to have our groceries delivered from the Co-op in Bishopsworth. There were no buses either, and no completed roads for them to go on. It was all higgledy-piggledy, but we accepted it, as we believed things were going to improve.' The services were finally laid on and the schools and shops were built, but the 20,000-strong Hartcliffe community still feels isolated south of the vibrant centre of Bristol.

It has experienced all the social problems associated with the lack of a proper local infrastructure ever since.

This approach to social engineering was unprecedented. Only a flattened country and a population used to being ordered about during the war would have gone along with it. The new replacement housing was the big political hot potato of its time. Governments were held strictly to account on their ability to house the nation. House-building statistics became the nation's bogeyman, just as inflation did in the 1970s, unemployment in the 1980s and interest rates in the 1990s. Questions would be asked every quarter in the Commons about recent housing targets. In 1951, the outgoing Labour government had built 195,000 homes. In 1950, the Conservatives had made the jaw-dropping promise that they would drive this figure up to 300,000. They erected 240,000 in 1952 and in 1953 actually achieved their target. In 1954, 340,000 homes were constructed.

Centralised government and the welfare state must, at last, have appeared to be living up to the initial post-war promise. This really was a new world, a world where the state was going to look after the people and never leave them exposed to want ever again. Free medical help? 'They' would give it to you. A new house? 'They' were building them. Baby needed orange juice? 'They' supplied it. It was time for a state-organised party.

One hundred years after the Great Exhibition, in the summer of 1951, the Festival of Britain spread colourfully across the south bank of the Thames. Built on land left unoccupied because of the war, it was part exhibition, part celebration, part funfair: 'a Tonic to the Nation'. There were pleasure gardens, restaurants, cafés and bars. Le Corbusier described the Festival in a BBC Radio broadcast in August 1951: 'It is healthy, it is solid, it is full of vigour and verve. It is full of diversity, it is full of unity.'

CHURCH UNITY

By the 1930s secularisation was increasingly discussed, as people realised that God could not prevent war or mass unemployment. In 1919 Nietzsche had said 'God is dead', and people were starting to agree.

But with the outbreak of the Second World War, religion took centre-stage once more, with Catholics, Anglicans and other sects pulling together as a Christian society. Fascism had led to a new influx of Jewish refugees from Europe, many of whom stayed after the war, becoming Zionists yearning for a nation state of their own (the State of Israel was formed in 1948).

After the war, the Church of England's attendance continued to decline. The Church questioned how it should move on; the answer, it was argued, was a return to proper Christian dogma. The Liturgical Movement stressed the total experience of worship, placing emphasis on the Eucharist.

And although the welfare state was now in place, the Church continued to wield its power in fighting social battles, such as the 1958 Campaign for Nuclear Disarmament, run from St Paul's Cathedral. In the 1960s the Church was surprisingly supportive of liberalising such laws as one making suicide a crime. However, it was against the 1967 Abortion Law (which was passed despite its protests).

In the 1950s the search for Christian unity was gaining momentum, and in the 1960s a series of talks were initiated between the Pope and the Archbishop of Canterbury. The Free Church, Anglicans and Evangelical Anglicans also tried to find common ground. This intensified quest for unity came in the face of competition, not from 'new religions' such as Hare Krishna and the US Mormons, but from the immigrants who left India from 1947 onwards – the Muslims, Sikhs and Hindus.

THE ILLUSTRATED
LONDON NEWS
FESTIVAL OF BRITAIN

THE EXHIBITION'S OPENING—SPECIAL NUMBER

Above: The Festival of Britain, despite its unreconstructed Modernist credentials, still had at its heart the classical allusion of Empire.

Opposite (top): Post-war Britain missed no opportunity to celebrate and the coronation of a young and beautiful Queen Elizabeth II in 1953 was ommemorated across the land.

Opposite (bottom): The cheap mass-produced plate that brought the spirit of the Festival of Britain into an optimistic home.

The public loved it. The war-weary British couple, him in his demob suit and her in a Utility dress danced outdoors to the sound of Joe Loss and his orchestra.

The Council for Industrial Design had proposed a design brief in 1949 which called for exhibits to be 'lively, and of today'. The Festival of Britain fulfilled this promise on many levels, with new and daring designs, always with a touch of fun, coherently used and repeated in the many pavilions, signs, pieces of furniture and even crockery. Everything seen at the Festival of Britain could be bought. On the day it closed, even the coffee tables of renowned designer Robin Day – now much sought-after collectors' items – were sold off for five pounds each.

The festival was centred on a number of important semi-permanent buildings. There were halls devoted to Transport, Sea and Ships, the Country and many other subjects. Visitors were as likely to encounter an exhibition of British tractors as a Barbara Hepworth sculpture. Ralph Tubbs designed the Dome of Discovery, and cartoonists Osbert Lancaster and John Piper the Battersea Fun Fair further up the Thames. The whole venture was masterminded by Gerald Barry, with Hugh Casson as Director of Architecture. Le Corbusier described them as men who 'did not have white hair and were not bald; it is astonishing, as usually we wait for hair to fall before giving such commissions.'

The location for the Festival Hall could not have been more inappropriate. The site was next to the racket of the Hungerford railway bridge. Leslie Martin and Peter Moro insulated the concert hall by putting it in a box suspended within the shell of the building: a box within a box. It was built in about eighteen months, and featured an amazing number of new scientific applications. The seats registered the same acoustic effect empty or full. The doors had sound-absorbent filters around their edge. Even the carpet was modern and distinctive enough to merit subsequent listing as Grade I. Frank Lloyd Wright said that the Festival Hall would never work; Le Corbusier described the interior as 'an extremely beautiful English creation', perhaps referring to the whimsical balconies, and declared that 'the whole world will admire it'. The Festival Hall still entertains and enthrals today.

Eight-and-a-half million visitors had a wonderful party at the Festival of Britain in the five-and-a-half months it was open. Overall, eighteen-and-a-half million people went to associated celebrations around the UK. Not long afterwards, in 1952, the nation was silenced by the death of King George VI, but re-energised by the coronation of his daughter Elizabeth II, which followed in 1953. The coronation was watched on television by an audience of twenty-five million; people either bought a set especially for the occasion, or went round to a neighbour's house to watch theirs.

In 1950, only 344,000 people had sets; just five years later this figure had risen to over four million. Through the 1950s as a whole, consumer spending went up by 115 per cent. It was time to buy anything and everything featuring the new motifs, designs and materials that had been showcased at the Festival.

This ray of optimistic sunshine would have had a hard job piercing the atmosphere of cooking smells, cigarette smoke and washing in the kitchen of Number 57. This room had become the centre of the Evans' family life. Who would wish to venture away from the warmth of the kitchen except for a quick scurry upstairs to a cold, damp bed? In its desire for informal living in one space, the kitchen, Number 57 was subconsciously adopting some Modernist thinking. There was another possible similarity. Mr and Mrs Evans could have dragged an old food safe

In Number 57's kitchen an attempt was made to arrange the room in a 'modern' way to keep up with the times. The oil lamp is a giveaway – the house still had no electricity.

and enamelled table out from the wall to create a division in the room. Now Mrs Evans could cook and still carry on a conversation across the divide to anyone eating in the 'dining' part of the dilapidated kitchen.

In 1955, 18 per cent of British households had a washing machine, 8 per cent had a refrigerator, and 1 per cent even had an early dishwasher, while 51 per cent had a vacuum cleaner. Many items in the contemporary style were finding their way into houses. The growth and near dominance of this futuristic design was well under way. In 1952 it featured on 4 per cent of wallpapers, and by 1956 this figure had grown to 20 per cent – by the end of the decade it was over 50 per cent. Similarly, one of the cheapest and best-selling ranges of crockery sold by Woolworths was also an absolute contemporary benchmark: the new 'Homemaker' range. It was made by Ridgeway Potteries and designed by Enid Seeney. It was decorated with images of fashionable 1950s home furnishings, including a picture of a Robin Day reclining armchair. Hugh Casson designed a chic range called 'Riviera' for Midwinter Tableware, while the young Terence Conran designed the more homely 'Nature Study' range. Similarly Pyrex, in the vanguard of heat-resistant glass production, was making its jolly ovenware. They also manufactured a Cona coffee maker designed by Abram Games, the designer of classic wartime posters and also the Festival of Britain emblem.

Much of this crockery was abandoning symmetry and going for abstract elliptical shapes. These were reminiscent of the orbit of a Sputnik satellite or a scientific peek at nature down a high-powered microscope. A connection was clearly drawn in an Institute of Contemporary Art exhibition in 1953 entitled 'Parallel of Life and Art'. It revealed that any asymmetric design, based on natural forms, could break the formality of the Modernist line; it offered a 'New Look' rather as Dior had done in the previous decade.

Other contemporary motifs included multicoloured balls resembling models of atomic structures, especially the 'Atomic Clock' by American designer George Nelson. The clock would have looked at home in a NASA control room, a laboratory or a living room. It combined a clear uncluttered face with futuristic hands, each numeral replaced by a molecule, seemingly straight from the DNA double helix discovered by Bernard Crick and James Watson in 1953. The popularity of the molecule or ball motif among designers was no surprise. Molecular biology had been one of the themes selected by the Festival of Britain organisers to stimulate designs. The ubiquitous balls appeared as the knob for racks or the feet for fruit bowls or wire plant holders. In similar vein, British designer Marianne Straub based the design for her 'Helmsley' fabric on the chemical structure of nylon.

These lively household goods would have sat upon other contemporary surfaces in the kitchen of 57 Kingsdown Parade. Formica could be stuck to an old second-hand Tudorbethan table in a spirit of wartime 'Make Do and Mend'. The old Georgian dresser, still doing stout service, could be covered in Fablon, an adhesive plastic sheeting that had jet-age graphics on it. Similar patterns, owing much to the linear asymmetrical paintings of Joan Miró, covered the plastic seats of new tubular metal chairs. This tube technology had been developed for use in wartime stretchers, and made chairs of all kinds immediately thinner and lighter than their wooden predecessors. Seats could be formed of plastic, or constructed using wartime plywood-pressing technologies.

Opposite: After years of deprivation and rationing. In the 1950s and 1960s domestic shelves were stacked with new trademarks and products thanks to a wave of marketing and advertising unthinkable just a decade before.

The newly defined 'teenagers' lived in bedsits and spent their comparatively large disposable income on winkle-pickers, transistor radios, Elvis Presley records and a popular mass-produced picture from Woolworths of an oriental Mona Lisa. There may have been more money and more consumer choice but in Number 57 home comforts still relied on a paraffin heater.

(The superbly strong and very light plywood Mosquito fighter-bomber flew at speeds well in excess of 350 miles per hour.)

While design ideas were changing, the entire economic and social face of the country was also being transformed. Now more people were getting married earlier, but they were having fewer children. The average family had 3.4 children in the first decade of the twentieth century; they now had only two. All these separate households required separate accommodation. Although the population of England and Wales went up by only 20 per cent to 48 million from 1921 to 1966, the number of private households leapt by 55 per cent to 15.7 million. This meant there was a need for smaller homes, and many more of them.

The way Number 57 was used as a home was about to change completely. The attic rooms had once been servants' quarters, then one of them was a workroom, and then they were used for family or lodgers' bedrooms. Now the attic was to become a separate living, eating and sleeping room. Bedsits were an answer to the demand for cheap accommodation, and were a financial godsend to large houses like Number 57, which always needed money for repairs. The only thing that had to be provided was a bed, a chair, a table and a gas ring on the landing.

The war had conditioned everyone to mucking in together in a culture of community, so now it was accepted that any house might have two or three families living in it. By 1958, thirty-seven dwellings in Kingsdown Parade and neighbouring Somerset Street had two or more families in them. Younger people could use this culture to their advantage, and move into cheap rented accommodation for a bit of independence. They could tell themselves that one-room living was Modern. In a reaction to wartime conformity, newly defined 'teenagers' practised disliking everything their parents liked. Their opportunities in life bore little resemblance to the world the previous generation had faced; now there were plenty of jobs for all. Real wages doubled in the same period and with low rents and little tax to pay, young people had a combined disposable annual

For a young couple to live in just one room was not ignominious. Formica, plastic and tubular steel crammed into one small place gave a post-war generation a sense of true independence and a new identity.

By the beginning of the 1960s, the upper landing of Number 57 was starting to show its age. The fabric of this once prized and valued house was on the path to decay and ruin.

income of £900 million by 1959. This was spent largely on leisure items: records, clothes and entertainment. In 1955 the first boutique opened in London's Carnaby Street with clothes just for them.

One of the main space-saving items in the bedsit was the bed-cum-sofa. This was a truly fashionable piece of furniture for its time, which did away with the traditional head-and-foot boards of a normal bed, and it had no wartime or Utility associations. It was not until the futon arrived in the late 1970s that a piece of furniture was so symbolic of a change in lifestyle and values. 'Square' parents, old-fashioned and out of touch, used their living rooms to drink tea with family members. 'Cool' teenagers invited their mates round for a cup of the new instant coffee, a fine brown powder which to today's palate would be unrecognisable as coffee.

One thing had not changed in Number 57's attic since Georgian times. Water still had to be carried upstairs, but this time by the tenants rather than a maid. Doing everything for oneself was now a badge of freedom – quite a reversal from the position only a hundred years earlier. However, damp and water penetration had really taken over

OUTDOOR AND INDOOR AMUSEMENTS

Until 1938 and the introduction of the Holidays with Pay Act, those able to afford holidays away from home were likely to be white-collar workers. A few manual workers were awarded paid holidays, but the granting of such a benefit was usually linked to good conduct and productivity. The Act stimulated the idea of taking a holiday, and about a third of the population began holidaying away from home, with town-dwellers hiking and rambling in the countryside and others heading for the seaside by train, motor coach and car.

Billy Butlin, a travelling showman born in South Africa, anticipated what the traditional seaside landlady and the inevitable British weather could not provide for the family. He built his first holiday camp in a disused sugar-beet field just outside Skegness in 1936, and transformed the British holiday experience for thousands for ever. The war years apart, holidaying during the summer months was a serious business.

Closer to home, many people enjoyed going to the 'flicks'. By 1939 there were nearly 5,000 cinemas in Britain, many with a seating capacity of more than 4,000, and over 20 million tickets were sold each week. The war years stimulated the cinema industry, offering not only imported American movies but also many from British studios, such as Laurence Olivier's *Henry V* and Noel Coward's *In Which We Serve*. The popularity of British films went on into the post-war years: Michael Balcon's

Ealing Studio comedies *Passport to Pimlico*, *Whisky Galore!* and *Kind Hearts and Coronets* were all made in the late 1940s.

By the late 1950s, however, the British film industry was in decline. Even the talents of Tony Richardson, Lindsay Anderson and John Schlesinger, who produced such gritty films as *The L-Shaped Room* and *A Kind of Loving* in the early 1960s, did not lead to sustained success. Much of the blame was pinned on the rise of television, the impact of which, as with the radio two decades earlier, had its critics. John Reith, the first Director-General of the BBC, assured its doubters that broadcasting would not be all entertainment as this would have been 'a prostitution of its powers'.

Indeed, as the number of purchased radio and television sets grew so did the sales of newspapers and books; 15,000 new book titles were published in the UK in 1939 compared with just 8,500 in 1914, and some 27 million books were sold in 1939 alone, reflecting a market stimulated by the introduction of Penguin sixpenny paperbacks first published by Allen Lane in 1935. Reading and owning good literature was no longer confined to the wealthy. Theatre too was becoming more 'accessible' with plays such as Sillitoe's 1958 *Saturday Night and Sunday Morning* appealing to a wider audience. Even the Royal Academy no longer required top hat and tails to be worn on 'private view days'.

by 1960 and the attic rooms became uninhabitable for even the most hardy. The occupied parts of the house were shrinking now to the few habitable rooms on the lower floors.

Downstairs, the sitting room had absorbed some of the trends of the late 1950s and early 1960s. All over the house the old Georgian panelled doors, alcoves and fireplaces were boarded over in an attempt to give the rooms a smooth-walled, modern look. Nylon curtains hung at the windows. They were colourful, and did not fade or need ironing. Television dramatically changed living-room furniture. The fashion was for the set to be placed on a side table, and furniture became more low-slung so it was easier to view the screen. Tables began to shrink in height so they were not in the viewer's way, becoming the ubiquitous coffee tables of the 1950s and 1960s. Picking up on the mixture of building materials in the construction of a modern house, Mr and Mrs Evans may have got hold of the end of a roll of some brick-effect wallpaper to distinguish the chimney breast in an otherwise plainly painted room. Instead of a dynamic overall wallpaper, colour could be added by a piece of Mondrian-inspired abstract-design fabric acting as an antimacassar on the broken-down brown sofa. A cheap print, a Festival of Britain mug or a coronation ornament made of unbreakable man-made Melamine could enliven a dusty shelf with a spot of colour. Plastic was also vacuum-formed into imitation Wedgwood bowls, only 120 years after the original ceramics had first made their appearance in the house.

The 'cosy corner' of a previous generation was now simply an opportunity to display the best modern objects the Evanses could afford.

It was becoming increasingly popular to buy furniture on the poor man's friend, hire purchase. In 1952 a survey for Mass Observation (an organisation that researched and analysed the nation's habits) found that 45 per cent of people used this facility for buying suites, carpets or televisions. New furniture could be foam-filled to make it lighter, softer and cheaper. The really striking developments in furniture were coming over from Scandinavia, rather as systembuilding had done. The Danes in particular favoured designs in wood, whereas the other major innovators, the Americans, favoured metal and plastic. 'G-Plan', founded by Ebenezer Gomme and manufactured in England, epitomised the break away from a three-piece-suite mentality towards interchangeable and matching chairs, recliners and sofas.

'Make Do and Mend' was mutating into 'Do It Yourself'. The Committee of Industrial Design encouraged *Woman* magazine (then read by 50 per cent of the female population aged between sixteen and forty-four) to publish articles on good design.

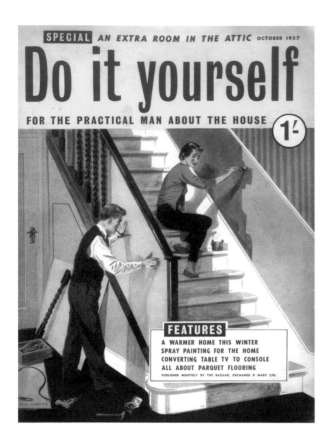

The picture on the cover of *Do it yourself* magazine could easily have been the staircase at Number 57. For a family to work to disguise the old building with hardboard and paint was a new way of bonding and brought a sense of achievement.

The periodical also changed its 'Home Makes' features into 'Tackle It Together' articles to get the man of the house involved. The BBC obligingly designed many sets for television dramas in line with Committee recommendations. Texas Homecare, a family business founded in 1911 in the United States, opened several shops in 1954 selling wallpapers and paint; it paved the way for the proliferation of home-improvement stores around today. In 1957 *Practical Householder* and *Do it yourself* magazine were published for the first time, aimed at firm-jawed, pipe-smoking handymen. Perhaps they were successful because the man of the house had tired of taking his instructions from his wife's magazines.

Outside Number 57 the threat of imminent destruction was getting ever closer. Nationally in 1954 there were 850,000 houses considered suitable for slum clearance. In 1955 members of the local authority housing department began to inspect Kingsdown and issue lists of houses that were to be classed as slums and unfit for human habitation. In 1958, nineteen houses in Kingsdown Parade and neighbouring Somerset Street were threatened with closing orders. This meant that unless the inhabitants (or their landlords) brought the house up to standard themselves, they would be compulsorily rehoused. This was not much of a choice for some. Why bother with DIY when neglect would only speed up the process of moving into a brand-new house that 'They' had built? Especially as house values were now so low that a roof replacement at £250 could easily cost more than a third of the value of the entire house.

In 1959 there were plans afoot for the redevelopment of Lower Kingsdown. Three- and four-storey terraces were to run along the contours of the lower part of the hill under Somerset Street. This was rejected by the Ministry of Housing as being too low in density to really address the problems of the area. There was also a proposal for a road that would slice directly through the gardens of Kingsdown Parade. So in 1962, when 'They' put a closing order on Number 57, Mr and Mrs Evans were probably relieved to get out. There was great uncertainty as to the fate of the area, and all they had to do was take their pick of three new council properties. By 1963, Number 57 was worth less than a thousand pounds. A new house in the area cost six times as much.

Demolition was seen as the only viable option. Number 57's distinguished Georgian pedigree counted for nothing. It was now seen as merely a tired old house, that nobody wanted. But this was nothing new. There had been a steady programme of demolishing aged buildings before and after the war. But now, the hatred of the old had risen to a new pitch. In 1963, London's old Euston station was demolished. Designed by Philip Hardwick in 1838, this vast structure was a monument to the power of the steam engine, which required a high and arching space to vent its steam and smoke. Now that these wondrous smoke-belching beasts were being withdrawn (the last ran in 1968), a new sort of station was perceived to be necessary for diesel engines and Prime Minister Harold Wilson's 1963 vision of the 'white heat of the technological revolution'. The only good thing to come out of this vandalism was the stirrings of a heritage movement. A vigorous but unsuccessful campaign was mounted to try to save the station by the nascent Victorian Society. The experience stood them in good stead, and the Society did save the Gothic splendour of St Pancras Station, which was the next scheduled for demolition.

The implications for Number 57 were obvious. Thirty years of neglect had taken a terrible toll. Philip Mann, who was eventually to buy Number 55, remembers the 'shabby depressed atmosphere' of the Parade in the early 1960s. He says that Number 57's sash windows lacked paint, and 'were propped up with things to stop the top sash falling down. The cast-iron gutters were rusty and hanging off, the roofs were in a poor state, and the gutters leaked and made stains down the front of the house. But there was a sad, majestic grandeur still there.' It seemed that there was no one to cry out in support its merits as a classic Georgian house and home, or see any reason to save it.

One possible gleam of light was the tiny Kingsdown Protection Association, which had been started in 1957 in the face of the huge changes proposed to Somerset Street. Sir John Betjeman had been moved to write to the newspapers on their behalf, and Somerset Street was saved. This success formed a bastion that protected Kingsdown Parade from being lumped in with Lower Kingsdown.

Philip Mann moved into Number 55 as the new development plan for Lower Kingsdown was proposing three sixteen-storey tower blocks separated by six-storey terraces. Higher Kingsdown was scheduled for similar development, and there were moves to build an extension of the local hospital on the west end of Kingsdown Parade. So Number 57 was under threat from three sides.

Thankfully, salvation was to come, in the shape of a young man who could have known nothing of the house's rich past, and could not have anticipated its destiny.

The dignified and grand staircase was now no more than an expedient way to climb between floors.

167

Chapter Six

PAST, PRESENT AND FUTURE:
1963 ONWARDS

At its lowest point Number 57 was an uninspiring eyesore in what had been a handsome Georgian terrace.

The last chapter in the history of 57 Kingsdown Parade is the only one with which I can directly relate. When the art and construction teams moved into the house for the last time (at least for now), they were not re-creating but creating domestic life as we now experience it. The stories seem more intimate and personal. This experience caused me to reflect on the domestic condition in which we all find ourselves today.

Historians are at home with the past but often ill at ease with the present and its immediate precedent. The past is available, discernible, measurable and as certain as can be. The present is a changing continuum. The responsibility for analysing, digesting and cataloguing its possibilities for future generations is a challenging task, requiring vision rather than hindsight. In the case of Number 57, this part of its story did more than hold up a mirror to life today; it made me look around the domestic environment and make the critical value judgements that escape the familiarity of the daily passing gaze.

Happily, 57 Kingsdown Parade turned out to be the perfect vehicle for our enthralling task of examination, enquiry and exploration. A smarter house, or a grander one, would have been cosseted and cherished throughout its life and, as such, would have been insulated from the tide of economic, social and political events that have left their mark on Number 57.

It remains a small but enduring miracle that throughout its long and eventful life not one of the host of people who lived there changed the building's fundamental form. Nor did they change the layout of its original design. John Britton's dining room is still there – more or less unchanged; it is the same room. He would still recognise it, as a space, but understandably would be either shocked or enthralled by the way it has been adapted, through time, to suit changing contemporary needs and aspirations.

I have never been back inside the house in Grantham in which I was born over fifty years ago. I have visited the house several times simply to reassure myself that it is still there, but I have never been inside since my family left it in 1955. In my mind our kitchen, scullery and dining room, and my bedroom, are as we left them almost half a century ago. But I know that the house is now some sort of management or education centre – no longer a family home. I find this thought a little unnerving. Maybe my small, intimate and endlessly reassuring bedroom is now an internet language resource facility. The thought is truly unsettling and, indeed, seems to cast some doubt on my cherished memory of times past.

LIVING TOGETHER

In the past few decades, an increasing number of couples have chosen to live together without the formality of a marriage ceremony, the term 'partner' being more common now than the word spouse. In 1996, there were about 1.6 million co-habiting couples in England and Wales – a number projected to double by 2021. Some partners opt for marriage when a child is born, while others, in an age where illegitimacy has lost its stigma, see no reason to change their status. (In the year 2000, almost two-fifths of all the births in the UK occurred outside marriage, a five-fold increase since 1970.) Given this state of affairs, there are periodic panics in the popular press about the death of marriage, yet as an institution it has proved itself to be remarkably resilient. Wedding parties still fill churches and registry offices alike – there were more than 300,000 in 1999.

The Church of England, still the nation's established Church, would of course prefer that man and woman live in holy matrimony according to traditional teachings. But just as it has had to absorb the seismic shock of women's ordination in 1992, it has had to accept the changing reality of personal relationships. The Church now christens the babies of unmarried parents; should it marry divorced people? (If the Prince of Wales, the future Defender of the Faith, wishes to marry his divorced companion in church,

this could well be a Reformation too far for many of the faithful.) Then there is the even more vexed question of homosexual unions.

But many people live their lives without reference to the wishes of any formal Church; the governing principle is choice. The choice may well be formal, heterosexual marriage, or co-habitation – committed or casual – without State or Church recognition. Same-sex couples may or may not wish to have their relationship acknowledged in a ceremony that calls on traditional values. These 'alternative' arrangements can enter a legal minefield when the relationship breaks down; conventional marriage has the accepted routes of divorce, but the law often lags behind individual lifestyles.

For couples who started living together, married or not, a specific 'starter home' evolved – economical, fully fitted and small (assuming the couple has not yet amassed the assorted junk of time). The more casual relationships of today ('Let's move in together') have given rise to an interesting design phenomenon. 'My things' and 'your things' form a relationship of their own. Furniture, pictures, ornaments and fabrics that were never planned to sit alongside one another do so without the slightest attempt at design coordination. To the observer, the result can be charming, confusing and amusing – or all three – depending on style sensibilities.

BEYOND THE GOGGLE BOX

At the beginning of the third millennium, the domestic entertainment industry has never been so multifarious and omnipresent. Technology has brought into the home an undreamed-off cornucopia of programmes to appeal to every taste, with the television set the focal point. At one time in Britain, just the one BBC channel in black and white satisfied the nation; viewers then could not have imagined the richness and diversity to come. Four more terrestrial channels arrived, first ITV in 1955, then BBC2 in 1964, followed by Channel 4 in 1982 and, most recently, Channel Five in 1997 – and all in living colour.

The choice has grown dramatically with satellite and cable stations, supplying something for everybody, with channels devoted to sport, film, music, history, nature, 'lifestyle', shopping... even reruns of old programmes first seen on television before some viewers were born. Digital technology will enable access to an even larger range of channels.

Yet the crucial conduit, the television set, and all the paraphernalia that goes with it, is a neglected piece of domestic hardware. The aged technology of Ceefax and Teletext has been available since the 1970s, but is hardly riveting entertainment or as comprehensive as the World Wide Web. As internet computer technology comes of age, the principal source of domestic entertainment could shift from the traditional big-name broadcasters to anything you want to watch from anywhere on the globe: scan the menu and click on a link.

Broadband cable systems are available to many homes in the UK, providing access to scores of television channels as well as a full telecommunications service, which allows high-speed internet access, and such facilities as home shopping and home banking. Meanwhile, the live web-cam has redefined the accepted language of television – it has enabled people to see things that are informal, unplanned, voyeuristic and often shocking and what we now see on terrestrial television has been strongly influenced by this capacity of a different medium.

The new generation of ultra-thin plasma screens will, before too long, hang like pictures on the wall throughout the house tuned to whatever you please. Television entertainment will, quite literally, become what many a jaundiced commentator has claimed it is already: wallpaper.

If the Tratman family, by some miracle, were to revisit their home at Number 57, I am confident that they would not suffer any of the unsettling emotion I feel about my old house. Their single, complete, self-contained family home is still just that. The impact of history has been as light and slight as the natural changes of the seasons, for Number 57 today is still fundamentally the same house it was over 200 years ago. The fabric, through time and tide, has been enriched and matured but not desecrated – which makes it a very special place indeed. In the beginning, when it was fresh and new, smelling of plaster, mortar, varnish and paint it was among the most fashionable, desirable and expensive houses in Bristol and, as Bristol was Britain's second largest city, in the country. They did not come much better than Number 57 in 1778.

It is that way again today. Bristol is once again a thriving city, with two universities, several theatres and the headquarters of many well-known financial and technological institutions. The houses in Kingsdown Parade are listed by estate agents as among the best in the city. Number 57's current boast of high social and financial value, along with its listing as a Grade II historic building, belies its recent past. In 1962 it suffered its nadir, when Bristol City Council placed the closing order on the house.

Beyond the dingy, damp walls of Number 57 – a house without electricity – the cultural revolution of the 1960s was under way: the contraceptive pill, the mini (skirt and car), Mary Quant, bobbed haircuts and the oddly boyish body of Twiggy. It was not just out with the old and in with the new; it was almost as if nothing from the past really mattered or even existed, a strange revival of early Modernist notions.

The changes were not just in superficial fashion. The Labour government, under prime minister Harold Wilson, was sponsoring an upheaval in social, economic and ideological values as fresh as those that stimulated the nation in 1951, courtesy of the Festival of Britain. Equal opportunities and social mobility appeared to provide a route upwards, outwards and onwards for all; crucially, there were university grants (not loans) for the children of the old working class. The Beatles were awarded MBEs; fashion designers, pop singers and film stars mixed freely with politicians and captains of industry. Even the union bosses who helped to govern the country over beer and sandwiches at Number 10 now seemed positively middle class.

Meanwhile, technology was surging forward. Bristol was seeing the first-hand development of Concorde, the supersonic passenger airliner that still flies today. On the global stage, the space age had begun when the Russians launched the first satellite, Sputnik, in 1957 – an achievement that was literally out of this world. The Americans caught up in 1958, with Explorer, and the space race was on, culminating in the first landing on the moon in 1969. These momentous events had a ripple effect on fashion and domestic design. Catwalk models wore mini-skirted space suits, and chrome, glass and curvilinear shapes in furniture brought outer space into the living room. Spherical televisions hung from ceilings as if defying gravity, while viewers reclined in strangely shaped chairs that seemed designed for aliens. Designers could have a field day with the material of the decade: synthetic plastic. It was versatile, shiny and available in any colour; by this time, there were no fewer than thirty-six different types available. The *Journal for the Society of Industrial Artists* welcomed the day that 'cutlery and furniture designs would swing like the Supremes'. The combination of mass culture and technological superiority celebrated an age in which anything seemed possible.

Not that anything positive seemed possible at the time for 57 Kingsdown Parade. Not until 1963, when the house's fortunes took an unlikely turn. A young Bristol jazz musician, John Macey, who played with the Avon City Jazz Band, was desperately looking for a house to buy for his family. Like most jazz musicians, he was hard up and, frankly, any house would do. As a former motor mechanic, John was good with his hands and ready to take on a house that needed work. The piano player in his band was a builder, and he mentioned that 57 Kingsdown Parade was derelict and vacant, if John was interested. He, the experienced builder, had decided to avoid it like the plague.

Above: In the late 1960s the kitchen at Number 57, was the height of fashion.

Below: Jazz musician turned home-improvement pioneer, John Macey.

The rise in 'Do It Yourself' was reflected in the media. The BBC's Barry Bucknell was the first television home-makeover man.

John did something that was exceptionally unusual for the day: he paid £880 for an uninhabitable house in an appalling state. Today, we take enthusiastic self-building and do-it-yourself for granted. For John Macey, it was a fundamental necessity: no personal elbow grease equalled no home for the family. The Poet Laureate John Betjeman would have thoroughly approved. He said, about the Kingsdown area of Bristol, 'Such a unique district can never be replaced. It should in the main be reconditioned rather than torn down.'

As soon as the house was his, John set to work restoring it, working every spare hour he had. He installed electricity, the first time the house had ever been wired. He replumbed it, including a central heating system (all the radiators were bought second-hand, and all were different), and installed the first ever bathroom. He employed a specialist only once, to lead the roof, for which he received a council renovation grant.

John actually found the pump and well that were mentioned in the deeds of the house 'to the rear of the said premises'. The pump was in a recess going up to the first storey, and the tank was beneath the kitchen floor. It was about four feet deep and ran the width of the room with an arched brick ceiling. There was crystal-clear rain water

FASTER AND FASTER FOOD

Over recent years, British eating habits have been transformed. Not so long ago, most meals were home-cooked and put on the table at set times, and the family sat down together to eat. Now, fewer people want to spend time and effort preparing every meal from scratch – one survey has estimated that only 28 per cent of households in the UK regularly do so. For most people, if they are in the kitchen at all, it is to microwave a ready-made meal. Some even avoid the kitchen altogether, eating a takeaway that does not even need heating up, such as a pizza delivered to the door.

When most meals were home-cooked, eating out used to be a very occasional treat with, for many people, a rather limited choice of restaurant – one serving traditional English food or, for the more adventurous, an Italian trattoria or French bistro. Now there are hundreds of restaurants of every type, serving food from all around the world, along with fast-food joints, that usually provide a takeaway service too. In the year 2000, there were no fewer than 45,875 such enterprises in the UK, with a total

turnover of £16.1 billion – a rise of 6.1 per cent on the previous year. One of the most popular fast-food outlets, McDonald's, opened its first restaurant in the UK in October 1974 and today has over 1,200, employing some 68,000 people. Consumers are evidently not put off by adverse publicity about BSE and annually spend about £2 billion on burgers alone.

There is a downside to all this convenience and instant satisfaction. Researchers have found that much of the takeaway and fast food we eat contain high levels of fat and sugar. Worryingly, the industry appears to spend large amounts of money on advertising during children's commercial TV programmes, presenting a grossly unbalanced nutritional message to young people among whom obesity is a real and growing problem. Also, with parents spending less time in the kitchen, and food technology lessons declining in schools, it is possible that some of today's young people may never learn to cook at all – providing a steady customer base for pizza parlours and burger bars, takeaways and ready meals.

in it, piped down from the roof. John found a second water-storage tank at the front of the house, lined with bitumen and with the down pipe from the outside of the house running into it. He discovered the kitchen still had its 1930s fireplace. He had hoped to find a range behind it, but instead he found bits of black cast-iron of unknown origin. Maybe these were pieces of the range that Mary Atherton had spent so much time blackleading over a hundred years earlier.

It is important to remember that all of John's efforts were at a time before the plethora of large warehouses dedicated to home improvements had sprung up and before the mass availability of power tools. John used all his imagination, manual dexterity and physical skill in the dedicated pursuit of one goal: to provide a home for his family. There was not the number of handy technical publications, magazines or television programmes that there are today; he was, quite literally, a pioneer in a field of human activity that now seems to all but dominate the British weekend.

At times he thought he was not going to succeed. His friends thought that he was out of his mind and would only waste his money on a building which the council would, in the end, claim for their own. It took two-and-a-half years of hard work before, finally, the closing order was lifted and John and his family were able to move in.

Downstairs the kitchen became a kitchen–living room, an open-plan arrangement separated by a breakfast bar. For the first time the kitchen was 'fitted', benefiting from all modern conveniences and with hot running water.

On the first floor, the drawing room of old was divided into two. One half accommodated the new bathroom; the suite was in fashionable pink with chrome fittings and the floor was black-and-white tiles. The other half of the old drawing room was used for storage, housing two freezers, a product owned then by only 4 per cent of householders. Such a use of this room seems absurd to us today, even sacrilegious. Despite the beginning of the return to favour of

GROWING OLD GRACEFULLY

Throughout history, some individuals have always lived to a great age compared to their peers. Whatever the average lifespan for a period, churchyards everywhere invariably record the passing of someone who has lived way beyond the traditional threescore years and ten. In our own time, the average age of death for a British man is seventy-five, and for a woman just under eighty: the highest in recorded history. In 1901, one person in twenty was aged sixty-five or over; in 2000 it was just over one in six. If this trend continues, by 2016 the number of people aged sixty-five and over in Britain will surpass those under the age of sixteen. It looks like an increasing number of centenarians can expect a telegram from Queen Elizabeth II and her successors.

The Queen's own mother lived to the ripe old age of 101, attended with every care throughout her long life until her death in 2002. Most of us do not have the privileges of royalty; as we age – and already in Britain half the population is over forty years of age – we will have to cope with living in dwellings that were often designed for the young and fit. Housing design in general makes few concessions to the needs of the aged. Much of the nation's housing stock is too large and expensive to run for those living on a small pension. The cost of heating alone can be daunting in a house where not used everyday. Steps, stairs and other obstacles are an accepted feature of most houses – indeed, they are often designed in as an indulgence. Those in the latter years of their life and with reduced mobility must learn to negotiate rather than enjoy their homes.

Imaginative designers should accept the challenge of designing specifically for the elderly. Primary schools are not just scaled-down secondary schools – the design philosophy is entirely different. Retirement homes do exist, but at the present time not in sufficient numbers to satisfy the demographic drift. In any case, many elderly people want to live in their own homes for as long as possible; adapting them with the inevitable hand-rails, stair-lift and specialised bath that appear clumsy add-ons. The seventh-age home of the future should be elegant, safe, convenient, easy to run and generally fit for its purpose.

Georgian houses in the 1960s, not all aspects of the style were appreciated. Interiors were often adapted to suit the Modern look: fireplaces were ripped out or boarded over; panelling and dados were removed; and sash windows were replaced by large picture windows. So John's approach to the house was par for the course.

The old dining room, the setting for the Alder family's beautiful Victorian Christmas, became a lounge that the Macey family rarely used. The main bedroom, on the second floor, was where John and his wife Doris slept. It was furnished with an old 1930s bedroom suite inherited from a relative. Their son Jim slept in the other bedroom. The attic rooms were used for storage, and Jim's Scalextric electric racing car track, a best-selling toy of the time.

Number 57 Kingsdown Parade was a family home once again, but John's work was far from over. As he puts it, 'That's the trouble with Georgian houses — you're forever repairing.' He likened his task to painting the Forth Bridge: no sooner have you finished something than something else needs doing.

While John Macey was breaking new ground with his personal crusade to make a home, designers were realising the economic potential of this new breed of happy homemakers. In 1964 the young Terence Conran opened his first Habitat store. It coincided with the time when the British were enjoying their first package holidays to Spain. He made it easy for them to buy contemporary continental furniture and fabrics that were relaxed and utterly in tune with the mood of the 1960s. At last shopping could be fun, a far cry from the penny-pinching restrictions of post-war austerity. And with this came the birth of shopping as an unlikely form of therapy.

Terence Conran's Habitat store fed the nation's increasing appetite for the simple, the modern and the Continental – and at an affordable price.

Conran is responsible for completely changing the face of British interior design in the second half of the twentieth century. Born in 1931, he studied textile design at the Central School of Arts and Crafts in London. In 1950 he joined the Rayon Centre as a full-time industrial designer. The following year, he worked with architect Dennis Lennon as a designer on some minor projects for the Festival of Britain. In 1952 he set up his own furniture-making business, creating the 'Summa' range, a squarer, more solid shape than the tapered-leg styles then prevailing from Scandinavia and Italy. He also designed the 'Nature Study' range for Midwinter Tableware, and founded the Conran Design Group in 1956.

Such bare facts pay little tribute to a man who single-handedly, it seemed, rescued Britain in the 1960s from a long sojourn in the design desert. His own philosophy is as straightforward as it is consistently brilliantly executed: 'My belief is simply that if reasonable and intelligent people are offered something that is well made, well designed, of a decent quality and at a price they can afford, then they will like and buy it. This is the abiding principle to which I hold, whether as a designer, retailer or restaurateur.'

Conran had developed this clear philosophy before opening the first Habitat in London's Fulham Road. He wanted to offer the best in Scandinavian and Italian furniture design, both practical and modern, at affordable prices. He pioneered flat-pack furniture. As he now says, 'You could go into Habitat and pick up your furniture in a package, strap it to the back of your Vespa, go home, assemble it and you've got instant gratification. Whereas if you ordered a piece of furniture from a shop it usually took sixteen weeks to be delivered. And then it was usually damaged.' Furthermore, taking a leaf out of the wartime Utility book, Conran also marketed a wide range of carpets, lamps, fabrics and coordinated household goods. The products were elegant, simple and functional, and you could pick and mix. They had no value judgements associated with them except that trendy young Terence, friend of the stars, had designed them, so they must be good. Everything was youthful, new, energetic, and all piled high to mimic the busy French markets Conran had seen on his trips abroad.

Habitat changed the face of Britain. Up to this point, a well-designed stainless-steel knife or plain white crockery was simply not available, at almost any price. Habitat went on to break new ground in the succeeding decades, bringing to Britain the duvet, and the wok. Conran was, belatedly, introducing the British public to Modernism with a strong Scandinavian influence.

By the 1960s the powerful lessons in design that had been taught by, and in small measure learnt from, the Festival of Britain had been all but forgotten. In mainstream architecture, post-war British Modernism came to an end on Thursday, 16 May 1968, when part of a tower block, Ronan Point in Tower Hamlets in London's East End, collapsed. One corner of the twenty-two-storey block fell down, killing five people and making a dramatic front page photograph. It showed eighteen floors of the building flapped down, floor upon floor, so exactly like a collapse of a house of cards that subeditors had little work reaching for a headline. In the *Guardian*, the picture ran opposite one of Parisian students tearing up the cobblestones to hurl at riot police. The literal fabric of society seemed to be crumbling. These images marked the abrupt wake-up call that ended the 1960s dream once and for all.

The first thing to remember about Ronan Point is the fact that the tower block did not fall down of its own volition; there was a gas explosion. The second is that the domino-like collapse of the floors would not have occurred if the joints holding the system-built structure together had been made properly. And the third is the fact that, far from being to blame for the failure of the building, the architects had not been closely involved in its design and construction.

On Thursday 16 May 1968 the collapse of a corner of the Ronan Point tower block in London's East End ended the British enthusiasm for concrete.

The system-building specification itself was immensely strong. The weak point was the nature of the joints holding the units together. It was not until joints in similar buildings were physically opened in 1986 that the pioneering architectural investigator Sam Webb was able to prove his theory; instead of being filled with dry-pack mortar to provide the necessary strength, the joints were filled with any rubbish that had been lying around on the building site. Whereas it used to be the architect who checked on such things, this role had now been assumed by the contractors themselves, often directly employing the consulting engineers. The latter approved the overall design criteria of the system, rather than the construction of a kit of parts on site. In other words, no one took it as their responsibility to see whether some likely lad was filling a joint to the crucial and precise standards demanded by the system for it to be safe.

This accurate analysis of the Ronan Point disaster took nearly two decades to research and compile. In the meantime, irreparable damage had been done to concrete: the word, the look and the method. Concrete went from Utopia to deathtrap in a few seconds. It was all too easy for the pundits to sum up. Concrete was bad, and pretty much anything else was good.

John Macey and his family lived at Number 57 for around a quarter of a century, finally moving out in 1990. By this time the area had been gentrified, with a growing population of professionals such as doctors and architects. The house was once again a sought-after residence, and John sold it for no less than £150,000, a fitting return on his superhuman efforts to successfully turn a dignified old wreck into a working family home.

The current chapter in the history of the house is not, any more, a mixture of hard fact, historical context and intelligent imagination; it is the reality of the way we live our lives today in a building designed for another age, for a time about which we fantasise and dream. For us today, Georgian is as fashionable a label as any to be found on London's Bond Street. Sometimes, but not always, the Georgian style is treated in the same ephemeral way as passing fashion: Georgian today and who knows what tomorrow?

Since the Maceys moved out, several families have lived at Number 57 but none stayed for a significant time. For a while it has been our house. But before it is returned to the mercy of the market, the television designers have the chance to strip it back to a blank canvas one last time as we examine how it will adapt to life today.

Our house still has the kitchen where it always was; it is the obvious place to put it. Today's kitchen is the heart of the home and no longer a purely functional space. In Georgian times, it was the domain of two servants, who would cook food on an open fire. It was not a place the gentleman owner would often visit himself. By the end of the nineteenth century, it had begun to benefit from new technology such as a gas stove and an ice chest to preserve food. Although the householder now spent time here, the kitchen remained a purely utilitarian space and decoration was minimal. By the 1950s, the kitchen had become a room for family eating, and was more consciously designed in the contemporary style. But it still was not a place in which to entertain. Now, more than any other room in the house, it is the one in which we show off.

The twenty-first-century kitchen is the pride of the home and the room on which we spend most money. It has taken over from the drawing room as the key statement of our sense of style and taste. Like the rest of the house, its fixtures and fittings become part of a conscious display intended to impress our friends and visitors, an attitude to domestic space redolent of the Georgian and Regency period. Modern conveniences abound, but in our contemporary house the kitchen also celebrates the past. The dresser is the same one that has stood there since Georgian times. The 1960s-inspired wallpaper brings a splash of retro style. The Regency dining table, now without a room of its own, takes pride of place. Even the up-to-the-minute cooker returns to the spot under the chimney breast where meals were spit-roasted 200 years ago. Nevertheless, the room is rooted in the present by a wall of cutting-edge kitchen units in stainless steel.

Stainless steel was developed as a by-product of gun manufacture during the First World War. It was quickly commandeered for domestic use because of its non-corrosive,

Number 57's kitchen, which has endured over two hundred years of change, can be seen either as a confusion of styles, or a sophisticated exhibition of contemporary taste.

Stainless steel, once a
necessity of industry, is
welcomed into John
Britton's original kitchen
without any sense of
respect for its intended use.

Three plastic bins beneath the copious sink show that today's family is enthusiastically embracing the new catechism of recycling.

hygienic qualities. Today it is no longer a purely functional material and has become a fashionable interior design statement that says we are more serious about our kitchens than ever. Some of the most expensive kitchens that I, as an architect, have been asked to design are meant to look like industrial restaurant kitchens. In the 1980s, restaurants began to create interiors in which their kitchens were an exposed feature and key to the overall look. In an era when chefs are celebrities whom both men and women seek to emulate, the look has extended into the home – although the owners seldom or never use the kitchen; they are always eating out at restaurants.

In the past, the introduction of gadgets to the house had been seen as a way of saving time and effort by mechanising common chores. Today we rely upon labour-saving devices more than ever, but our appliances are also statements of our taste. In an age where designer branding affects every product we own, even the lemon squeezer and the tea strainer display our sense of style.

Above the kitchen, on the first floor, is the principal room in the house. What used to be the Regency withdrawing room becomes the twenty-first-century living room. This space has always been the style leader in the house. In the early 1800s it displayed the fashion and elegance of the Regency period. By the middle of the nineteenth century it was a cluttered treasure-trove of Victorian innovation and curiosities. Since then it has been an Edwardian parlour and a 1950s lounge.

Opposite: An object from outer space or simply a lemon squeezer?

In today's living room, all of these looks are part of the broad choice available. Number 57's television designers, tackling this room for the last time, were able to

The drawing room became the parlour, the parlour the living room; and today it is a cross between a home-entertainment centre and a display cabinet for all that is considered to be fashionable. In keeping with Post Modern eclecticism, the original late-Georgian fireplace remains in tact.

borrow elements from a variety of styles, to create a brand-new contemporary look. Despite the spectrum of choice available at our fingertips today, most would consider that this living room is surprisingly simple. The walls are plain and the furnishings are low and informal. The surfaces are uncluttered and the overall look is one of calming emptiness. Hints of the room's past remain – the dado rail and shutters are still there.

Despite the comparatively sparse look, this new living room has a somewhat confusing sense of style, accommodating both public show to impress guests, and private indulgence – a new comfort zone for the overworked and stressed owners. It is a place for lazing, listening and watching – not people but television. It lacks the genuine care and commitment given to the room by, say, the Tratmans for the simple reason that we have the financial wherewithal and a bewildering array of good-value products to change its looks as often as we change our clothes. While it took John Macey two-and-a-half years to make Number 57 his home, today we can remake ours in as long as it takes us to read some incomprehensible flat-pack furniture instructions and conjure up a 'look' that will remain that way for the length of an haute couture season and little more than that. Here today, changed tomorrow – and we are proud of it.

Although the owners of Number 57 today will certainly value its Georgian style and credentials, they probably, albeit subconsciously, hanker after the very summit of today's desirable domestic space – the loft. The trend for loft-living grew out of 1950s Manhattan, where artists recycled industrial buildings to create spaces in which to live and work. Most famously, Andy Warhol ran his Pop Art 'Factory' from a New York warehouse conversion. Loft living hit the United Kingdom with the beginning of the renaissance of London's Docklands in the early 1980s. Warehouse conversions answer our twenty-first-century quest for light and space. Furnishings and ornamentation are minimal, emphasising a sense of emptiness. Despite this minimalism, this ultimate contemporary living space gets its distinctive aesthetic from its past, as industrial architectural features such as bricks, beams and columns become part of its look.

Not for the first time, the owners and designers of Number 57 find it difficult to compete with the ultimate domestic fashion of the time. John Britton had a fine Georgian dining room, but it was a far cry from the spacious elegance of style leaders of the day like that at Number 1 Royal Crescent in Bath.

The dining room, the lesser of the two rooms on the first floor of Number 57, has been a living space from the very beginning – at least until today. This elegantly proportioned room has been ransomed to a new domestic requirement: the home office. This title in itself has a built-in contradiction; maybe it is appropriate to make this contradiction manifest by a singular disregard for the dignity of this historic room.

When I was an architectural student in the 1960s, we were taught that the corporate office building would be a thing of the past by the third millennium. It was anticipated that the march of technology would mean that we no longer had to commute long distances to gather in one place for a regimented working day which, in its structure, organisation and social nuances had changed little since the end of the nineteenth century. Creative architects, planners and designers speculated that the future, vested in a technology as yet only dreamed of, would free us for a simpler, more flexible lifestyle

The flat-screen computer, which brings work firmly into the home, sits on a table that is where there was once a candle-bedecked Victorian Christmas tree.

based around our homes. The concept became known as the Electronic Cottage. In short, we would all work from home, and home would no longer, necessarily, be in or around our great towns and cities. In the minds of the big thinkers, the highlands of Scotland, the fells of Yorkshire and the dales of Derbyshire would be sprinkled with individual hives of activity where captains of industry would mix work, relaxation and pleasure in a new seamless confection of a better life. The wires and airwaves would link together through an untiring web all those who would no longer stress their minds or bodies with the superfluous need to gather together.

It was a great dream that gave rise to some truly original architectural thinking, and speculation about what the home of the future would be like. Manifestly, though, this idealistic dream has not turned into a dominant reality, although an increasing number of people are finally calling the bluff of the system and are earning their living without stepping outside their front door. However, our cities are still dominated by cranes; society at the beginning of the third millennium seems to continue to have an insatiable appetite for offices.

PLURALISM AND LIBERALISM IN RELIGION

The last thirty years have seen a growing religious pluralism in England. While the majority of people still consider themselves Christian, less than 20 per cent attend church. Pentecostal churches, set up to meet the spiritual needs of Afro-Caribbean Christians with an emphasis on evangelism, prophecy and healing, are now the third largest denomination of churches in England after Roman Catholic and Anglican.

There are over 2 million Muslims, Sikhs and Hindus in Britain. The number of Muslims who attend regular worship is roughly the same as those who attend Church of England services, and schools – including Church schools – increasingly teach a pluralistic view of religion.

New sects such as the Mormons and Jehovah's Witnesses continue to offer alternative views of Christianity, promoted through door-to-door visits. Other 'new' religions have punched above their weight through the media: the Unification Church – the Moonies – with tales of brainwashing, and the orange-robed Hare Krishna members, who have received negative publicity for their Hindu beliefs adjusted for a western world. The interest among young people in these and other sects seems to point not to increasing secularisation, but to a fundamental problem within the mainstream faith. Like the soldiers returning from the First World War, they find that the Church no longer meets their needs, and they are looking for belief systems elsewhere.

There is continued debate between the Catholic and Anglican faiths, but unification seems unlikely while such differences of opinion on issues such as birth control and homosexuality remain. Similar differences have created a rift between Orthodox and Liberal Jews.

The Church of England's decline has stopped, and its modernisation included the ordination of women ministers in 1992 – the Church is working to admit them as bishops, and the new Archbishop of Canterbury, Rowan Williams, is in favour of women's equal status in the Church. And while the head of the church is still the Crown, Prince Charles's role of 'Defender of the Faith' is one he has suggested modifying to 'Defender of Faith', as an indicator at the highest level that the Church and Crown welcome a pluralistic religious environment in Britain.

There is one element, though, of the Electronic Cottage idea that has come true more generally. Today we expect our home to be a portal to the outside world through telephone, fax, e-mail and the Internet. As if a day in the office in front of a computer display screen was not enough, we seem to want more when we get home. The enthusiasm for this new aspect of the domestic round has gone so far that the home office now seems indispensable.

We like to believe that the office at home is our domestic control-centre where we sit proudly at the bridge of a time machine that knows no geographical or physical boundaries. We turn on, tune in but, unlike the 1960s, do not drop out; we drop in to the all-consuming and time-devouring realm of the electronic universe. The home-office is not the control centre; it is the out-of-control centre. We bring into our homes an uncoordinated clutter of technology which, if we bothered to step back and look, has the same naïve sense of self-importance as the horn on the Nashes' first gramophone. The average home-office desk has a clutter of screens, keyboards, wires, plugs, adaptors and transformers. Some of the equipment duplicates the functions of its neighbour as we dutifully assimilate the hard-sell products of the twenty-first-century electronics industry.

This state of affairs will not last for long. The Japanese electronics giants have already started work on a programme to persuade us to rationalise the electronics in our homes. Every single piece of electronic equipment we have, from the microwave to the television remote to the comparatively simple portable mini-disc player, has at its heart a microprocessor. Most of these things incorporate a visual display screen of one sort or another. Again, most of this equipment incorporates a digital timing device. The goal is to link them all together and network them into one mainframe home computer. The Japanese know, and we merely need to be convinced, that a centralised grey box tucked away in the cupboard under the stairs or in the garage linked by radio-waves to every room in the house could save the wires, save the profligate consumption of electronic components and

transform the domestic condition more dramatically than any change in the history of Number 57. Perhaps, while we are getting used to that, we will also take in our stride other imminent inventions, such as paint that can actually conduct electricity, and windows that can automatically darken, doing away with the need for curtains or blinds.

Our home office does its best to accommodate what is a run-of-the-mill arrangement of home electronics. The period curved shelves on either side of the chimney breast can be used for storage. The new desk, fitted beneath the windows so that those long hours labouring at home may at least be leavened by a pleasant view of the garden, is made of varnished plywood fashioned into a smooth organic curve.

The desk occupies a small part of the room. There is then a stool designed on ergonomic principles to encourage the correct posture for keyboard work. The science of ergonomics was introduced during the 1960s. By studying human behaviour and anatomical geometry, it proved possible to design household gadgets and furniture that fitted more comfortably into the natural rhythms and physical possibilities of the human body. Ergonomics changed the kitchen for ever. The height of worktops, depth of wall

In the home office we seem to accept a lack of coordination and a discomfort that we would find unacceptable in the workplace.

189

From bedroom to bathroom. From a simple desire for cleanliness to an obsession with a pampered body beautiful.

units and size of their doors were all determined by ergonomics in the 1960s. It was a thoroughly worthwhile new science, some of whose wisdom has sadly been lost today. We all know that there are wonderful office chairs, like the one at the desk in Number 57, at which we kneel rather than sit and which undoubtedly are the best possible thing for bad-back sufferers. But all too often we sacrifice long-term benefit to short-term exigency.

Just as technology makes its clumsy debut in the house of today, so house-owners in the past have been equally confused about how to assimilate changes in plumbing and drainage. John Britton, although a gentleman through and through, would openly relieve himself in a chamber pot in the corner of the dining room. At least there was a cupboard into which he could put the pot to give a veneer of respectability to an otherwise basic function. In Victorian times there was an outside privy that sometimes leaked into the house. Even after a kitchen tap was fitted in the 1870s, servants would have to boil water and carry it through the house. As late as the 1950s, at least in 57 Kingsdown Parade, a tin bath was the best that was on offer. John Macey introduced the first bathroom less than forty years ago. Then it was a purely functional space.

Just as a perfectly decent room has been entirely given over to an office, so a room on the second floor that was designed as a bedroom – and indeed has been used as such for over 200 years – has been mortgaged to our insatiable appetite for cleanliness and bodily self-indulgence. It is now a bathroom, considered to be one of the most important rooms in the house. We take running hot and cold water for granted. We consume 100 litres of water per person per day. It takes 80 litres for a bath and 35 litres for a shower and, worst of all, 10 litres every time we flush the WC. The bathroom is no longer just about cleanliness; it is about self-indulgence, pampering and relaxing.

Once again, the look of the room is eclectic. The original Georgian fireplace and bare boards form the backdrop. The hearth, decorated with an array of candles, offers a convenient and disposable twist on a

His and hers wash basins – another sign of the extravagant luxury of the modern home.

period feature. In our obsession with cleanliness, colour has been rejected in favour of clinical white ceramic, which has been brought up to date with sleek fittings finished in chrome. Two separate wash basins are an indulgence but are excused by apparently offering a way of creating efficiency in our time-starved lives. His and hers basins (which have in fact been around since the 1960s and always seemed to feature in James Bond movies) are there to cater for the unlikely moment when he and she, at exactly the same time, decide to wash their face or brush their teeth.

The major design influence on our bathrooms today is the booming industry in health clubs and spas. In our frantic culture, rituals of cleansing and well-being help us to unwind, and interiors combining hygienic white surfaces with sensuous accessories create the perfect ambience. The extravagance of today's bathroom would impress the most fastidious of Ancient Roman senators, or indeed that eminent Aesthete Lord Leighton. We are more than happy for our guests to perform their bodily functions in our bathroom as they will return impressed, not just by our choice of toiletries, but by the conspicuously extravagant use of space and narcissistic preoccupation with our bodies.

In the 1950s (and I can say this from personal testimony), most people bathed only once a week. Few homes had readily available running hot water, so bathtime was an effort. After all, most people only changed their undergarments once or twice a week, cosmetic deodorant did not exist and dry-cleaning seemed to be a contradictory impossibility (which, in any event, was available only in the larger cities). Nevertheless, nobody complained about the smell of another. Those in historical times did not, either. There was a long tradition of being sewn into your undergarments for the winter and, for most in the early history of Number 57, one bath a year was more than enough.

It has been adequately proved scientifically that excessive washing is bad for our skin and our overall health. Once again, our perverse behaviour ensures that for the time being there is no indication that we will change – any more than John Britton could have anticipated for one moment that his successors in title at Number 57 would be able to dispose of their excrement at the push of a lever and that they would bother to bathe every single day.

FOR EVER CHANGING FASHION

After the swinging 1960s came disillusionment. Youngsters escaped the materialistic society through romantic clothes typified by idealist designer Laura Ashley or by becoming hippies. Hirsute men and women wore long ethnic robes and strings of beads, with flowers in their hair and painted on their faces symbolising peace and love.

In the 1970s fashion followed flower power with flares, skin-tight shirts with long pointed collars and kipper ties, but it was a mixed-up decade. Increasingly, post-war fashion came from the street not couture houses – the East End Teddy Boys, the 1960s Mods and Rockers, the Skinheads. In the late 1970s, Punk swore itself in. As a reaction to conformist Britain, young people from all classes dyed and spiked their hair, pierced their noses with safety pins and wore tattered black clothing held together with studs and chains.

The 1980s was the 'Gimme Decade', where Yuppies wore Armani suits with red braces or tight short skirts with shoulder-padded jackets. Some preferred idealism again, and followed Spandau Ballet as frilly-shirted New Romantics. But the legacy of the 1980s was sportswear.

The *Fame* generation had lounged in legwarmers, Lycra leggings and the cotton 'body', but in the 1990s sportswear became streetwear. Shellsuits led to branded tracksuits and £100 trainers. For 1990s sportswear companies and their clientele, image was everything.

Catwalk outfits have become more spectacular (and unwearable). The couture fashion icon has shifted from Princess Diana to sexy songstress Kylie Minogue in her crocheted backless Julien MacDonald dresses and bondage stage wear. (With the fashion for barely there dresses, women's underwear has followed suit – transparent single-hook bras and tiny thongs are popular.)

Fashion increasingly follows celebrity style, with male icons such as David Beckham influencing menswear, a growing market. The male skirt is yet to catch on, though.

The contemporary idea of bedroom luxury is exemplified by the largest bed that money can buy set contrastingly alongside a fireplace that provided only meagre warmth hundreds of years ago.

The other room on the second floor of the house is still true to its original function, as a bedroom. The twenty-first-century bedroom is one of the few truly honest spaces left in the home. We tend not to show it off to friends and visitors (unless there is something new in the way of decoration or furnishing). It is the real 'living' room. We do not take our clothes off only in preparation for sleep; we may pause for a moment to take in our appearance in a full-length mirror with the inevitable dissatisfaction with our body shape. During the history of the house, mirrors have previously been an expensive luxury. Up until Victorian times the principal source of reflection for the lady of the house would have been a small hand-held mirror. Victorian glass technology meant that large mirrors became a great deal cheaper. Nevertheless, the full-length mirrors of today, which allow us to look at our entirety literally from head to toe, are now taken for granted – albeit often concealed on the inside of a wardrobe door in case we would rather not know the truth about how we look.

The room is now no longer simply known as the main bedroom but the master bedroom – a title presumably intended to confer upon it some innate sense of grandeur. For a short time during the nineteenth century it was a hygienic nursery with clean metal beds and a lino floor. Throughout, its function has remained the same: a room in which to sleep, store clothes, dress, undress and generally make ready for a public day. Then, of course, when the bed is shared by a couple, there is the sexual element – not that it is possible to do more than speculate about bedroom behaviour throughout the ages, records and testimonies being notoriously unreliable. Suffice to say that the bedroom was, and still is, the most private and personal of all rooms.

Stylistically, the room is more single-minded than the rest of the spaces in the house of today. Its principal pieces of furniture are of plain, simple, Scandinavian Modernist design – with, inevitably for a twenty-first-century interior, the essential glances back to the past, with the exposed fireplace and an original 1950s chair.

There is a return to bright colours on the wall, but they are balanced by more neutral tones. The overall sense in the room is of space and light. The bed is lower than it has ever been before, showing the influence of the Japanese bed pallet, the futon, if not in its original form.

The bed, along with the wardrobe (which these days is more of a storage unit, providing more than just space for hanging clothes), may look like high design when, in fact, they are surprisingly cheap and cheerful. The defining look of this room is created thanks to self-assembly furniture, one of the biggest influences on our homes today. The occupants of Number 57 at the beginning of a new millennium will make the pilgrimage to the new interior design mecca, the IKEA store.

IKEA is the largest furniture chain in the world, with 143 stores in twenty-two countries. Its annual catalogue has a huge print-run second only to the Bible. Combining manufacturing production processes with economical materials, it produces Scandinavian-style Modernist furniture for the masses – and is immensely popular. The company made its mark in Britain in the 1980s, and now in this country alone more than 650,000 people shop at IKEA every week, choosing from its 12,000 lines.

Among the most popular items at IKEA and other outlets are what are usually referred to as 'storage solutions'. Indeed, such is the unstoppable pace of consumerism

A trip to a flat-pack furniture emporium seems to be a modern addiction, at least for the 650,000 people who visit the twenty-two British IKEA stores every week.

today that accumulations of 'stuff' do present a problem. Despite the fact that we buy more and more things we do not need, using money we do not have, we still find it hard to discard that which we were supposed to have replaced. So to achieve the desirable clutter-free interiors of today, all our junk — that we will never use again or seldom even see — has to be secreted using increasingly ingenious storage facilities.

One piece of bedroom furniture that seems to have lost much of its appeal is the dressing table. As far back as Regency times in Number 57, this was a shrine to female beauty, remaining so through Victorian and Edwardian times. Today we seem disinclined to designate a special item of furniture for the process of personal grooming and make-up. Certainly some modern bedrooms are too small, and a mirror on top of a chest of drawers suffices. In a house such as Number 57, the luxurious bathroom has become, along with the bedroom, a place in which to relax and combine luxury dressing-table-type activities alongside the essentials of personal hygiene. Nevertheless, it is all too familiar a sight to see a young woman applying her make-up in a train, on the underground or even in a car while stationary at traffic lights.

All in all, the new look to the second floor of Number 57, with the combination of master bedroom and a space that can hardly be referred to simply as a bathroom, adds up to a reflection of a more luxurious lifestyle provided by greater affluence.

The top floor of the house was traditionally reserved for servants — the two plain, cheerless rooms giving a little respite from incessant labour. While some households today may have domestic help, few people have live-in cooks and cleaners. Those two top rooms would now be seen as flexible extra space, their garret-like appearance setting them apart from the rest of the house stylistically. They could be guest rooms, or bedrooms for children (in which case one might be reserved for a nanny or au pair).

Throughout the four floors of the house, nothing seems of a piece. It is random, confused, superficial, transitory and contradictory. But that is precisely the point. The twenty-first-century domestic interior is a conscious statement of Post Modern intention. Post Modernism is a world view that maintains that all world views are equally valid and equally valuable. So anything goes. Confusion shows style and taste, not ignorance of style or wanton indecision. So this entire contemporary domestic look is easily explicable. The stainless-steel kitchen is set against a Regency dining table; a perfectly elegant Georgian room is a cluttered office; another is a room with a bath and a great deal more. The historic drawing room is chock-full of stylistic borrowings, and the bedroom's sophisticated and contemporary look is achieved through a combination of ephemeral catalogue choices.

Despite today's approach to interior design and decoration, Number 57 is strong enough to take this brief period in its long and distinguished history in its stride. To contemporary eyes, with current taste, the house of today is as desirable as it was two hundred years ago. Judging today's style, fashion and taste is a task for the strong-minded and resolutely opinionated. As I have said, I was brought up to believe that everything Victorian was beyond redemption. I have changed my view. I would like to see this change of opinion as a strength that has grown out of a deeper and possibly more mature understanding of the past. Future generations may – almost certainly will – look back on Number 57 as it was in 2002 with respect and admiration. They can do nothing else; hindsight is ultimately forgiving.

Although there could have been no original intention that Number 57 would last for over 200 years, there is now little doubt that, as a Grade II listed building in good structural condition, it could last another 200 years.

This story has been but a snapshot of the rich and enduring life of a modest house that exemplifies the three architectural virtues set out by the Roman architectural historian Vitruvius in the books he wrote for Julius Caesar: firmness, commodity and delight. In today's language, that translates as structural stability, usefulness and aesthetic pleasure. Number 57's history, and the story of the lives of those who have lived in it, enriches our understanding of our own place in the continuum of domestic time. Our own home (wherever or whatever it is) is a mirror of Number 57; it too leaves a permanent for those in the future with as much inquisitiveness as those on the team that have told this house's story.

In today's secular society we seek means other than religion to give a context to our lives. There is an increasing enthusiasm for rooting ourselves in the history of our family. Genealogy gives us a sense of continuity and permanence. It enriches our fleeting lives – it makes us, now, part of an enduring continuum. The story of 57 Kingsdown Parade teaches us that knowing the history of the places in which we work out our lives adds further richness and certainty to our passing tenure of the buildings that belong to history and, for a time, are ours.

Opposite: 225 years on, the staircase remains.

The genealogy of place should be our next absorbing and reassuring muse.

SUPPLIERS' DIRECTORY

This is an introductory list of good quality suppliers of elements to get you started as you restore or recreate a period home. Most of the suppliers listed offer websites and brochures to help you select the most appropriate products. Details are correct at the time of going to press but we cannot accept any responsibility for the service provided by the suppliers listed.

Exploring local antiques markets, fairs and sales can be invaluable for locating more unusual items. *The Antique Trader* is available from newsagents and gives details of forthcoming events.

An addictive website to visit is www.ebay.co.uk which calls itself 'the world's online marketplace'. This auction website has sections for collectables (including kitchenalia) antiques and architectural salvage.

▲ = brochure available   ● = mail order available

ARCHITECTURAL RECLAMATION

The London Architectural Salvage and Supply Company ▲
Tel: 020 7749 9944
www.lassco.co.uk

The kings of architectural reclamation, Lassco has grown into five companies: St Michael's, a church filled with architectural antiques; Lassco Warehouse specialising in architectural salvage; Lassco Flooring supplying reclaimed wood floors; Lassco RBK selling original and reproduction radiators, bathroom fittings, period kitchen furniture and kitchenalia and Lassco House and Garden selling replica friezes, door furniture, fireplaces and mirrors.

Olliffs
21 Lower Redland Road
Bristol BS6 6TB
Tel: 0117 923 9232
www.olliffs.com

Olliffs' fascinating website has sections for new stock and 'offers invited' on old stock. They also have a shop in Bristol and will try to find items for you that they do not have in stock.

Retrouvius
2a Ravensworth Road
London NW10 5NR
Tel: 020 8960 6060
www.retrouvius.com

Retrouvius specialises in both reclamation and design, selling only items the owners, Adam Hills and Maria Speake have 'rescued' themselves. Warehouse visits are by appointment only. They also host related exhibitions.

DOORS AND WINDOWS

Arnold & Oakley ▲ ●
Architectural Ironmongery
28 Kyrle Street
Ross-on-Wye
Herefordshire HR9 7DB
Tel: 01989 567946
www.arciron.co.uk

This company produces an extensive range of door furniture and fittings including a mind-boggling selection of black iron antique-style fittings and Art Nouveau cabinet handles.

Barron Glass ▲ ●
Unit 4 Old Cola Yard Farm Estate
Northleach
Glasgow GL54 3HE
Tel: 01451 860282
www.barronglass.co.uk

Barron Glass produces Victorian-style pine doors with decorative glass panels based on original designs. The etched glass patterns include stars, fleur-de-lys and Gothic styles and they also provide a sandblasting service to customers' own designs. Plain panel doors as well as those with glazed panels are available in Gothic, Georgian and Victorian styles.

Clayton Munroe ▲ ●
Kingston Workshop
Staverton
Totnes
Devon TQ9 6AR
Tel: 01803 762626
www.claytonmunroe.com

This company produces premium-quality door furniture and cabinet fittings, the majority of which are handmade to give the most authentic finish. Traditional, rustic and contemporary designs are all included.

The Fingerplate Company ▲ ●
The Limes
Coles Oak Lane
Dedham
Essex CO7 6DR
Tel: 0870 765 0100
www.fingerplates.com

Between 1850 and 1950 most interior doors had door-plates, also known as finger- or push-plates. This small company produces brass or copper reproductions of Victorian, Edwardian and Art Nouveau door-plates. Plates are hand-finished and are available lacquered or unlacquered, which gives a duller, more aged effect.

The Original Box Sash Window Company ▲
The Joinery
29–30 The Arches
Alma Road
Windsor
Berkshire SL4 1QZ
Tel: 01753 858196
www.boxsash.com

Specialists in wooden sash windows, constructed by joiners using traditional wooden replacements to ensure buildings retain their period character. All styles from seventeenth-century to Edwardian can be replicated.

The Shutter Shop ▲ ●
Unit 2/8 Chelsea Harbour Design Centre
Chelsea Harbour
London SW10 0XE
Tel: 020 7351 4202

Unit 3 Taplins Court
Church Lane
Hartley Wintney
Hampshire RG27 8XU
01252 844575
www.shuttershop.co.uk

The Shutter Shop offers a wide range of slatted louvres and solid shutters that can be custom-made to fit arched or tapered windows and stained or painted to your own specification.

FIREPLACES, PANELLING AND DETAILS

The Cast Iron Shop
394 Caledonian Road
London N1 1DW
Tel: 020 7609 0934 and 020 7700 3007

Specialists in cast iron with thousands of castings in stock from Georgian to contemporary designs. They can also copy castings if you have a sample pattern or old casting to match.

Hallidays ▲

The Old College
High Street
Dorchester
Oxfordshire OX10 7HL
Tel: 01865 340028 and 01865 340068
www.hallidays.com

Hallidays is a long-established family business specialising in handmade period design for panelled room schemes, fire surrounds, corner cupboards, bookcases, mantels, radiator covers and even home offices that disappear behind bookshelves. Using traditional woodcarving and carpentry skills, they reproduce classic designs of the Georgian and Regency periods.

Locker and Riley ▲

Capital House
Hawk Hill
Battles Bridge
Essex SS11 7RJ
Tel: 01268 574100
www.lockerandriley.com

Award-winning creators of fibrous plaster mouldings using designs from their impressive collection of over 7,000 antique moulds from neo-classical Georgian to High Victorian and Edwardian designs. Cornices, panel mouldings, ceiling roses, corbels, dado rails, niches, friezes and arches to order.

Nostalgia

Hollands Mill
61 Shaw Heath
Stockport
Cheshire SK3 8BH
Tel: 0161 477 7706
www.nostalgia-uk.com

Specialists in antique fireplaces and bathroom fittings, Nostalgia have over 1,400 fireplaces ranging from the eighteenth to the twentieth century in their massive warehouse. They also supply gas coal-effect fires to suit their fireplaces.

Thistle & Rose

5 Anne St
Edinburgh EH4 1PL
Tel: 0131 315 4254

Manufacturers of facsimile neo-classical Adam-style mantelpieces using pine and gesso. They can trace the lineage of their designs to specific rooms in Old College Edinburgh and other grand Georgian houses in the Scottish borders. The chimney pieces are manufactured from authentic material using traditional techniques. All gesso ornamentation is formulated from original workshop recipes and timber comes from renewable sources.

BATHROOMS

Aston Matthews ▲

141–147a Essex Road
London N1 2SN
Tel: 020 7226 7220
www.astonmatthews.co.uk

With over 2,000 lines in stock, Aston Matthews offers stylish contemporary bathrooms and accessories as well as traditional bath fittings, deco-style sinks and reproduction roll-top baths.

Chadder and Company ▲

Bleinheim Studio
London Road
Forest Row
East Sussex RH18 5EZ
Tel: 01342 823243
www.chadder.com

Martin Chadder has been collecting and restoring antique baths and fittings for many years. Chadder and Company not only reproduce Victorian roll-top baths, but also a large range of Victorian taps and shower fittings. They also offer a Bathshield enamelling service to renovate chipped or stained cast iron baths and refurnish taps and fittings.

Stiffkey Bathrooms ▲ ●
89 Upper Giles Street
Norwich
Norfolk NR2 1AB
Tel: 01603 627850
www.stiffkeybathrooms.com

Specialists in antique bathroom furniture and
manufacturers of period bathroom accessories based
on original designs. All products are made of solid
brass and are available in brass, chrome and nikel
finishes. Styles include Victorian, Edwardian and
Art Nouveau.

KITCHENS AND KITCHENALIA

Alan and Kathy Stacey
PO Box 2771
Yeovil
Somerset BA22 7DZ
Tel: 01963 441333
www.antiqueboxes.uk.com

Specialist dealers in quality tortoiseshell, ivory,
shagreen, mother-of-pearl and exotic timer tea
caddies and boxes. Visits to their showroom
by appointment.

Formica ▲
Coast Road
North Shields
Tyne and Wear NE29 8RE
Tel: 0191 259 3000 for nearest stockist
www.formica-europe.com

Formica is the trade name of an American laminate
popular since the 1950s.

www.grannyscupboard.co.uk
This web site offers a wide range of kitchenalia
including flour and bread bins, breadboards and
knives, scale measures as well as original packaging
and trade boxes starting at a few pounds.

Magnet ▲
Tel: 0845 123 6789 for nearest showroom
www.magnet.co.uk

Magnet makes a wide range of kitchens, many of
which have traditional influences. Ranges include
Shaker style, Victorian style and the Edwardian style
such as the Bloomsbury and Aldersley. They also
have some contemporary styles from cool stainless
steel to bright and funky.

Smallbone of Devizes
Tel: 020 7589 5998 for nearest showroom
www.smallbone.co.uk

Smallbone offer Arts and Crafts, Edwardian and
Victorian kitchens. Unfitted kitchen elements are also
available such as court cupboards, pastry dressers,
apothecary drawers and parlour cupboards.

FURNITURE

Aram
110 Drury Lane
London WC2B 5SG
Tel: 020 7557 7557
www.aram.co.uk

A massive store on four floors of a converted
warehouse that offers both design classics and
contemporary furniture, kitchenware, lighting and
bathroom accessories.

Dodge and Son
28–33 Cheap Street
Sherbourne
Dorset DT9 3PU
Tel: 01935 815151
www.dodgeandson.co.uk

Specialists in good reproduction Hepplewhite
and Chippendale furniture, especially dining tables
and chairs.

G Plan

24 Rosyth Road
Glasgow G5 0YD
Tel: 0141 300 7300 for nearest stockist
www.gplancabinets.co.uk

The fabulously named Ebenezer Gomme founded G Plan in 1898. During the 1960s and 1970s it became famous for introducing Scandinavian-inspired teak modular furniture to Britain, including the Form Five and Fresco ranges.

Habitat ▲

Tel: 0845 601 0470 for nearest store

Recently, Habitat have been reintroducing classic 1950s and 1960s designs by Robin Day and Vernon Panton as well as commissioning contemporary designers.

Fritz Hansen

Tel: 020 7837 2030 for nearest stockist
www.fritzhansen.com

This Danish company produces many of Arne Jacobsen's furniture designs dating from the 1950s and 1960s including his famous Series 7 and Ant dining chairs and the Swan and Egg armchairs. Available in a range of woods, fabrics and leathers.

Hepple ▲

11 Market Street
Hexham
Northumberland NE46 3NS
Tel: 01434 602260
www.hepple.co.uk

Producers of handmade traditional upholstered furniture constructed from hand-built frames, horsehair and coir fibre. They also produce a large range of wing and button back tub chairs with traditional brass and ceramic castors. Fabric options include kilim, Aubusson needlepoint, leather and ostrich skin.

Isokon Plus ▲

Turnham Green Terrace Mews
London W14 1QU
Tel: 020 8994 0636
www.isokonplus.com

Founded in 1935 by Jack Pritchard, Isokon made modernist plywood furniture by leading designers of the day including Marcel Breuer and Ernest Race. These ranges included sofas, armchairs, dining chairs and the famous Isokon Penguin Donkey book-and-magazine rack. Contemporary designs in a similar modernist tradition have been added to the collection including sideboards and chests of drawers by Michael Sodeau and shelves, dining and coffee tables by Barber Osgerby.

The Original Bedstead Company ▲

Tel: 01536 410700 for nearest stockists
www.obc-uk.net

This company uses its extensive archive of original designs to craft beds that replicate the heritage of the originals. Cast iron and brass beds include traditional British styles and opulent four-posters. There are also childrens cast iron bed designs in a range of colours.

Scandecor ▲

20 Castle Street
Brighton
East Sussex BN1 2HD
Tel: 01273 820208

This company specialises in reproducing leather art deco-style sofas complete with contrasting trim as well as other designs from the 1950s and 1960s. Ranges have such evocative names as the Bogart, Roxy, Odeon, Ritz and Swing Time, to create the appropriate 1930s feel. These are based on authentic designs including copies of sofas and chairs from the great French art deco ocean liner the SS *Normandie* – the great French art deco ocean liner. Solid beech frames and distressed leathers are available for a more authentic look.

SCP

135–139 Curtain Road
London EC2A 3BX
Tel: 020 7739 1869
www.scp.co.uk
(also concessions in branches of Selfridges)

This company is one of the leading manufacturers of contemporary furniture – commissioning the design classics of tomorrow. They also sell a collection of design classics from 1900 to 1969 and contemporary lighting and accessories.

Seventh Heaven ▲

Chirk Mills
Chirk
Wrexham
North Wales LL14 5BU
Tel: 01691 777622
www.seventh-heaven.co.uk

Seventh Heaven boasts that they have the largest selection of antique beds in Europe. All beds are restored by them and they can extend narrow antique beds while maintaining the original style.

Skandium

72 Wigmore Street
London W1U 2SG
Tel: 020 7935 2077
www.skandium.com
(also concessions in branches of Selfridges)

The shop for the best in Scandinavian modernism including fabric by Marimekko, tableware by Stelton, lighting by Louis Poulson and glassware by Orrefors.

Twentytwentyone

274 Upper Street
London N1 2UA
Tel: 020 7288 1996

These real enthusiasts offer original post-war furniture classics by Eames and Jacobsen as well as classic designs by less well-known names.

V&A Upholstered Furniture

The Mid Way
Dunkirk
Nottingham
NG7 2TS
Tel: 01332 811666

Showroom of upholstered furniture inspired by objects from the furniture and textile collections of the Victoria and Albert Museum.

PAINTS, WALLPAPERS AND FABRICS

Cath Kidston ▲ ●

8 Clarendon Cross
London W11 4AP
Tel: 020 7221 4000

8 Elystan Street
London SW3 3NS
Tel: 020 7229 8000 for telephone orders
www.cathkidston.co.uk

Cath Kidston has single-handedly rehabilitated the quintessentially English floral print designs of the 1940s and 1950s. She now has a range of 126 fabrics and wallpapers and over 670 products in the catalogue.

Cole and Son

Chelsea Harbour Design Centre
London SW10 0XE
Tel: 020 7376 4628 for nearest stockist
www.cole-and-son.com

Cole and Son provided many of the wallpapers seen in Number 57. They have an amazing archive and base their wallpapers on their collection of wooden printing blocks of over 1,750 designs representing all styles from the eighteenth to the twentieth century. They are renowned for their hand-blocked Pugin-designed wallpapers for the Houses of Parliament and have provided wallpapers for many historical houses including Buckingham Palace.

Crown ▲

Tel: 0870 241 6457 for nearest stockist
www.historic-colours.co.uk

Crown offer six ranges of historical colours drawn
from the collections of the Royal Institute of British
Architects and based on colours from original
drawings – Palladian, Neo-Classical, Gothic Revival,
Victorian Eclectic, Arts & Crafts and '50s Sketchbook
– and with authentic finishes.

Dulux ▲

Tel: 01753 550555 for stockists
Tel: 0891 515222 (premium rate) colour advice line
www.dulux.co.uk

Dulux produce three ranges of 'heritage colours' –
Georgian, Victorian and Edwardian & Art Deco – all
available in a range of interior and exterior finishes.

Farrow and Ball ▲ ●

Tel: 01202 876141 for nearest stockist
www.farrow-ball.com

Farrow and Ball are manufacturers of traditional
wallpapers and paints. Their colour chart a has
description of each paint colour, with details of the
date where possible, and suggestions for use to help
with accurate restoration.

Ian Mankin ▲ ●

271 Wandsworth Bridge Road
London SW6 2TX
Tel: 020 7371 8825

109 Regent's Park Road
London NW1 8UR
Tel: 020 7722 0997 for mail order

Established in 1983 by Ian Mankin, the company is
renown for its simple striped utility fabrics including
blazer stripes, checks, plaids and tickings in cotton
and linen suitable for curtains and upholstery.

The Imperial Home Décor Group

Tel: 01254 870700 for nearest stockist
www.ihdg.co.uk

The heavily embossed wallpaper beloved by the
Victorians and Edwardians is still produced today
in a wide range of patterns. Designs date from
1898 to 1979 and all patterns include the dates
when they were first introduced.

Laura Ashley ▲ ●

Tel: 0800 868100 for nearest store
www.lauraashley.com

Laura Ashley is renowned for its floral prints and has
an impressive collection of wallpaper, fabrics, curtains,
paints, bed linen, carpets, lighting and home
accessories in both traditional and contemporary styles
some of which can be made to measure.

Sanderson

Tel: 01895 830044 for nearest stockist
www.william-morris.co.uk

Sanderson produce a home furnishings collection
based on the archive of William Morris and Co.
Wallpapers and curtains are available in nine of
his famous patterns including Chrysanthemums,
Honeysuckle and Willow Boughs. Other designs
include Pugin Velvet and Voysey. The paint
collection is available in thirty-six colours that use
natural dyes to complement the fabric and
wallpaper ranges.

Zoffany ▲

Tel: 01923 710680 for stockists
www.zoffany.com

Zoffany produce coordinated wallpaper, fabrics,
carpets, furniture and paint. They have collaborated
with the National Trust to create a collection of fabric
and wallpapers based upon those found in some of
Britain's historic houses.

FLOORING

Brintons
Tel: 0800 505055 for nearest stockist
www.brintons.net

Established in 1783, this company is the largest
manufacturer of high-quality woven Axminsters from
traditional patterns to contemporary cards and
plain tufteds, tartans, plaids and Persian designs.
Its National Trust collection includes Osterley,
inspired by a Robert Adam ceiling, Uppark based
on an eighteenth-century shutter carving and
Petworth reflecting the Rococo styling of an
eighteenth-century carpet.

Bruce Hardwood Floors ▲
Tel: 01235 515102 for nearest stockist
www.bruce.com

The world's largest manufacturers of hardwood
floors. Oak and maple are the standard woods
used, available in a wide range of stains and
crafted in a variety of widths and shades. Parquet
flooring and crafted wood-tiled floors with borders
and patterns are also available.

The Downs Stone Company Ltd ▲
Lower Buildings
Lyneham Road
Sarsden
Oxfordshire OX7 6PN
Tel: 01608 658357
www.downstone.com

The Downs Stone Company was established –
upon the acquisition of a small quarry – to process,
supply and build with the finest-quality genuine,
Cotswold stone. Ranges include traditional flagstone
flooring including stones that have been 'antiqued' for
restoration projects and limestone tiles with contrasting
cabochons suitable for hallways. They can also make
stone sinks to client specifications and replicate
Cotswold stone fireplaces.

Kelaty
Kelaty House
First Way
Wembley
Middlesex HA9 0JD
Tel: 020 8903 9998 for nearest stockist
www.kelaty.com

Kelaty's 200,000 rugs are all handmade. They have
a collection of Eastern rugs that is second to none due
to partnerships with manufacturers from China to Iran.
Their Aubusson tapestry designs are faithful
reproductions of eighteenth-century French designs and
they stock needlepoint and kilim rugs. They also deal
in antique Caucasian and Persian carpets. They have
an antique finish which after special washing
accurately reproduces classic antique Chinese carpets.

Marmoleum ▲
Forbo-Nairn
PO Box 1
Kircaldy
Fife KY1 2SB
Tel: 0800 731 2369
www.marmoleum.co.uk

Marmoleum is an updated version of linoleum made
from natural materials and is environmentally friendly
and hygenic. It is completely bio-degradable. As well
as a large range of mottled colours, classical
chequer, vine and Greek key borders, and a range
of inserts are also available. It comes as tiles or as
larger sheets.

Paris Ceramics ▲
583 Kings Road
London SW6 2EH
Tel: 020 7371 7778
www.parisceramics.com

Leading specialists in sourcing and reclaiming antique
stone and terracotta from all over the world. Ranges
include flagstones, limestone, 'aged' limestone,
mosaics, Cosmati (geometric patterned marble),
handmade terracotta and decorative tiles.

Woodward Grosvenor & Co. Ltd ▲
Stourvale Mills
Green Street
Kidderminster
Worcestershire DY10 1AT
Tel: 01562 820020
www.woodwardgrosvenor.co.uk

Woodward Grosvenor has an archive of over 20,000 designs dating back to their founding in 1790 and can produce these as tufted, Axminster and Wilton carpets.

LIGHTING

Brooklands ▲ ●
Tel: 01483 267474 for nearest stockist

Brooklands specialise in quality solid brass lighting including Regency-style wall lights, a Georgian range and ornate Victorian designs.

Christopher Wray ▲
Tel: 020 7751 8701 for nearest showroom
www.christopherwray.com

Established in 1964, Christopher Wray is known for its comprehensive range of reproduction and contemporary lighting including crystal chandeliers in all sizes, Chrome Deco and Tiffany styles. They also stock a range of original antique lamps and can convert, repair and restore customers' own lights.

CTO Lighting
Unit 102a Belgravia Workshops
157–163 Marlborough Road
London N19 4NF
Tel: 020 7686 8700 for nearest stockist
www.cto-lighting.co.uk

CTO specialises in elegant, clean-lined contemporary lighting. They also create cushion designs for top boutique hotels.

Olivers Lighting Company ▲ ●
The Udimore Workshops
Udimore
Rye
East Sussex TN31 6AS
Tel: 01797 225166
www.oliverslighting.co.uk

Olivers make period light switches and coordinating electrical accessories. Each order is individually hand-finished to the customer's specifications to combine traditional materials with modern technology.

MIRRORS

Reproduction Mirrors ▲ ●
1 David Terrace
Tucker Street
Wells
Somerset BA5 2DX
Tel: 01749 674219

Specialists in fine reproduction handmade and traditional over-mantel and pier-wall mirrors. They also restore antique mirrors and frames. This company produce thirty different designs including simple reeded over-mantels, over-mantels with friezes and plain Victorian style arch top mantels.

CLOCKS

The Clock Clinic
85 Lower Richmond Road
London SW15 1EU
Tel: 020 8788 1407
www.clockclinic.co.uk

A family-run business established in 1971 selling English long-case and bracket clocks. All clocks are overhauled and come with a year guarantee. They also repair and restore mechanisms and cases for customers' own clocks.

P. A. Oxley Antique Clocks

The Old Rectory
Main Road
Cherhill
Near Calne
Wiltshire SN11 8UX
Tel: 01249 816227
www.british-antiqueclocks.com

Specialists in seventeenth, eighteenth and nineteenth-century clocks and barometers with four showrooms and a well-illustrated website.

CUTLERY AND SILVERWARE

Chimo Holdings

White Rose Works
61 Eyre Lane
Sheffield S1 3GF
Tel: 0114 249 0969
www.chimoholdings.co.uk

Chimo Holdings have a large collection of cutlery patterns in sterling silver, silver plate and stainless steel, all made in their Sheffield factory. They also have some more unusual cutlery ranges featuring bone and mother-of-pearl handles.

Don Alexander ▲

475 Ecclesall Road
Sheffield S11 8PP
Tel: 0114 268 5701
www.sheffield-made.com

This shop offers a choice of some of big names in Sheffield-made pewter, silver and steel and a large range of traditional-pattern cutlery classics like the Regency 'French Leaf', 'Harley' – a 1920s design – and 1960s designs by Robert Welch. They can source designs to order from the Sheffield area. The shop also sells an assortment of miscellanea including carving knives, corkscrews, picture frames, napkin rings and tankards.

Lincoln House Fine English Silver & Cutlery ▲

Clayworth
Near Retford
Nottinghamshire DN22 9AD
Tel: 0800 328 3694
www.silvercutlery.com

Lincoln House in Nottinghamshire has over 150 cutlery designs available in sterling silver, silver plate and stainless steel, and some of the finest patterns from the last five centuries. They offer a free sample service and a personalising service whereby your family emblem can be engraved on handles or blades of the cutlery. They also sell decorative tableware, including sterling-silver candlesticks and Georgian-style cruet sets.

United Cutlers ▲

Cutlery Works
Herries Road
Sheffield S6 1QU
Tel: 0114 243 3984
www.cutlerysets.com

United Cutlers offer a large selection of classic cutlery patterns. A small family business, all United Cutlers' cutlery is crafted by hand in their Sheffield workshops from sterling silver, silver plate and stainless steel. There is also a range of canteens, cabinets and rolls available in which to keep your silver cutlery in mint condition. They also offer a free sample service and can even offer tips on the correct table settings for any occasion.

W. Wright Cutlery and Silverware ▲ ●

7–11 Copper Street
Sheffield S3 7AG
Tel: 0114 279 6568
www.w-right.demon.co.uk

W. Wright are one of the few remaining, original, small cutlery manufacturers left in Sheffield and have been making cutlery in the city for over 100 years. They have a fine collection of designs available, from classic to contemporary.

INTERESTING PLACES TO VISIT

A La Ronde
Summer Lane
Exmouth
Devon EX8 5BD
Tel: 01395 265514
www.nationaltrust.org.uk

An unusual sixteen-sided house completed in
1796 for Jane and Mary Parminter, which now houses
the collection of objects brought back from their
Grand Tour.

Arley Hall
Near Northwich
Cheshire CW9 6NA
Tel: 01565 777353
www.arleyestate.zuunet.co.uk

Built in the Victorian Jacobean style in 1840, Arley
Hall has an adjoining private chapel designed by
Anthony Salvin (1799–1881).

Arlington Court
Arlington
Near Barnstable
North Devon EX31 4LP
Tel: 01271 850296
www.nationaltrust.org.uk

Arlington Court was built for the Chichester family in
the neoclassical style in 1822 and contains much of
the original furniture from the period.

Arthur Lodge
60 Dalkeith Road
Edinburgh
Scotland EH16 5AD
Tel: 0131 667 5163
www.stately-homes.com

Arthur Lodge was designed by Thomas Hamilton
(1784–1858) and was completed in 1827 as a
Greek revival neoclassical villa.

Arundel Castle
Arundel
West Sussex BN18 9AB
Tel: 01903 883136
www.arundelcastle.org

Arundel Castle was built at the end of the eleventh
century by Roger de Montgomery (1022–94) and
has been open to visitors for the past 200 years.

Belmont Park
Throwley
Faversham
Kent ME13 0HH
Tel: 01795 890202
www.gardenvisit.com

Belmont Park is a late eighteenth-century country
mansion designed by Samuel Wyatt (1737–1807).
It contains original furniture from the period,
mementoes brought back from India and a substantial
clock collection.

Berrington Hall
Near Leominster
Herefordshire HR6 0DW
Tel: 01568 615721
www.nationaltrust.org.uk

Berrington Hall was designed and built between
1778 and 1781 by leading English Georgian architect
Henry Holland (1745–1806). Holland enjoyed a
fruitful partnership with the gardener, Lancelot
'Capability' Brown. Key interior features include a
Victorian nursery and laundry and a Georgian dairy.

British Architectural Library

21 Portman Square
London W1H 9HF
Tel: 020 7580 5533
www.architecture.com

The collection at the British Architectural Library includes over 600,000 architectural drawings dating from c.1500 onwards.

Brobury House

Brobury
Herefordshire HR3 6BS
Tel: 01981 500229
www.broburyhouse.co.uk

A Victorian country gentleman's house and gardens.

Brodsworth Hall

Brodsworth
Near Doncaster
South Yorkshire DN5 7XJ
Tel: 01302 722598
www.microart-ukheritage.co.uk

Brodsworth Hall was built between 1861 and 1863. Its contents have survived almost intact and reflect the sharp contrast between the opulent state rooms and the austere servants' quarters.

Broughton House

High Street
Kirkcudbright
Scotland DG6 4JX
Tel: 01557 330437
www.nts.org.uk

An interesting late eighteenth-century house which became the home and studio of the artist A. E. Hornel, one of the 'Glasgow Boys' painters. Examples of his work are on show in the house.

Biddulph Grange Garden

Grange Road
Biddulph
Stoke-on-Trent ST8 7SD
Tel: 01782 517999
www.nationaltrust.org.uk

A restored High Victorian garden which features an Egyptian court and a miniature Great Wall of China.

Brooking Collection

Greenwich University
Oakfield Lane
Dartford
Kent DA1 2SZ
Tel: 020 8316 9897
www.buildingconservation.com

A collection of architectural detail from the sixteenth to twentieth century including examples of windows, doors, fanlights and fireplaces.

Bryn Bras Castle

Llanrug
Caenarfon
Gwynedd
Wales LL55 4RE
Tel: 01286 870210
www.medievalcastles.net

Built in 1830 in the neo-Romanesque style and attributed to Thomas Hopper (1776–1856), who also worked on Penrhyn Castle.

Caerhays Castle

Caerhays
Gorran
St Austell
Cornwall PL26 6LY
Tel: 01872 501310
www.caerhays.co.uk

An example of one of the few castles left standing designed by John Nash (1752–1835).

Coggles Manor Farm Museum
Church Lane
Witney
Oxfordshire OX8 6LA
Tel: 01993 772602

Although the manor house belongs to a much earlier age, the rooms have been furnished in a late-Victorian style.

Cowper and Newton Museum
Orchard Side
Market Place
Olney
Bedfordshire MK46 4AJ
Tel: 01234 711516
www.mkheritage.co.uk

Small museum in the home of William Cowper (1731–1800), poet, letter-writer and translator of Homer. The museum contains belongings of both Cowper and his close friend, John Newton (1725–1807). There is a recreation of a Victorian country kitchen and a wash house inside.

Clumber Park
Worksop
Nottinghamshire S80 3AZ
Tel: 01909 476592
www.nationaltrust.org.uk

The house that once stood here was demolished in the late 1930s, but what remains is a fine example of a Gothic-revival chapel finished in 1889. There is also parkland with what is reputed to be the longest double lime avenue in Europe, a huge lake and a Victorian apiary.

Cragside
Rothbury
Morpeth
Northumberland NE65 7PX
Tel: 01669 620333
www.nationaltrust.org.uk

Designed and built by Sir Norman Shaw (1831–1912) for the first Lord Armstrong as a family home and a showcase for his art collection.

Dennis Savers House
18 Folgate Street
Spitalfields
London E1 6BX
Tel: 0207 247 4013
www.dennissavershouse.co.uk

Perhaps the only house left in London still lit by gas, this is a fully furnished early Georgian home. Dennis Savers created this still-life drama to evoke a time when a family of master silk weavers occupied the house.

Design Museum
Shad Thames
London SE1 2YD
Tel: 020 7403 6933
www.designmuseum.org

This museum was the inspiration of Sir Terence Conran (1931–) and opened in 1989 to demonstrate the social, cultural and economic reasons for contemporary design.

Dunham Massey Hall
Altringham
Cheshire WA14 4SJ
Tel: 0161 929 7508
www.nationaltrust.org.uk

An example of an early Georgian house containing artefacts from various periods. The interior was remodelled during the Edwardian period and is thought to be the finest example of its type in Britain. The extensive grounds contain a Georgian orangery and a Victorian bark house and well house.

Eltham Palace
Eltham
London SE9 5QE
Tel: 020 8294 2548
www.english-heritage.org.uk

A medieval palace and modernist country house surrounded by moated grounds. During the 1930s the wealthy Courauld family had the substantial apartment built and decorated in a fascinating period style.

Fairfax House

Castlegate
York YO1 1RN
Tel: 01904 623332
www.fairfaxhouse.co.uk

A fine example of a large Georgian town house, fully furnished with eighteenth-century decorations and furniture. The dining-room table is even laid for dinner.

Fasque

Fettercairn
Kincardineshire
Scotland AB30 1DJ
Tel: 01561 340202
www.theheritagetrail.co.uk

This house, completed in 1809, was the home of William Gladstone (1809–98).

Geffrye Museum

Kingsland Road
London E2 8EA
Tel: 020 7739 9893
www.geffrye-museum.org.uk

Period-room displays tracing the history of English domestic interiors over the past 400 years.

The Georgian House

7 Charlotte Square
Edinburgh
Scotland EH2 4DR
Tel: 0131 225 2160
www.nts.org.uk

A Robert Adam (1732–94) neoclassical palace-fronted town house. Every room is furnished in the style that it would have been in 1796.

Georgian House Museum

7 Great George Street
Bristol BS1 5RR
Tel: 0117 921 1362
www.bristol-city.gov.uk/museums

An example of a town house built in 1790 for a local wealthy businessman. The house is furnished to illustrate life above and below stairs.

Georgian Theatre Royal

Victoria Road
Richmond
North Yorkshire DL10 4DW
Tel: 01748 823710
www.georgiantheatre.com

This working theatre first opened in 1788, and has been beautifully restored.

Gilbert White's House

The Wakes
High Street
Selborne
Alton
Hampshire GU34 3JH
Tel: 01420 511275

This house was the home of the Reverend Gilbert White (1720–1793), author of *The Natural History of Selborne*, and a is fine example of an eighteenth-century country home.

Gunnersbury Park Museum

Gunnersbury Park
London W3 8LQ
Tel: 020 8992 1612
www.rothschildarchive.org

A museum of social history with furnished rooms and kitchens from the original house, which was refurbished by Sidney Smirke (1781–1867) for the Rothschild family.

Highclere Castle
Newbury
Hampshire RG20 9RN
Tel: 01635 253210
www.highclerecastle.co.uk

Highclere Castle was built in the 1830s by Sir Charles Barry (1790–1860) who was also working on the Houses of Parliament at the time. Gothic, Moorish and rococo revival styles are all represented.

Hill House
Upper Colquhoun Street
Helensburgh
Scotland G84 9AJ
Tel: 01436 673900
www.nts.org.uk

Built in 1902, this is perhaps the finest example of the domestic creations of the architect and artist Charles Rennie Mackintosh (1868–1928).

Hill of Tarvit Mansionhouse
Cupar
Fife
Scotland KY15 5PB
Tel: 01334 653127
www.nts.org.uk

A large country house, built in 1906 by architect Sir Robert Lorimer (1864–1929). Contains a collection of French, vernacular and Chippendale furniture and a restored Edwardian laundry.

Historic Dockyard
Chatham
Kent ME4 4TE
Tel: 01634 812251
www.chdt.org.uk

A unique Georgian and early Victorian dockyard with an 80-acre working museum.

Holbourne Museum of Art
Great Pulteney Street
Bath BA2 4DB
Tel: 01225 466669
www.letsgothere.co.uk

Georgian house, set in beautiful gardens and containing important paintings, majolica ware, glass, etc.

Hughenden Manor
High Wycombe
Buckinghamshire HP14 4LA
Tel: 01494 532580
www.nationaltrust.org.uk

Red-brick house built in the Gothic style for British prime minister and novelist, Benjamin Disraeli (1804–81), who spent the last 33 years of his life here. The interior is a good example of a fine, comfortable Victorian home.

Ickworth House
Horringer
Bury St Edmunds
Suffolk IP29 5QE
Tel: 01284 735270
www.nationaltrust.org.uk

Large country house built for the Earl of Bristol in 1795, consisting of a central rotunda with curved corridors. Important paintings from various periods and a magnificent Georgian silver collection are on display.

Ironbridge Gorge Museums
Ironbridge
Telford
Shropshire TF8 7AW
Tel: 01952 433522
www.ironbridge.org.uk

The exhibits at Ironbridge Gorge include a reconstructed Victorian village dedicated to the history of the British Industrial Revolution. Abraham Darby's famous iron bridge of 1779 spans the river Severn nearby.

Kedleston Hall
Quardon
Derby
Derbyshire DE22 5JH
Tel: 01332 842191
www.nationaltrust.org.uk

Kedleston Hall was built between 1759 and 1765. The Robert Adam interior has hardly been altered and there is a fine collection of original furniture and paintings.

Kelmscott Manor
Kelmscott
Near Lechlade
Gloucestershire GL7 3HJ
Tel: 01367 252486
www.kelmscottmanor.co.uk

Kelmscott was the home of William Morris (1834–96) from 1871 until his death. The house contains many examples of Morris' work: furniture, textiles, carpets and ceramics. The house is now owned by the Society of Antiquaries.

Killerton House
Broadclyst
Exeter
Devon EX5 3LE
Tel: 01392 881345
www.nationaltrust.org.uk
A large family house built in 1778 with furniture from various periods and an interesting Victorian laundry. The house also contains the Paulise de Bush costume collection dating from the eighteenth century.

Knighthayes
Bolham
Tiverton
Devon EX16 7RQ
Tel: 01884 254665
www.nationaltrust.org.uk

This Victorian Gothic house was designed in 1869 by William Burges (1827–81).

Leighton Hall
Carnforth
Lancashire LA5 9ST
Tel: 01524 734474
www.leighton-hall.co.uk

This large, imposing house and chapel from the eighteenth century are fronted by a neo-Gothic façade. Leighton Hall also contains a collection of Gillow of Lancaster furniture.

Leighton House
12 Holland Park Road
London W14 8LZ
Tel: 020 7602 3316
www.rbkc.gov.uk/leightonhousemuseum/

Leighton House was built for Frederick Lord Leighton (1830–96) and finished in 1879 as a house for entertaining and as an ornate studio. Its centrepiece is the magnificent Arab Hall with mosaic frieze and fountain.

Linley Sambourne House
18 Stafford Terrace
London W8 7BH
Tel: 020 7994 1019
www.rbkc.gov.uk/linleysambournehouse

A late-Victorian town house with a substantial amount of original decoration and furniture. This was once the home of Linley Sambourne (1844–1910), chief cartoonist of *Punch*, and examples of his work are on display in the house.

Little Holland House
40 Beeches Avenue
Carlshalton
Surrey SM5 3LW
Tel: 020 8770 4781
www.sutton.gov.uk

The artist Frank Dickinson (1874–1961) designed, built and furnished this house as his own home. He was influenced by William Morris (1834–96) and John Ruskin (1819–1900).

Manderston
Duns
Berwickshire TD11 3PP
Tel: 01361 883450
www.manderston.co.uk

Large Edwardian country house built between 1903 and 1905, which incorporates a magnificent silver staircase. Manderston was the location for the successful Channel 4 series 'The Edwardian Country House'.

Mentmore Towers
Mentmore
Near Leighton Buzzard
Bedfordshire LU7 0QH
Tel: 01296 662183
www.touruk.co.uk
Built in 1855 for Baron Meyer Amschel de Rothschild, this house was designed by Sir Joseph Paxton (1803–65) and is Victorian Jacobeathan at its best. The large entrance hall is dominated by a white marble staircase and the dining and sitting rooms are in an ornate gilded style.

Mount Stuart House
Isle of Bute PA20 9LR
Tel: 01700 503877
www.mountstuart.com

Impressive High-Victorian Gothic-revival house designed by Sir Robert Anderson (1834–1921).

Mr Straw's House
7 Blyth Grove
Worksop S81 0JG
Tel: 01909 482380
www.nationaltrust.org.uk

A modestly-sized Edwardian semi-detached house which has remained unaltered in decoration and content since the 1930s.

National Monuments Record Centre
Kemble Drive
Swindon
Wiltshire SN2 2GZ
Tel: 01793 414600
www.english-heritage.org.uk

The national collection of photographs, drawings and texts relating to architecture, archaeology, air photography and maritime sites.

Normanby Hall
Normanby
Scunthorpe
Lincolnshire DN15 9HU
Tel: 01726 720588
www.touruk.co.uk

This Regency mansion, designed by Sir Robert Smirke (1781–1867), contains Regency, Victorian and Edwardian furniture and a comprehensive costume collection.

Nostell Priory
Doncaster Road
Nostell
Near Wakefield
Yorkshire WF4 1QE
Tel: 01924 863892
www.nationaltrust.org.uk

Nostell Priory is the work of the English architect James Paine (1717–89) with some of the staterooms decorated later by Robert Adam (1728–94). The house contains one of the best collections of Chippendale furniture, including an eighteenth-century doll's house.

Osborne House

East Cowes
Isle of Wight PO32 6JY
Tel: 01983 200022
www.tourist-information-uk.com

Italian villa designed by Prince Albert (1819–61) as a rural retreat for Queen Victoria and their family. The original furniture is still in situ and visitors can take a ride in an authentic Victorian carriage around the grounds.

Quarry Bank Mill

Styal
Wilmslow
Cheshire SK9 4LA
Tel: 01625 527468
www.nationaltrust.org

A working cotton mill built in 1784 by Samuel Greg (1758–1834), an early pioneer of the factory system. The mill is powered by a 50-ton waterwheel and the 1830 beam engine demonstrates how steam complimented water power during the Industrial Revolution.

Rodmarton Manor

Cirencester
Gloucestershire GL7 6PF
Tel: 01285 841253
www.rodmarton-manor.co.uk

Rodmarton Manor took over 20 years to build from 1909 onwards and is one of the last country houses to be built in local stone by local craftsmen.

Rossendale Museum

Whitaker Park
Rawtenstall
Rossendale
Lancashire BB4 6RE
Tel: 01706 217777
www.aboutbritain.com/RossendaleMuseum

This house at Rossendale, built in 1840, was once a nineteenth-century mill owner's home and is now a museum for furniture, costumes and fine and decorative arts.

Number 1 Royal Crescent

Bath BA1 2LR
Tel: 01225 428126
www.bath-preservation-trust.org.uk

This was the first house in the Royal Crescent, built between 1767 and 1774. It was designed by John Wood the Younger (1728–81) and was the inspiration for town-houses for decades to come.

Royal Pavilion

Brighton
East Sussex BN1 1EE
Tel: 01273 603005
www.royalpavilion.brighton.co.uk

In 1787 the architect Henry Holland (1745–1806) built a neoclassical villa which was transformed between 1815 and 1822 into what we see today. The personal architect to the Regent, John Nash (1752–1835), remodelled the villa in the Chinese and Hindu style with opulent staterooms.

Saltram House

Plympton
Plymouth PL7 1UH
Tel: 01752 333500
www.nationaltrust.org.uk

This is the sort of house that inspired the builders of Number 57 Kingsdown Parade. Saltram was built during the reign of George II and has two rooms decorated by Robert Adam (1728–92). It contains period furniture, china and pictures by, among others, Joshua Reynolds (1723–92) and Angelica Kauffmann (1741–1807).

Sir John Soane's House

13 Lincoln's Inn Fields
London WC2A 3BP
Tel: 020 7405 2107
www.soane.org

The eminent architect Sir John Soane (1753–1837)
designed this house and he lived here for the last 25
years of his life. Finished in 1812, the interior
employs mirrors, folding walls, double-height rooms
and top-lighting through coloured glass.

Sion Hill Hall

Kirkby Wiske
Thirsk
North Yorkshire YO7 4EU
Tel: 01845 587206
www.sionhillhall.co.uk

An Edwardian mansion designed by Walter Brierley
(1862–1926), who was influenced by the Arts and
Crafts movement and was a leading exponent of the
'Wrenaissance' style.

Standen

East Grinstead
West Sussex RH19 4NE
Tel: 01342 323029
www.nationaltrust.org.uk

The house at Standen was designed by the architect,
Phillip Webb (1831–1915), with original
decorations and furnishings by Morris and Co.

Stott Park Bobbin Mill

Lower Stott Park
Ulverston
Cumbria LA12 8AX
Tel: 01539 441288
www.theheritagetrail.co.uk

Built in 1835, Stott Park Bobbin Mill provides
demonstrations of the machinery and techniques used
during the Industrial Revolution.

Sunnycroft

200 Holyhead Road
Wellington
Telford
Shropshire TF1 2DR
Tel: 0870 608 1259
www.nationaltrust.org.uk

This house is typical of the type of villa built for
middle-class Victorians in the suburbs of towns and
cities. The contents and decorations remain
unchanged from when the house was first built.

Tatton Park

Knutsford
Cheshire WA16 6QN
Tel: 01625 534400
www.tattonpark.org.uk

A Palladian mansion designed by James Wyatt
(1746–1813) which is filled with works of art from
various periods and commissioned Gillow furniture.

The Tenement House

145 Buccleuch Street
Glasgow
Scotland G3 6QN
Tel: 0141 333 0183
www.nts.org.uk

A gaslit tenement flat furnished as it was in 1892.

Theatre Royal

Westgate Street
Bury St Edmunds
Suffolk IP33 1QR
Tel: 01284 755127
www.nationaltrust.org.uk

A rare example of a late-Georgian theatre.

Victoria and Albert Museum

South Kensington
London SW7 2RL
Tel: 020 7942 2000
www.vam.ac.uk

The national museum of applied and decorative arts, with thousands of exhibits from all over the world. Also known as 'Britain's attic'!

Waddesdon Manor
Waddesdon
Near Aylesbury
Buckinghamshire HP18 0JH
Tel: 01296 651236
www.nationaltrust.org.uk

Renaissance-style chateau built between 1874 and 1889 to house Baron Ferdinand de Rothschild's collection of eighteenth-century works of art. Magnificent parties were held here with guests including Queen Victoria and the Shah of Persia.

Wallace Collection
Hertford House
Manchester Square
London W1V 3BN
Tel: 020 7563 9500
www.the-wallace-collection.org.uk

Hertford House dates from the late eighteenth century with substantial additions carried out in 1872 by the architect Thomas Ambler. In 1900 the house was opened as a public museum, displaying the substantial collection of art and furniture amassed by Sir Richard Wallace.

Watts Gallery
Down Lane
Guildford
Surrey GU3 1DQ
Tel: 01483 810235
www.wattsgallery.org.uk

Purpose-built gallery in the house of the nineteenth-century artist G. F. Watts.

Wilberforce House
High Street
Hull HU1 1EP
Tel: 01482 613902
www.hullcc.gov.uk

This museum tells the story of William Wilberforce's struggle to abolish slavery, as well as housing some other interesting displays – notably a Victorian parlour and a set of Georgian rooms.

William Morris Gallery
Lloyd Park
Forest Road
Walthamstow
London E17 4PP
Tel: 020 8527 3782
www.lbwf.gov/wmg/home.htm

William Morris (1834–96) was born very close to this building which houses a comprehensive collection of his work.

2 Willow Road
Hampstead
London NW3 1TH
Tel: 020 7435 6166
www.nationaltrust.org.uk

This was designed and built as a terrace of three houses, one of which was the home of architect Erno Goldfinger (1902–87). Goldfinger was influenced by his time in Paris during the 1920s where he was friends with Max Ernst and other Surrealists.

Wimpole Home Farm
Arrington
Royston
Hertfordshire SG8 0BW
Tel: 01223 207257
www.wimpole.org

Model farm created in 1794 by Sir John Soane (1753–1837). Adjacent is Wimpole Hall which features the work of Soane, James Gibbs and Henry Flitcroft.

INDEX

PICTURE CREDITS